Music For Silenced Voices

Music For Silenced Voices

Shostakovich and His Fifteen Quartets

WENDY LESSER

Yale UNIVERSITY PRESS

New Haven & London

Published with assistance from the Mary Cady Tew Memorial Fund.

Yale University Press books may be purchased in quantity for educational, business, or promotional use. For information, please e-mail sales.press@yale.edu (U.S. office) or sales@yaleup.co.uk (U.K. office).

Endpapers: After the premiere of the ballet *The Bolt,* 1931. Reproduced by permission of the St. Petersburg State Museum of Theatre and Music.

Set in Adobe Garamond type by Integrated Publishing Solutions, Grand Rapids, Michigan.
Printed in the United States of America.

Library of Congress Cataloging-in-Publication Data

Lesser, Wendy.
Music for silenced voices : Shostakovich and his fifteen quartets / Wendy Lesser.
p. cm.
Includes bibliographical references and index.
ISBN 978-0-300-16933-1 (hardcover : alk. paper)   1. Shostakovich, Dmitrii Dmitrievich, 1906–1975. Quartets, strings.   2. String quartet.   I. Title.
ML410.S53L47 2011
785'.7194092—dc22   2010038140

A catalogue record for this book is available from the British Library.

This paper meets the requirements of ANSI/NISO Z39.48–1992 (Permanence of Paper).

10 9 8 7 6 5 4 3 2 1

BOOKS BY WENDY LESSER

Room for Doubt

The Pagoda in the Garden

Nothing Remains the Same

The Amateur

A Director Calls

Pictures at an Execution

His Other Half

The Life Below the Ground

The Genius of Language (editor)

Hiding in Plain Sight (editor)

For Martin and Barbara Bauer

For not only is an odd man not always a particular and isolated case, but, on the contrary, it sometimes happens that it is precisely he, perhaps, who bears within himself the heart of the whole, while the other people of his epoch have all for some reason been torn away for a time by some kind of flooding wind.

—FYODOR DOSTOYEVSKY,
preface to *The Brothers Karamazov*

Contents

Dramatis Personae: A Selective List

Nina Varzar: his first wife

Margarita Kainova: his second wife

Irina Shostakovich*: his third wife

Galina and Maxim* Shostakovich: his children

Maria and Zoya Shostakovich: his sisters

Ivan Sollertinsky: his best friend

Isaak Glikman: his close friend and informal secretary

Vissarion Shebalin (composer), Pyotr Vilyams (painter and set designer), Levon Atovmyan (composer), Grigori Kozintsev (director), Mikhail Zoshchenko (writer): old friends of his from before the Second World War

Moisei Weinberg (composer) and his wife, Natalya Mikhoels (linguist): longtime family friends of his and Nina's

Ilya Slonim (sculptor), his wife, Tatiana Litvinova (translator), and her sister-in-law, Flora Litvinova (biologist): family friends made during the wartime evacuation

Mstislav Rostropovich (cellist) and his wife, Galina Vishnevskaya (soprano): younger close friends from the postwar period

Yelena Konstantinovskaya (translator), Galina Ustvolskaya (composer), Elmira Nazirova (composer and pianist): some of his girlfriends and muses

Yevgeny Mravinsky: Leningrad Philharmonic conductor who premiered most of Shostakovich's symphonies

Kurt Sanderling*: assistant to Mravinsky during the 1940s; later, conductor of the (East) Berlin Symphony Orchestra and a leading interpreter of Shostakovich symphonies

Dmitri Tsyganov, Vasily Shirinsky, Vadim Borisovsky, and Sergei
Shirinsky: original members of the Beethoven Quartet; Shostakovich's
old friends and collaborators

FROM A YOUNGER GENERATION

Galina Shirinskaya*, pianist: daughter and niece of original Beethoven
Quartet players
Olga Dombrovskaya*: curator of the Shostakovich archive and museum
in Moscow
Larissa Chirkova*: curator of the Shostakovich house museum in St.
Petersburg
Helga Landauer*: co-director of the film *A Journey of Dmitry Shostakovich*
Ignat Solzhenitsyn*, pianist and conductor: son of Aleksandr Solzhenitsyn

MEMBERS OF STRING QUARTET GROUPS WHO PLAYED SHOSTAKOVICH'S QUARTETS

BEETHOVEN QUARTET
Dmitri Tsyganov (first violin)
Vasily Shirinsky (second violin)—replaced by Nikolai Zabavnikov
Vadim Borisovsky (viola)—replaced by Fyodor Druzhinin
Sergei Shirinsky (cello)—replaced by Yevgeny Altman

BORODIN QUARTET
Rostislav Dubinsky (violin)
Yaroslav Alexandrov (violin)
Rudolf Barshai (viola)—replaced by Dmitri Shebalin
Valentin Berlinsky (cello)

FITZWILLIAM QUARTET
Christopher Rowland (violin)
Jonathan Sparey (violin)
Alan George (viola)
Ioan Davies (cello)

EMERSON QUARTET
Eugene Drucker* (violin)
Philip Setzer* (violin)
Lawrence Dutton (viola)
David Finckel (cello)

ALEXANDER QUARTET
Zakarias Grafilo (first violin)
Frederick Lifsitz* (second violin)
Paul Yarbrough (viola)
Sandy Wilson* (cello)

VERTIGO QUARTET
José Maria Blumenschein* (violin)
Johannes Dickbauer* (violin)
Lily Francis* (viola)
Nicholas Canellakis* (cello)

*interviewed for this book

⋛ I ⋚

Elegy

In him, there are great contradictions. In him, one quality
obliterates the other. It is conflict in the highest degree.
It is almost a catastrophe.

—MIKHAIL ZOSHCHENKO,
in a private letter about Shostakovich, 1941

I t is hard to say whether he was extraordinarily fortunate or
profoundly unlucky. Even he would probably have been
unable to decide, for in regard to his own situation and his
own character, he was often dubious and always divided. He was
a self-acknowledged coward who sometimes demonstrated great
courage. A born survivor, he was obsessed with death. He had an
excellent sense of humor and an equally strong streak of melancholy. Though reserved in outward demeanor and inclined to
long silences, he was subject to bouts of intense passion. Mentally and physically he tended to be either lightning fast or practically immobilized. He was both a generous man and an embit-
tered one. Immensely loyal to his friends, he was repeatedly

guilty of disloyalty to his own principles. He cared a great deal for words, and he signed his name to documents he had never read. He was a modernist who officially despised modernism. He was a baptized unbeliever with a strong affection for the Jews. As for his country, he both hated and loved it—and the mixed emotion was returned, it seems, for he became at different times a prominent beneficiary and a prominent victim of his nation's cultural regime. He was an essentially private person who lived out his existence on a public platform. He wrote music that pleased the many, and he wrote music for the very few: perhaps, finally, only for himself. We know a great deal about him, and he remains largely invisible to us.

In this last respect, Dmitri Shostakovich is like all subjects of artist biographies, only more so. You are drawn to the life because you love the art, and you imagine that knowing more about the life will bring you closer to the art, but for the most part the life is a smoke screen getting between you and the art. You pick up threads and clues, searching for a pattern that explains the whole, forgetting that a great deal of life (and art) depends on chance events. You can never definitively find the hidden springs of an artwork; you can only attempt to grasp the results as they gush forth, and with music, which is nearly as changeable and bodiless as water, that grasp will be especially tenuous.

Nevertheless, there is a desire to connect the human being who once lived to the still-living music, which seems to have a human voice behind it—*does* have a human voice behind it, if only one could hear it properly. For me, and I think for many other avid listeners, Shostakovich's own voice is most clearly audible in his fifteen string quartets. He became famous in his lifetime for the symphonies and operas, and it is through these larger-scale works that most people know his name today, but those are precisely the works of his that were most subject to interference by the Soviet authorities. The interference was internal as well as external: that is, Shostakovich often censored *himself*, distorting and suppressing his own talent in order to write the kinds of pieces that were demanded of him as a public artist. But nobody at the top of the Soviet Union's cultural hierarchy paid much attention to what he was doing in his smaller-scale, under-the-radar chamber music. So whereas the symphonies can be bombastic or overblown or afflicted with moments of bad faith, the quartets are amazingly pure and consistently appealing. Taken individually, each represents a major contribution to the string quartet literature; taken as a whole, they stand as one of the monuments of twentieth-century music. And as a key to Shostakovich's own preoccupations—as a kind of "diary" that records "the story of his soul," as his widow put it—they offer unparalleled access to the composer's inner life.

Musicians who play Shostakovich's string quartets can read that diary through the music: that is how they manage to perform the quartets, even if they know little or nothing about the composer's life. You can get the whole story from the fifteen quartets themselves, if you are alert enough. But I am not alert enough, and I am not a musician, so I have had to go about it backwards, by way of the life first and then the music. Only after learning something of the biography have I been able to hear what was there all along in the quartets.

When we nonmusicians listen to music, we respond with an awareness of logic and pattern and history, but also with our emotions and imaginations, and to put these responses into words is not an easy matter. In speaking about Shostakovich's quartets, I have sometimes borrowed from the languages of literary and art criticism, both of which have a stronger tradition of impressionistic response than one usually finds in academic music criticism. I have tried to remain faithful to the specific demands of music, which by its very nature is less imitative of reality, less "naturalistic" or "figurative" than literature or painting. Still, my approach to Shostakovich's music is essentially that of a writer, and this entails certain pitfalls. To hazard an interpretation, in the literary sense of the word, is to venture an opinion (some might even call it a guess) about what was intended or accomplished in a work of art. The line between correct interpretations and incorrect ones is bound to be fuzzy and inconstant; even the artist is not the ultimate authority in this regard, for he may well have given rise to something that is larger than his own intentions. (In fact, if he is a good artist, he has almost certainly done so.) But there *are* wrong interpretations, wrong assumptions, wrong pathways in approaching an artwork—or, for that matter, a life story. To say that opinions can vary is not to say that anything goes. And in dealing with Shostakovich it seems especially important to keep the known facts in mind at all times and to adhere to them, precisely because falsehood, dishonesty, and misrepresentation were such devastating issues in his life.

To uncover the truth about a dead artist is always difficult. Many things stand in the way: jealous colleagues who lie about their competitor to make him look worse; sycophantic followers who lie about their hero to make him look better; innocently inaccurate memories, which get the facts wrong and compound the myths; contemporary reviews, which are often silly and always subjective, then as now; and the artist's own secretiveness, or evasiveness, or simple inability to articulate what he is doing in his art. But to these normal layers of obfuscation, Shostakovich's case adds many more. Silence was at the heart of his enterprise. It is there in his music (which, especially toward the end, seemed to be pulling the notes out of a deep silence, or sending them back into it), and it is there in his personality (there are numerous stories about his sitting in silence, even in the company of friends), and it is there, most particularly, in the conditions of his twentieth-century Russian life. To speak, in those circumstances, was to betray, and to speak the truth was to betray oneself. Even private letters could be intercepted; even private words could be conveyed to the wrong ears. History got rewritten every few years, and no one was safe from the sudden switchbacks. So the wise kept their own counsel and didn't put anything down on paper, except nonsense and distractions. People learned to speak in code, but the codes themselves were ambiguous and incomplete. Nothing that emerged from that world (or perhaps, indeed, any world) can be taken at face value.

This is why the uproar over Solomon Volkov's *Testimony*—which purports to be the unmediated truth about Shostakovich's experiences and opinions, as told to Volkov by Shostakovich himself—is finally so pointless. Perhaps the controversy had some meaning when the book first appeared in 1979, with Shostakovich only a few years dead and the Soviet Union still alive; perhaps it seemed significant then that Shostakovich could say nasty things about Stalin, the Party, and the whole Soviet machine. After all, his *New York Times* obituary had described him as "a committed Communist," and though people within Russia might have been aware, even at the time, of his uncomfortable relationship to authority, no one on the outside spoke of it. But now we have numerous other kinds of evidence—the oral testimony of the composer's friends and relations, recently published letters to and from him, analogous instances in previously unprintable novels, stories, and poems, and our own increasingly informed sense of how life in that time was lived—to suggest that Shostakovich could never have been the placidly obedient Party apparatchik he was sometimes made to seem. So Volkov's central and rather doubtfully obtained revelation is no revelation at all. And, perhaps more importantly, nothing is gained by this sleight-of-hand effort to transform the reluctant public figure into a secret dissident, for the Volkov portrayal of a resentful, self-righteous Shostakovich is far less appealing and finally less persuasive than the tortured and self-torturing man it replaces.

As for the rest of the book, well, anyone who has ever read a bad transcription of a poorly conducted interview will recognize in *Testimony* the feeble efforts of the speaker's voice to make itself heard over the static generated by the interviewer's biases and preconceptions. Some elements of his own opinions do probably make it through, which is why we Shostakovich-seekers are all tempted to mine *Testimony* for the fragments that are personally useful to us. But we need to recognize that in doing so we are essentially choosing at random, with no certainty about the veracity of our selections. We could be quoting Shostakovich, or we could simply be quoting Volkov—a character straight out of Gogol or Dostoyevsky, rubbing his hands with oily fake-servitude as he announces proudly in the preface that Shostakovich called him "the most intelligent man of the new generation." Even this remark needs to be taken as coded (if indeed it was ever spoken at all), seen as a typically dark joke, similar to the one Shostakovich made annually when he offered as his New Year's toast, "Let's drink to this—that things don't get any better!"

Whatever I may have heard or known of Shostakovich's work in the period when he was alive—a period that overlapped with my childhood and youth—his music did not really come into focus for me until the third decade after his death. A dozen years had passed since the collapse of the Soviet Union, and I was living in Berlin, along with a substantial number of the USSR's former citizens, when Valery Gergiev and the Mariinsky Opera and Orchestra came to town in the autumn of 2003. On their performance schedule were several works by Soviet-era composers, including the Shostakovich opera *Lady Macbeth of the Mtsensk District*. I couldn't get tickets for *Lady Macbeth* (uncharacteristically for Berlin, it had sold out far in advance, mainly to the hordes of Russian immigrants), but I did manage to capture two good seats to a performance of Shostakovich's Fourth Symphony.

What I didn't understand at the time was how cunningly Gergiev had constructed his programs. *Lady Macbeth of the Mtsensk District* was Shostakovich's second (and, as it turned out, last) major work in operatic form; it was also the first piece to bring him widespread national attention. He was twenty-four when he began writing it—basing the plot on a story by Nikolai Leskov—and only twenty-seven when it premiered at Leningrad's Maly Opera Theater in January of 1934. The new opera, which received a nearly simultaneous Moscow premiere at the Nemirovich-Danchenko Theater, was so successful that within two years it had earned a couple of performances abroad, had been given a new production at the Bolshoi, and overall had appeared more than two hundred times in Moscow and Leningrad. Shostakovich had dedicated *Lady Macbeth* to his new bride, Nina Varzar, and he remained fond enough of its music to quote from a key aria in his "autobiographical" Eighth Quartet, written over a quarter century later.

But by that time *Lady Macbeth of the Mtsensk District* had come to be associated with one of the bleakest moments in Shostakovich's career. Throughout his twenties he had been a rapidly rising star, praised in all the journals and celebrated by all the official institutions, and *Lady Macbeth* seemed at first a continuation of that success. But in January of 1936 Iosif Vissario-novich Stalin unexpectedly attended one of the Moscow performances, and neither the Party leader nor any member of his entourage stayed to the end. Two days later an unsigned commentary called "Muddle Instead of Music" appeared in *Pravda*; some even said it was written by Stalin himself, and though that is probably untrue, it might as well have been, given its effects.

The article condemned *Lady Macbeth of the Mtsensk District* for its bourgeois formalism and its vulgar naturalism (two charges that would seem to be completely at odds, but consistency was never the hobgoblin of these particular little minds). It criticized the score for assaulting the audience with "a stream of sounds that is—by design—inharmonious and chaotic," and argued that if *Lady Macbeth* had been popular abroad, that was because "the opera's twitching, clamorous, neurotic music titillates the perverted tastes of bourgeois audiences." The critic also complained that "the music wheezes, groans, pants, and gasps for breath in order to present love scenes as naturalistically as possible. And 'love' is smeared all over the opera in the most vulgar manner." Above all, the writer was concerned that the "apolitical" *Lady Macbeth*, with its patent rejection of "simple, accessible musical speech," represented a dangerous move away from the stated goals of Socialist Realist art. Instead, "the ability of good music to grip the masses is sacrificed to petit-bourgeois formalism, which pretends to be original while merely indulging in cheap playacting. This is a game of unintelligibility that can end in tears," the article warned darkly.

When this bombshell fell, Shostakovich was a little over half-way through writing his Fourth Symphony. He completed it as he had intended to, without conceding anything to the *Pravda* critique, and it was scheduled for a first performance by the Leningrad Philharmonic on December 11, 1936. Shostakovich was well aware of the cloud that hung over him during this time: he had been publicly criticized by the Composers' Union, his popularity in the music-reviewing press had plummeted, and it was clear that he was no longer safe from the sudden political arrests that were beginning to impinge on his friends and family. But terrified as he was of the possible effects of the performance, he was still deeply dismayed when, shortly before the scheduled premiere, a high-ranking bureaucrat visited the Philharmonic building and urged the composer to withdraw his symphony. This he did (under what degree of pressure, we do not know), and the Symphony No. 4 in C Minor—an extremely ambitious, unconventional work that Shostakovich would later view with regretful longing as the beginning of a road not taken—remained unperformed until 1961, eight years after Stalin's death.

What Gergiev did, in his October 2003 performance in Berlin, was to pair this symphony with Prokofiev's *Cantata for the Twentieth Anniversary of the October Revolution*, another work composed in the same period, but a much more politically calculated one (though the calculation apparently didn't succeed: Prokofiev's piece, too, was rejected for being insufficiently conventional). Because I wasn't aware of the full history at the time, I didn't realize how carefully Gergiev had chosen and placed the symphony. It was the perfect pendant to the unfairly criticized *Lady Macbeth*, that other grandly inventive work Shostakovich had undertaken before his thirtieth birthday. And the Fourth Symphony, coming so close upon the heels of its predecessor, was marked by the knowledge of what had happened to the composer of *Lady Macbeth*; its final fade to nothingness signals a darker, gloomier perspective than anything *Pravda* could have found to criticize in the opera. The largely Russian audience in Berlin understood all this—understood exactly the game Gergiev was playing in his pairing of the pro-Lenin cantata with the banished Fourth Symphony. So whereas the Prokofiev vocal piece was greeted, that Berlin night, by a rather frightening chorus of politically inspired boos, the Shostakovich symphony's final silence was met with an equal silence on the part of the audience, and then with deafening applause.

I had taken in Shostakovich's music, and I had been moved by it, but I had not really understood what I had heard. Eventually I was to hear all the quartets—performed, in a concentrated five-concert series, by the Emerson Quartet—and, somewhat later, most of the symphonies. And then, in the spring of 2007, I attended a Brooklyn recital by the extremely young Vertigo Quartet. On the program was Shostakovich's Twelfth Quartet. As I listened to it and watched the musicians play, I found myself thinking back to the Emersons' program notes and recalling everything about Shostakovich's life that had been associated with this quartet. The second violin was absolutely silent for the first few minutes of the piece, and that, I remembered, was not only because the Twelfth was dedicated to the first violinist of the Beethoven Quartet (the group that had premiered all of Shostakovich's quartets from the Second onward), but also because the second violinist had died not long before; this was, in essence, his ghost sitting there. Much of the rest of the piece seemed to be about death, too. How was it that such young players could perform it so well? And how was it that I found this dark, difficult music welcoming and warm, rather than frightening or off-putting? It was something to do with how personal it felt—how much of Shostakovich's own voice could be heard behind the quartet, as it could not be in even the best of the symphonies. A secretive figure behind a public mask, he had chosen the string quartet, it seemed, as his vehicle of self-revelation. And what he was revealing was not just his own personality, but all the suffering, awareness, and shame that had come to him through his peculiar placement in history.

It would be an exaggeration to say that Shostakovich's quartets gave me my first real affection for twentieth-century music. But let us say that I was finally ready for the quartets at the moment they planted themselves in my life. I was prepared to listen to something that reflected, rather than alleviated, my own anxiety, and I was willing to learn from an artist who had lived through difficult times, both personally and politically. I was going through a difficult period myself in 2007, and so was my whole country. The sympathetic, glimmering melancholy I perceived in Shostakovich's quartets seemed to offer, if not an answer, at any rate a reasonable accompaniment.

It was the experience of his own dark times, I am convinced, that brought forth Shostakovich's string quartets. Before he became the master chronicler of despair, or desperation, or whatever the emotion is that agitates all the quartets, Shostakovich was a brilliant, excitable, successful, ambitious Soviet composer. There is nothing wrong with this. Even the First Symphony, composed when he was only seventeen or eighteen as his graduation exercise for the Leningrad Conservatory, shows how enormously talented Shostakovich was from the start. And there are undertones, even in this early work, of the anxious melancholic he was to become: it is not all sweetness and light, there in the First Symphony. But in this case the nervousness seems just another jazzy tool at his disposal, and the intimations of death lean toward the enjoyable grotesque rather than the unbearable truth. It was not until much later that these dark qualities were to move to the center of his personality, and of his music.

And that makes sense, for his early years seem, by Russian standards, to have been comparatively easy. His father, Dmitri Boleslavovich Shostakovich—a Russian of Polish descent—was an engineer employed by the Bureau of Weights and Standards; he was one of those rare people who did essentially the same work after the revolution as before, so the family's style of living did not change radically in 1917, except to the degree that all

St. Petersburg residents were faced with new difficulties and restrictions. Shostakovich's mother, Sofia Vasilyevna, had trained
as a musician at the St. Petersburg Conservatory, and though she
gave up her musical career to marry and raise a family, she made
sure, by giving the lessons herself, that each of her three children
learned the piano, and she also supervised Shostakovich's later
musical development. Both parents had grown up in Siberia,
and both had radical politics in their family pasts, as well as ac-
tivists, thinkers, writers, and artists among their intelligentsia
friends. So, to the extent that we can now untangle real history
from Party-line whitewash, it would seem that the Russian Revolution was largely a welcomed rather than a feared event in the
Shostakovich household. When the October/November revolution took place, Shostakovich, who had been born on September
25, 1906, was just over eleven years old.

At the time of the revolution, the family was living in a large
top-floor flat at 9 Nikolaevskaya Street (later renamed Marat
Street, or Ulitsa Marata in Russian). The five of them had moved
there in 1914 from the somewhat smaller apartment in which
Shostakovich had been born, just down the street at 16 Nikolaevskaya, and he himself was to remain in the 9 Marat apartment well into adulthood. He did not leave it, in fact, until
around the time of the *Lady Macbeth* premiere, in late 1933 or early
1934, and the twenty-year period he spent there was to prove the
longest time he ever lived anywhere in his life. Speaking in 2006 at
the opening of an informal Shostakovich Museum in this space,
the soprano Galina Vishnevskaya—who met Shostakovich much

later in his life, becoming close friends with him through her husband, the cellist Mstislav Rostropovich—commented about the 9 Marat flat: "I think that only here was he really happy."

Built to pre-war standards of comfort and elegance, the family home was significantly more attractive than most of his subsequent accommodations: the ceilings were high, the rooms spacious and pleasingly proportioned, with solid walls and old-fashioned moldings. The L-shaped apartment boasted seven rooms plus kitchen and bath, enough so that one small room could be allocated to a servant, another used as a study, and two assigned to the three children (Shostakovich, as the only boy, probably had his own bedroom). The dining room was grand but rather dark; the main reception room, however, was a large, nearly square space, beautifully lit in the daytime by tall windows facing out onto Marat, and at night by a large crystal chandelier. Flanked by two equally pleasant but much smaller rooms, this reception room was to remain the flat's long-term heart and soul: you can catch a glimpse of it in the 1931 photo taken after the premiere of Shostakovich's ballet *The Bolt*, when twenty-six people, including the composer, his mother, one of his two sisters, a famous short-story writer, a comparably famous music critic, and some soon-to-be-famous ballerinas (one of them draped across Shostakovich's lap), plus an assortment of other men and women, all crowded into the family flat to celebrate.

But by that time this grand room had become one of only three inhabited by Shostakovich's family. When he was fifteen—that is, in February of 1922—his father died suddenly of pneumonia, and the family was plunged into relative poverty. His mother had to go out to work for the first time in her life (she took a job as a cashier), and his older sister, Maria, gave piano lessons to supplement the family income. But even this was not enough to maintain the household at its former level. The servant was let go, and four of the original seven rooms were rented out to tenants, who then shared the kitchen and bathroom with the Shostakoviches. Only the reception room and the two adjoining rooms remained in the family's possession, which meant that Sofia Vasilyevna, her two daughters, her son, and a baby grand piano all had to occupy this formerly elegant, now cramped space.

Though Shostakovich was shocked and saddened by his father's unexpected death, most accounts suggest that he remained comparatively insulated: from emotional distress at the death itself, because he was able to find an outlet in music (he composed one of his earliest chamber pieces in memory of his father); and from the household's financial burden, because his mother insisted that he continue his studies at the Petrograd Conservatory and not go out to work. Even at this stage, Shostakovich was being treated as a cherished genius, and not only by his relentlessly overprotective mother. There are stories of faculty members at the Conservatory procuring extra government-subsidized food for this anemic, tubercular, highly promising young musician, and other tales of that sort.

But this story of relative insulation is countered by another story, one that Shostakovich told to a close friend much later in his life. Flora Litvinova, who met Shostakovich during the Second World War and remained friendly with him for decades, at one point tried to explain what she saw as his unusual degree of fearfulness and anxiety. "Where this fear sprang from originally I don't know," she said. "Once he spoke about the despair he experienced after his father's death, when he suddenly found himself alone in a hostile world. A frail boy, he had to shoulder the responsibility of caring for his mother and sisters." And it is true that Shostakovich did eventually have to take a job, as a piano player in three successive silent-movie houses on nearby Nevsky Prospect. Still, even this drudgery—comparable, in some respects, to Charles Dickens's equally short-lived and equally formative drudgery at the blacking factory—turned out not to be an unmitigated burden. The experience of playing along with, and at times improvising to, the juddery action of these early silents gave free rein to the narrative aspect of his musical imagination; it also allowed him a semi-public space in which to try out new compositions. And in any case that difficult period at the cinemas, which he deeply and vociferously resented, lasted less than two years.

From May of 1926, when the nineteen-year-old Shostakovich heard the premiere of his Symphony No. 1 in F Minor at Leningrad Symphony Hall, up to the sudden appearance of "Muddle Instead of Music" in January of 1936, fate seemed to be smiling on the young composer. By the time he was twenty-nine, he had collaborated with many of the most stimulating artists of his period, had composed two more symphonies that received respectful if forgettable premieres, and had written a great deal of ballet, film, and incidental theater music (including the score for the first performance of Vladimir Mayakovsky's *The Bedbug*, staged by Vsevolod Meyerhold in 1929). Prior to *Lady Macbeth*, he had completed one full opera—*The Nose*, with a libretto based on Gogol's story and a startlingly innovative score—and had begun work on one or two others. He had traveled outside the Soviet Union, to Warsaw and Berlin, and had met a number of international musical luminaries, including Darius Milhaud, Alban Berg, and Arthur Honegger. By his late twenties he had fallen deeply in love several times, engaging in serious affairs that spanned a number of years and often overlapped with each other. He had met, married, divorced, and then remarried the smart, attractive Nina Varzar, a scientist who came from an even more accomplished and artistic family than his own, and who was to provide the stalwart center of his life. He had a best friend, the brilliant scholar and critic Ivan Sollertinsky, from whom he was nearly inseparable, and a wide circle of friends and acquaintances in Leningrad and Moscow. In short, he was part of the exciting artistic ferment that marked the first decade or two of post-revolutionary Russia, and he was as comfortable in that world as he would ever be anywhere.

It may be useful to contrast this artistic existence with that of another twentieth-century figure, just a year older than Shosta-kovich, who was also from St. Petersburg. Alisa Rosenbaum—or Ayn Rand, as she was to become—was born in 1905, the child of a Jewish pharmacist. Her father's St. Petersburg business was confiscated by the Bolsheviks after the revolution, and though he moved his family to the Crimea and opened a new shop, that too was eventually taken over. In February of 1926 (around the same time Shostakovich was quitting his final movie-house job and preparing for the performance of his First Symphony), Ayn Rand took leave of her family, sailed to the United States, donned her new name, and moved to Hollywood. There she rapidly worked her way up from wardrobe assistant to author of screen-plays and plays. Eventually she was to write the grimly libertar-ian best-selling novels *The Fountainhead* and *Atlas Shrugged*, both of which celebrated rampant individualism and free-market capitalism over any kind of cooperative, collaborative, socialist ethic. The result of contemplating her own life story had been to make her not only a fierce anti-Communist, but a fierce oppo-nent of anything that seemed weak or modulated or in any way ambiguous. "Contradictions do not exist," says the tycoon hero of *Atlas Shrugged*, transparently a mouthpiece for his author's views. "Whenever you think that you are facing a contradiction, check your premises. You will find that one of them is wrong."

The life story that shaped Shostakovich's sensibility, on the other hand, was one in which contradictions were essential and unavoidable. One could be delighted by certain aspects of "pro-gram music" and filled with disgust at others, so that serving the needs of the clamoring audience was both a privilege and a chore. One could be a solitary composer and also a member of a collaborative group, and neither role necessarily excluded the other. One could be in love with two women at the same time; one could be grateful for but also annoyed at the excessive inter-ventions of a doting mother. One could thrill to the excitement of a revolutionary new political and artistic world, and one could also laugh mordantly at the shortcomings of that world, in a way that brought laughter very close to pain.

Mikhail Zoshchenko—the well-known writer who was present at the *Bolt* celebration, a man with whom Shostakovich played poker for a time, and whose writings he greatly admired—was perhaps the chief exemplar, in print, of this sort of painful laughter. He wrote short, witty, enormously popular pieces that were published mainly in periodical form throughout the 1920s and well into the 1930s. Reading his stories, we can still get a sense of the kind of wild, risky truth-telling that was possible in the pre-Stalinized Soviet Union. In "The Galosh," for instance (perhaps Zoshchenko's most famous story, and certainly one of his best), the unnamed narrator describes losing a single one of his pair of galoshes on the city tram. The galoshes are old and worn, but they are his only pair, so he really needs to get that second one back. He goes to the lost and found department of the tram company, where he learns that his galosh is indeed among the many that have been found and filed—but he can't get it back until he has a written statement from his landlord saying he has lost a galosh. Fearful of sticking his neck out, the landlord won't give the written statement until he receives a written request for it from the tram company, which in turn cannot initiate the action . . . and so on. Eventually, after overcoming enormous bureaucratic obstacles, the narrator manages to retrieve his single galosh, and then promptly loses the other.

The dark humor of the story lies not just in its Kafkaesque

depiction of the tiny individual lost amid the governmentally imposed regulations, but also in the antic, colloquial language of the narrator. It is an idiosyncratic, personal idiom, and as such it rings clearly against the ludicrous rigidities of the rule-defining vocabulary and sentence structure, so that the two kinds of language barely seem to have any functions in common. From the title itself (can there be a single galosh? not in English, at any rate), Zoshchenko's ear for the oddities of speech gives him an instantaneous way into the maze of Soviet life: the individual, flawed human versus the unyielding, insisting-on-its-own-perfection administrative machine; the expansive, conversational, somewhat hapless tone of the narrator heard in relation to the predigested pap of the governing rules. Neither of these two forms of language, as Zoshchenko reproduces them, sounds anything like standard "literary" speech: they are at once more realistic and less beautified than that, and contemporary Russian audiences responded with rueful delight to both recognizable idioms. What they were appreciating, above all, was Zoshchenko's ear for the false note—a crucial appendage for any Soviet artist with a grain of sense and humor.

In Shostakovich's case, the false notes were much more literal than that. He had a remarkable talent for detecting, even in the most unlikely circumstances, the sound of something going wrong in the music. There are many stories demonstrating this unusual ability of his, but I will offer only one, taken (as are many of my direct quotations) from Elizabeth Wilson's marvelous compendium of voices, *Shostakovich: A Life Remembered.* Here is an anecdote reported by the conductor Yevgeny Mravinsky, who worked closely with Shostakovich on almost all his symphonies from the Fifth to the Twelfth:

> We were rehearsing the Eighth Symphony. In the first movement, not long before the general climax, there is an episode in which the cor anglais has to go up quite high into the second octave. The cor anglais is doubled by the oboes and the cellos and is almost indistinguishable in the general sound of the orchestra. Taking this into consideration, the player decided to put his part down an octave, so as to save his lip for the important long solo which comes straight after the climax. It was almost impossible to hear the cor anglais amidst the overpowering noise of the orchestra and to expose the player's little trick. But suddenly, from behind me in the stalls, Shostakovich's voice rang out, "Why is the cor anglais playing an octave down?" We were all stunned. The orchestra stopped playing, and after a second of complete silence applause broke out.

That Shostakovich had an extremely delicate ear was never in doubt. But the surprising thing was how he used that ear. Like Zoshchenko, he used it to *create* the false note as well as to detect it. Shostakovich's music is filled with moments where a seemingly stable melody begins and then breaks down into dissonance, or where our expectations have been set up to hear a particular turn of phrase and instead we get something very slightly off from that. Even Mravinsky could be fooled by this, as the violinist Yakov Milkis makes clear in his story about another rehearsal:

> In the break Mravinsky turned round to us and said, "Do you know, I have the impression that in this place Dmitri Dmitriyevich has omitted something; there's a discrepancy between the harmonies of these chords as they appear here and where they appear elsewhere . . ."

Just at this moment, Dmitri Dmitriyevich himself came up to Mravinsky, who put the question to him without further ado. Dmitri Dmitriyevich glanced at the score: "Oh dear, what a terrible omission; what an error I have committed. But you know what, let's leave it as it is, just let things stay as they are." We then understood that this "error" was deliberate.

A great deal of Shostakovich's manner and style is displayed in this anecdote. There is the doubleness, the irony, whereby he says one thing ("Oh dear, what a terrible omission") and at the same time lets his listeners know that the opposite is the case. There is politeness in his response, but there is also firm resistance. And then there is the musical method itself—the deliberate "error," confounding the ear of the listener and making him doubt his own expectations.

Even the author of "Muddle Instead of Music" could hear this, though he interpreted it as a flaw rather than a method. "If once in a while the composer accidentally stumbles upon a simple, comprehensible melody," the anonymous *Pravda* critic complained, "then immediately, as if frightened by the prospect, he throws himself into dense thickets of musical chaos, at times the purest cacophony." This was vastly overstated, of course, but the perceptions were not completely wrong, though what was made of them turned out to be dangerously wrongheaded.

Shostakovich may have believed at first that he could ignore the threat contained in that *Pravda* article. In the end, though, he was compelled to submit to it. The lesson of the Fourth Symphony had been too much for him. By the time he withdrew it, in December of 1936, he had become a man with a family: his and Nina's first child, a daughter named Galina, had been born in May. He was no longer the coddled son in his mother's elegant (if reduced) apartment. Now he and Nina had their own place in a far less convenient and luxurious part of town, north of the Neva on Kirovsky Prospect, and for the first time in his life he was wholly responsible for the rent. That he occasionally had trouble meeting this responsibility, due mainly to his frequent and excessive gambling, is signaled by the fact that his mother had to arrange the sale of his piano to her friend Klavdia Shulzhenko, sometime after he and Nina moved to the Kirovsky apartment, so as to pay off his gambling debts. But by late December of 1936, Shostakovich's problems were more than just financial. What was at stake, in the ominous threats to his career, was not just his livelihood but his life.

The choice must have been a terrifying one: stop writing music entirely, or try to write in a way that would not alienate the public authorities. By 1936, leaving the country legally was no longer possible, as it had been for earlier émigrés like Prokofiev and Stravinsky; and illegal defection, which would have put his wife and young daughter at risk, was not an option for Shostakovich. Even during the years when emigration had been allowed, he had been an unlikely candidate for it, in part because of his own deep attachment to the Russian landscape and the Russian language. Besides, it was not at all clear that he could make a living as a composer outside of Russia. Everything about the way he had learned to practice his art, including the method of its financial support, was peculiar to the Soviet environment. So the choice was narrowed to silence or capitulation. And again, that kind of silence was never a real possibility for him. If he was not a composer, he was nothing.

The decision was not just about self-preservation, not, at least, in the sense we usually mean the word "self." There was also the matter of an artist's responsibility toward his work. This notion had a Soviet meaning, and that may have weighed with Shostakovich too, but I suspect he also thought about the idea in a larger, older context. The parable of the buried talents, though it was not attributed to the New Testament in Russia's post-revolutionary curriculum, had already entered the language sufficiently to become a colloquialism, and besides, Shostakovich "knew his Bible," as his friend Isaak Glikman tells us. In any case, the biblical tale's point—that it is wrong to hide or withhold your gifts instead of using them—would have been instinctively apparent to any true artist, religiously educated or not. Shostakovich already, at the age of thirty, knew himself to be a significantly original composer; he knew, in other words, that he was capable of producing valuable, lasting work that was unlike anyone else's. This knowledge entailed certain obligations (one might even call them ethical obligations), and one of these was that he try as hard as possible to keep writing music. It would have been pretentious and morally dubious of him to have used this argument in self-defense, and he never did so, but I am invoking it on his behalf.

Among the many things he was trying not to betray (this, too, not always successfully) was his talent.

He must have imagined that he could obey the rules and at the same time reserve something of himself, so that his essential core would remain unaltered despite the outward show. In this he proved to be both correct and incorrect. Shostakovich the artist survived the experience of having his arm twisted and went on to become a great composer with a distinctive voice of his own. But it was never exactly the same voice that it had been before. "You ask if I would have been different without 'Party guidance'?" he reportedly said to Flora Litvinova during their last conversation, a few years before his death. "Yes, almost certainly. No doubt the line that I was pursuing when I wrote the Fourth Symphony would have been stronger and sharper in my work. I would have displayed more brilliance, used more sarcasm, I could have revealed my ideas more openly instead of resorting to camouflage; I would have written more pure music."

But it was, in fact, the "pure music" of the quartets that ultimately emerged from this forge of repression. And in typical Shostakovich fashion, it was the experience of success, rather than the experience of failure, that made him realize how severely he had been repressed.

During the four months that followed the December non-premiere of the Fourth Symphony, the composer wrote virtually no serious music. The only exception was a set of *Four Romances on Texts by Pushkin* for bass voice and piano, which he considered so chancy that, after playing them for a few listeners, he

stuffed them in a drawer for many years. Shostakovich was suffering tremendous anxiety during this period: he was rightly
convinced that he could be detained and possibly even killed at
any moment. His sister, brother-in-law, and mother-in-law had
all been arrested or exiled (or both) by the spring of 1937, and he
himself had been questioned and nearly arrested—the only
thing preventing his detention being the sudden arrest of his
interrogator. These were hardly the ideal conditions under which
to produce a reputation-restoring work.

But in late April of 1937 he began work on the Fifth Symphony, and by the end of the summer he was done with it. It was
perceived by contemporaries, and in fact described by Shostakovich, as a much more conventional work than the Fourth, with
four movements culminating in a rousing Finale "*fortissimo* and
in the major," as the composer put it. The Largo movement had
enormous emotional appeal in a register that might, perhaps,
have been taken as too gloomy; and there were one or two ec-
centricities hidden elsewhere in the piece, such as an allusion to
the married surname of a recent girlfriend (she had married a
man named Karmen, so Shostakovich quoted from Bizet), or an
even more obscure reference to the as-yet-unheard *Four Romances*. But these were just Shostakovich's minor gestures in
the direction of a private language. Outwardly the Fifth was a
straightforward work in the symphonic tradition, sufficiently
melodious to please the Soviet critics, and carrying a program
note that described the implied narrative as "a lengthy spiritual
battle, crowned by victory."

The symphony received its late-fall premiere from the Leningrad Philharmonic, performing under the baton of Yevgeny Mravinsky. A young and practically unknown conductor at the time, Mravinsky had worked for months with Shostakovich, trying to get him to define everything from the intention behind particular passages to the precise tempo of whole movements. He found the composer distinctly unforthcoming in response to his direct questions, but he learned to use indirection to get the answers he needed, and in the end they arrived at a performance they could both be pleased with.

On November 21, 1937, the large, airy, elegantly columned Leningrad Philharmonic concert hall was packed for the premiere. Besides the excited throng that took up every seat on the slightly raked main floor, there were people filling the benches along the sides and peering down from the upper-level galleries. When the symphony ended, the crowd erupted into wild and unabating applause, at which point Mravinsky raised the score above his head and waved it as a salute to the composer. During the ensuing half-hour standing ovation, Shostakovich was called repeatedly to the stage. In fact, his friends were so worried that this spontaneous outpouring of support might be taken as a political demonstration that they hustled the victorious composer out of the building before the energetic clapping had completely died down.

The critical response was a little slower in coming, mainly because Shostakovich had been such a non-person for so many months that no one was willing to speak before the official verdict was known. At first there was some attempt by a couple of

Party nudniks to get the Leningrad premiere declared a fake victory, on the grounds that the applause was engineered by a pro-Shostakovich claque brought in from Moscow. But this demonstrably false rumor failed to take root, and in the end the positive reviews began to appear. The Symphony No. 5 in D Minor was declared a triumph of Socialist Realism, written in a vein that everyone in the Soviet Union could appreciate, with a clear narrative line showing the "formation of a personality"; and Shostakovich, in turn, was restored to his stature as a highly respected, politically approved composer. He even went along with the emerging theories about the work, describing it as a partially autobiographical symphony about "the suffering of man, and all-conquering optimism." And though he muttered a bit in private ("I wonder, what would they be saying if I had finished it *pianissimo* and in the minor?"), he seemed glad enough that the sword had been lifted from over his head.

Not everyone was enthusiastic about the Fifth Symphony. Prokofiev, in a friendly note to Shostakovich written some months after the premiere, celebrated the arrival of a "real and fresh piece of music" but felt that it was being praised for the wrong virtues. The exiled poet Osip Mandelstam—who illegally spent the night in Moscow, risking his soon-to-be-ended life, in order to hear Shostakovich's latest work—labeled it "tedious intimidation." And Ivan Sollertinsky, Shostakovich's best friend and most trusted adviser, reportedly felt that the new symphony had been cobbled together out of the "waste matter" of the Fourth. The fact that the Fifth Symphony was and remained one of Shostakovich's best-loved pieces would not have prevented the composer from feeling this criticism keenly.

Or from generating it himself. From this point in his career onward, it is never entirely clear what he thought about the works he was producing. There was the public statement about the music, and then there was the music itself, and if they didn't entirely fit together, that was not his concern. He did his best to cover his tracks, allowing other people to develop their own theories about what the music meant, and if those theories served the Soviet authorities' purposes, so much the better for his own sense of personal safety. For instance, a journalist came up with a tagline for the Fifth Symphony—"the practical creative answer of a Soviet artist to just criticism"—which stuck with the piece forever, so much so that it was taken by many people to be the subtitle Shostakovich himself had given to the work; and though Shostakovich had not originated this phrase, he made no efforts to disown it or to dissociate it from the symphony. On the contrary: he learned from this success how to have other, similar successes, complete with misleading taglines and ostensibly patriotic subjects, for almost all his subsequent symphonies until the Thirteenth.

And yet it must have broken something in him, for he did not compose anything, except a bit of incidental music for theater and film, for nearly a year following the completion of the Fifth. Shostakovich was an active, indeed antic, personality, and it was completely out of character for him to lie fallow for so long; he rarely did it again, even when he was old and ill. Perhaps the immediate relief of the successful premiere accounted for some of the pause—that is, he was probably worn out, and the release of tension could well have caused him to collapse into exhaustion.

But even that phase had to come to an end, and life had to move on somehow. On May 10, 1938, Shostakovich's second child, a son named Maxim, was born. And later that same month—on the morning of his daughter's second birthday, to be exact—he began work on his First String Quartet.

≥ 2 ≤

Serenade

Shostakovich's bust is Slonim's best work. However, the then
chairman of the Committee for the Arts wasn't pleased with it.
"What we need is an optimistic Shostakovich." Shostakovich
was fond of repeating this phrase.

—TATIANA LITVINOVA,
in *Shostakovich: A Life Remembered*

Having children of your own causes you to recall the
child you once were. Shostakovich was no different
from other parents in this respect, and Maxim's birth
would have been especially likely to remind him of his own
childhood, for with the addition of this infant son, the composer's family took on exactly the contours of the September
1906 household in which Dmitri Boleslavovich, Sofia Vasilyevna, and their first daughter, Maria, greeted the arrival of the
newborn Dmitri (or "Mitya," as he was called for short). But
even without this perceived parallel—which could well have remained unconscious—Shostakovich's thoughts in May of 1938
would naturally have returned to his own earliest years.

The documentary evidence about what those memories might have been is scanty and mostly suspect. In 1966, for instance, an article called "Autobiography" was published under Shostakovich's name in the journal *Sovetskaya muzyka*. It is not clear that any of it is true, or even that Shostakovich wrote it. (He was in the habit of getting friends, particularly the devoted and obliging Isaak Glikman, to fulfill such tedious assignments for him.) Still, the material is too tempting to leave aside, especially when Shostakovich refers to his earliest musical memories.

"Until I started to play the piano," he says, "I had no desire to learn, although I did show a certain interest in music. When our neighbors played quartets I would put my ear to the wall and listen." So at the heart of one of his crucial childhood memories lies the music of a string quartet. In the pre-revolutionary Russia into which Shostakovich was born and to which this memory dated back, the amateur performance of string quartets at home would have been an accepted feature of life in certain bourgeois households, just as it was in Europe. By the time Shostakovich recalled this event, however, such private chamber music performances would have become so rare as to be almost nonexistent, in part because of the space limitations of Soviet life.

This early musical memory was also, quite pointedly, a memory about eavesdropping. Listening through walls, spying through keyholes, peeking through windows—for the adult Shostakovich, as for all Eastern Europeans of his era, these were to become terrifying, life-destroying tactics. But to a child, eavesdropping means something else entirely. It is his primary method of gaining access to the mysterious adult world that surrounds and controls him. It is a way of participating while also remaining passive and indeed hidden. It is how he learns about what adults do, and therefore about what he himself might someday want to do. Concealed in that small body, beneath the attention of most adults, the child is perfectly designed for this secretive work, this curiosity-fulfilling task, this pleasurable act of eavesdropping. Even to know that he is excluded from the observed activity affords part of the strange thrill, for it reinforces his sense that he is special, and solitary—a rare pleasure for a second child, particularly in the crowded conditions of urban family life.

One of the few other stories we have about music in Shostakovich's childhood also hinges on the idea of secret observation, though here it entails peeking rather than eavesdropping. The memory comes from Shostakovich's aunt Nadezhda, his mother's sister. She dates it to 1916, but it probably took place in 1915, when Shostakovich, at the age of nearly nine, had just started to take piano lessons with his mother. Victor Seroff, who interviewed Shostakovich's family members when he wrote the first English-language biography of the composer in 1943, reports that

> Nadejda remembers very well the first time Mitya improvised for her. He sat down at the piano one evening and, with an absorbed expression on his handsome little face, started to make up a story.
>
> "Here is a snow-covered village far away"—a run and the beginning of a little tune accompanied his words—"moonlight is shining on the empty road—here is a little house lit by a candle"—Mitya played his tune and then, looking slyly over the top of the

piano, he suddenly flicked a high note in the treble—"Somebody peeks in the window."

To be on the outside, and yet to enjoy vicariously the intimacy of a cozy, candlelit family life; to have the melancholy pleasures of solitude as well as the warmer engagement with a connected group of people; to go to the hiding place deep within oneself, and at the same time to escape oneself entirely: these are among the rewards that the string quartet was to bring to Shostakovich, even at the very beginning. Many years later he was to say of the First String Quartet, "I tried to convey in it images of childhood, somewhat naive, bright, springlike moods." But naive and spring-like did not come easily to Shostakovich. He had to pare down his naturally resonant, emphatic, dark-toned symphonic style to an almost unrecognizable point to get to that childlike simplic-ity. And even then, the brightness and joy were not immediately apparent.

The String Quartet No. 1 in C Major—that simplest, most un-adorned of keys, which uses only the piano's white notes—starts with a slow-paced Moderato movement that is quiet, diffident, almost fearful in its tentativeness. The diffidence is not just that of a composer new to a form; melodically and rhythmically, this whole movement evokes a sense of shyness, novelty, and hesi-tant emergence, like that of a solitary child exploring a strange, new place. The rhythm skips and hops, changing its mind about whether it wants to move forward at a regular pace or dawdle in the shadows. And the melody itself is hardly the direct, cheerful sound we might expect from the key of C. This is a major key made to sound darker and more unsettled, a trick accomplished partly through the frequent insertion of those habitual "wrong" notes: for instance, a sharp or flat where our ear has been led by the previous measures to expect the unmodified natural, which in turn produces a mood of deflation or slight depression. Shostakovich alleged at the time that this quartet was meant to be "joyful, merry, lyrical," and one can almost hear the laughs in a series of chortle-like arpeggios, but they have more the tone of a wizard's scary cackle than a child's delighted one. If there is a fairy-tale feeling behind this quartet, it is as much the dark story of a small boy wandering alone in a forest—perhaps while "moonlight is shining on the empty road"—as it is the kind of tale that has a happy ending.

(I realize that to talk about a "tale" at all, in regard to these clearly plotless works, is to do some violence to Shostakovich's freedom as a composer. The quartets, after all, were a way for him to get away from storytelling program music and politically meaningful symphonies. Very little that he ever wrote was closer to "pure music," in the sense of being free from the daily require- ments and risks of verbal significance. And yet Shostakovich's narrative impulse was so strong, and his connection to fiction, drama, and other forms of literature so profound, that one can't help hearing elements of plot even in these works. All his life he was to comment that many of his best, most perceptive reviews came not from the official musicologists and music critics but from writers. He was deeply attached to Russian literature, of the past as well as of his own time, and his mind was filled with long, memorized passages, page after page of Chekhov or Gogol or Zoshchenko, which he could unfurl at appropriate moments. It would hardly be surprising to find that some of these fictional, dramatic elements had invaded even his purest musical compositions. So when I occasionally imagine story lines behind parts of the quartets, I hope I am not just imposing my own sensibility, but that I am also answering to something in the music itself: that is, a pressure toward meaning, a pressure of an almost literary kind.)

The Quartet in C Major's second movement begins with a viola solo—a haunting, enticing tune, slightly plaintive and melancholy in the way that many Russian folk songs tend to be. The melody, which eventually moves to the first violin, culminates in a moment of actual cheer: a sequence of triplets, mainly carried by the higher strings, that sing out in a fluid, soaringly dancelike manner. This small outburst is truly a case of optimistic Shostakovich, with nothing forced or ironic behind it, as if the clouds had briefly parted to reveal the quietly gorgeous late-afternoon sun. But, perhaps because it is so brief, the moment fails to reassure, and—after a short series of irregular, harsh, disruptive notes—we are returned to the original haunting tune, played, as at the beginning, on the viola. This time the voice is not completely alone, for it is accompanied by regular pizzicato beats on both the higher and lower instruments. Rather than making us feel, though, that the solitary traveler has been joined by other people, this rhythmic accompaniment suggests something else— perhaps that the lone human figure, whistling to himself in the dark, has suddenly become inordinately aware of the hollow sounds of his own footsteps and heartbeat.

The pace of the last two movements is faster but not necessarily any cheerier. At the beginning of the third movement, a seemingly endless series of repeated notes on the viola turns that instrument from a voice into a mere source of rhythm—capturing it and imprisoning it, so to speak, while the second violin and then the first alternately take up the new melody. The feeling is as much agitation as excitement, as if someone had been given all the freedom in the world to dance as he wished, but none to get away. That equivocal lightness persists in the final Allegro movement, where the cheerful melody is now carried by the first violin. This is definitely the most "positive" of the four movements, but—in contrast to the purely lyrical triplet passage that came earlier—this optimism has a slightly manic, forced quality. I would not go so far as to call the mood cynical, but there is something working underneath the skittery melody (perhaps, among other things, the rather martial 2/2 meter) that pulls the last movement in the direction of anxiety. This feeling rises to the surface when the harsh bow strokes that were later to become a Shostakovich trademark make their first brief but startling appearance. If this is spring, it is not without its thunderstorms.

And though the First Quartet ends emphatically, rather than

with the dying-out notes that close its first three movements, that too may have been a kind of whistling in the dark. Certainly Shostakovich did not always foresee the piece ending on an upbeat note. "In the process of composition I regrouped midstream," he wrote to his friend Sollertinsky shortly after finishing this quartet. "The first movement became the last, the last first. Four movements, in all. It didn't turn out particularly well. But, you know, it's hard to compose well. One has to know how."

That is to say, at the age of thirty-one he had purposely returned himself to a condition of not knowing how—a condition alien to him since at least his late teens—by choosing a medium that was unfamiliar to him. He was looking for a clean slate, but if he was to achieve this radical renewal, he couldn't make things easy on himself: "After all, the quartet is one of the most difficult musical genres," he noted at the time. And if the bare, revealing string quartet was difficult in itself, Shostakovich used it in a way that offered even less room than usual for the composer to hide his faults. He opted for a medium that was already self-exposing and then he made it more so, by stripping down the nineteenth-century luxuriant sonority of the string quartet (as used by Brahms, for instance) to something much starker and sparer, rather in the way the visual artists of his youth—Kazimir Malevich, El Lissitzky, and others—had stripped down painting to its most basic geometric forms. That in choosing the string quartet he was throwing himself into competition with giants like Haydn, Mozart, Schubert, and Beethoven could not have made the trial any easier. But what began as a tentative new venture, something that could be tossed away unfinished if it didn't work out, "captivated" him, and he completed the quartet in less than two months.

He could not have been as dissatisfied with the results as he professed to Sollertinsky, because he allowed the piece to be premiered in Leningrad by the Glazunov Quartet on October 10, 1938. Perhaps because it was his first foray into a new genre, or perhaps because he was the recently reconstituted hero of the Fifth Symphony, even this small chamber piece, conceived in part as a way of getting him out of the limelight, received a great deal of attention. But this time the attention was all positive. The official critics, apparently, were soothed by the joyful-spring label, not to mention the seemingly untroubled key of C major. And the audience response was utterly warm and enthusiastic, so much so that when the Beethoven Quartet gave the Moscow premiere that November, the musicians had to play the entire quartet over again as an encore.

If the string quartet gave Shostakovich a route back to his childhood, it also offered him an escape from his previous musical history. He had been a noted concert pianist since his teens and a regular performer of his own Piano Concerto No. 1 since its 1933 premiere. Aside from a very early composition for string octet, his op. 11 from 1924—and, among the non-opus-number-worthy, a couple of arrangements of pre-existing material that he produced for the Vuillaume Quartet in 1932—all of his previous chamber works had included the piano. In choosing to embark on a string quartet, he had temporarily abandoned his own instrument in favor of three he couldn't play. The fact that the violin, the viola, and the cello were not Shostakovich's instruments may have had something to do with the childlike simplicity of the First Quartet: that is, not having worked closely with a string quartet group before, he might have felt a bit uncertain about the musicians' and instruments' capacities and strengths. (In later years he was to question individual members of the Beethoven Quartet and other performers about whether a given passage was too fast or too complicated for their particular instrument, and, thanks in part to his early and well-learned lessons in instrumentation, he would almost always be told that it was not. Even toward the end of his life, when he was writing his most complicated and personal quartets, he reportedly asked the string players whether a particular passage was too difficult to play—to which the violist Fyodor Druzhinin responded, "You should write whatever you want; our business is to play it.")

Perhaps more significantly, the switch to the string quartet meant that he was setting aside the vast universe of the symphony for a more limited world inhabited by four equal players, and in doing so he was entering a kind of metaphorical democracy. If the full orchestra can be seen as a mass society in which the performers risk losing their individuality, while the solo recital represents an essentially narcissistic arrangement, then the string quartet might be viewed as an ideal society in which the musicians look to each other for guidance. By eliminating the massive and hierarchical orchestral structure, Shostakovich was attaining a measure of practical relief—from the need to rehearse in a large, public space, with intrusive questions flung at him by a conductor and with every move potentially watched by interfering officials—but he may also have been pursuing a symbolic goal as well. As a totem placed in front of the musicians and granted the power to order them all around, the conductor might possibly have struck the erstwhile persecuted, lately pardoned Shostakovich as a figure altogether too much in the Stalin mode. And if the Athenian democracy represented by the string quartet was an impractical model that could never exist in the real world of politics . . . well, so much the more reason for Shostakovich to seek it out in his private life, and in his music.

It's true that in the eighteenth century, early in the history of the string quartet's development, the four-member ensemble was dominated by the first violin, the in-house leader to whom the other players were expected to look for signals about starts, stops, sudden rhythmic changes, and so on. And it was also the first violin, in Haydn's newly invented medium, whose voice led the music, carrying the highest or most noticeable melody. But even Haydn began to vary this formula in his later quartets, and as the string quartet came into Mozart's hands, the pattern was already changing. By the time of Beethoven's late, great quartets, the structure had broken wide open, and the leading voice could as easily be a viola or a cello as a violin.

What Beethoven had taken to an extreme in his last quartets—that is, the strange alternations of sound and silence, harshness and melody—Shostakovich picked up and began to use for himself. In a Shostakovich quartet (and this is already true for the

Quartet No. 1), some of the instruments may sit silent for lengthy periods while just one or two others play. Moods shift quickly, and tempos and even keys seem to change from measure to measure. What's more, the obsessive repetition, expressive pizzicato, and harsh multiple-string bowing all work to eliminate the old-fashioned distinction (one that was already breaking down in the nineteenth century) between melody-carrying and rhythm-carrying voices. Even in this earliest of his ventures into the medium, Shostakovich was working toward a new sound for string quartets, one that did not fit at all neatly into the officially sanctioned "simple and popular music language accessible to all." But like a young child managing to eavesdrop unseen, he was doing it unobtrusively, in a genre that was too unimportant and too small-scale to bother about.

From the modern perspective, the First Quartet is generally seen as the weakest link in the chain of fifteen quartets. Critics tend to view it as a mere forerunner of what was to come, a not-yet-Shostakovich work signaling his transition to a new genre. And it is true that, despite its evident charms, the First does not have quite the complexity or idiosyncrasy of the later quartets. Still, the Quartet in C Major sounds more like Shostakovich than it does like anyone else. Even in this simplified form, we can hear his distinctive voice, and if we had never received any other quartets from Shostakovich, we would still cherish this one as something quite special.

For the next six years, from 1938 to 1944, Shostakovich didn't produce another quartet. These were very busy years in the composer's life, and they also included the war years, which meant that he was suffering major disruptions and deprivations during that time (though not to the extent that the average Russian did, for Shostakovich was already in a special category). But neither the activity nor the distraction sufficiently accounts for his failure to return to the string quartet. It was more, I think, that he had nothing to say in that medium, for the present—nothing that he needed to express in that intimate, collusive, slightly alienated, extremely private genre. He had successfully written one quartet, but that didn't necessarily mean he would ever try any more.

Actually, he did make one foray into a similar venture quite soon after completing the First Quartet. In 1940 Shostakovich and the four members of the Beethoven Quartet premiered his Piano Quintet in G Minor—a quartet, as it were, with a fifth role for himself written into it. The Piano Quintet is a manifestly thrilling piece of music, and it won the Stalin Prize for its year (two completely unrelated facts, but both no doubt encouraging to the composer). Still, it does not really lead into or out of the fifteen real quartets, in that it mostly avoids the introverted, private-language feeling of the quartet cycle. Aside from the second movement, which begins as a very quiet, mournful solo and then turns into a subdued duet, the Piano Quintet shows Shostakovich in a more public, performing-for-an-audience, self-conscious guise than the compositions for string quartet alone. It is as if the very presence of the piano—or perhaps the presence of the composer himself *on* the piano—changed this from a mainly interior to a primarily outward-looking work.

Certainly Shostakovich's motive in writing it was outward-looking, or so he alleged in a conversation he had at that time with his friend Isaak Glikman, as reported by Glikman himself. "Do you know why I wrote a piano part into the quartet?" Shostakovich said to him. "I did it so that I could play it myself and have a reason to go on tour to different towns and places. So now the Glazunovs and Beethovens, who get to go everywhere, will have to take me with them, and I will get my chance to see the world as well."

At this Glikman and Shostakovich both burst out laughing, and then Glikman said, "You're not serious?" To which Shostakovich responded, "Absolutely! You're a dyed-in-the-wool stay-at-home, but I'm a dyed-in-the-wool wanderer." ("It was hard to tell from the expression on his face if he were serious or not," Glikman adds.)

That conversation took place in the summer of 1940, and within a year nobody was wandering anywhere, because the Germans had invaded the Soviet Union, and Leningrad was under siege. For quite a while—for much longer than his friends, his colleagues, and the authorities deemed advisable—Shostakovich stuck it out in Leningrad, refusing to leave his native city and evacuate to safety. Eventually, though, he and his immediate family were sent to Kuibyshev (also known as Samara), a southeastern city where a number of Party officials and many of the nation's cultural eminences waited out the war. Glikman got evacuated even farther, to Tashkent, and Sollertinsky was sent to Novosibirsk with the Leningrad Philharmonic, to which he was the musical adviser. So in addition to the other wartime problems of a displaced person—that is, long uncomfortable train rides to unknown places, lost or abandoned possessions, extremely cramped housing with no room for privacy, and so forth—Shostakovich was subjected to the absence of his closest friends; and indeed this, more than anything else, was what he complained about during the war.

Initially Shostakovich, Nina, and the two children were assigned a single room in Kuibyshev, just as all the other families were. Soon, however, they were upgraded to two rooms, one of them containing a piano, and it was in this precious second room that he proceeded to finish his Seventh Symphony. His Sixth Symphony may have failed to win him any useful degree of official approval (it had been severely criticized, after its late-1939 premiere, for its backsliding inaccessibility), but Shostakovich was still the great hope of the Soviet composing industry, and the powers that be were determined to continue stoking the system until he yielded up the desired results.

This he did in late 1941, in the form of the "Leningrad" Symphony, which is how the Seventh almost immediately became known: and "known" is the operative word here. No single work by Shostakovich—no piece of music by anyone in the world, during that time—was listened to by more people with more intense emotion than the Leningrad Symphony in its wartime performances. The circumstances were the stuff of legend, with scores being flown behind the lines, soldier-musicians assembled from the front, and war-ravaged civilians gathering bravely together in makeshift concert halls just to hear this one inspiring composition. In a public relations move that made the composer the Soviets' most valuable international export (and gave him, one presumes, several extra years of privilege and protection), the Leningrad Symphony was even broadcast on the NBC Radio Network in America, under the baton of Arturo Toscanini. The week before it went out over the airwaves, in July of 1942, *Time* magazine featured Shostakovich on its cover, portraying him as a heroic figure in a fireman's helmet (an outfit he had worn during his brief Leningrad period of voluntary service, before he was evacuated). Within the USSR, after its initial March 5 performance in Kuibyshev, the symphony was played in every town and city that could muster the necessary number of musicians, nowhere more movingly than in besieged Leningrad itself, where the concert was a powerful symbol of resistance as well as a real consolation to its listeners.

Shostakovich had every right to be proud of his achievement, and he might well have been moved by the nationwide flood of enthusiasm and approval that washed over him as a result. He must also have been pleased with the symphony's practical effects, not only on the spirits of his compatriots but also on his own family's well-being. His mother, sister, and nephew were finally evacuated from Leningrad to Kuibyshev during the early rehearsals of the Seventh Symphony, and his in-laws followed soon after. That the composer now had a whole brood of Shostakoviches and Varzars to support would not have been as daunting as the anxiety of worrying about their fates. Nor did he (or anyone else, as far as I know) ever voice the suspicion that these relatives had been held hostage until he had produced the requisite masterpiece. The flow of power and privilege and disaster and deprivation was too erratic, in the wartime Soviet Union, for such calculation to seem likely.

If anything, Shostakovich would have felt complicatedly guilty at how well he was being treated. It was good to have enough room in which to compose, and enough food for his extended family, not to mention the travel privileges that allowed him to go to Moscow, Novosibirsk, and elsewhere for performances of the Seventh. But it was also painful for him to feel the differences between his position and that of others, as he did whenever he sought to help his friends. Of the many stories about Shostakovich's legendary generosity, what follows is a fairly representative example.

The sculptor Ilya Slonim, his wife, Tatiana Litvinova, and her sister-in-law Flora Litvinova had all been evacuated to Kuibyshev from Moscow, and there they became very friendly with the Shostakoviches, who lived right below them in the same apartment building. Early in their acquaintance, Slonim asked if he could sculpt a bust of Shostakovich, and the composer readily agreed, arriving promptly at eleven every morning for the sittings. "My husband and I were in love with Shostakovich," Tatiana Litvinova later said. "Between his daily sittings we talked only about him." But after only four or five of these sittings,

Slonim informed Shostakovich that they would not be able to meet again: he'd been told to report to the recruiting office the very next day, there to be sent to the front. "Dmitri Dmitriyevich didn't seem to react to my husband's announcement in any way," Tatiana went on.

> But an hour later he came back and asked "Ilya Lvovich, do you need any money?" We were touched. But what followed was totally unexpected. It turned out that, directly upon leaving us, Shostakovich had gone to the State Committee for the Arts. There he announced that the sculptor Slonim was working on his bust, and it was therefore desirable that he should be exempted from army service. The Shostakovich of the moment was a Big Noise. To appreciate what he had done, one must realize how squeamishly humble he was, how he detested any contact with the powers that be. My husband was accordingly exempted and enlisted in the so-called "golden heritage of the creative intelligentsia."

There is no doubt that Shostakovich was an extremely generous friend, both in wartime and in the harsh political times that preceded and followed the war. But even true generosity can be a corollary of a bad conscience. It was not Shostakovich's fault that he had an eminently useful talent. Still, the narrow, slippery path along which he had to slither in exercising that gift must occasionally have made him feel rather wormlike. A man of lesser sensibility and greater capacity for self-delusion might, perhaps, have accepted the situation more easily, but this was hardly consolation: Shostakovich was too honest, too intelligent, and too morally alert to derive any comfort from his own sense of guilt.

The war years, in any case, only confirmed what the late 1930s had forecast—that Shostakovich's fate was to be a man in hiding, a secret self behind a public face. If the psychoanalytic ideas of D. W. Winnicott have any validity (and experience leads me to believe that they do), then all the rewards and public satisfactions accumulated by Shostakovich's "false" public self would have done nothing to assuage the needs and sadnesses of the "true" self locked inside. Shostakovich was of course a special instance of this, since, rather than being the victim of an unwilled neurosis, he had consciously constructed the public version of himself as protective armor. But he had been assisted in that construction by Stalin, and *Time* magazine, and all the other enormous external forces that made him both a celebrated hero and a shivering wreck. "Nobody who saw him taking his bows on the platform after his music was performed could forget his crooked figure, his grimace of misery and the fingers that never stopped drumming on his cheek. . . . There was something robot-like in his movements," reported one friend, and it was a description that was echoed by many others. But even if the public figure couldn't always successfully disguise the private one, Shostakovich insisted on keeping the mask in place.

Still, he relied on his friends to see through it. In a letter written on December 31, 1943, he sent mordant New Year's greetings to Glikman. "It will be a year of happiness, of joy, of victory, a year that will bring us all much joy," he wrote. "The freedom-loving peoples will at last throw off the yoke of Hitlerism, peace will reign over the whole world, and we shall live once more in

peace under the sun of Stalin's Constitution. Of this I am convinced, and consequently experience feelings of unalloyed joy."
This is typical of the kind of ventriloquism Shostakovich would
routinely perform in his letters, and I always wonder why I, an
American reading these passages more than sixty years later, can
decipher the code when the Soviet censors could not. But perhaps that was not the point. The sentiment behind the words
might have been obvious, but the words themselves were not
prosecutable. And in any case disaster, when it fell, would arrive
with nearly random unpredictability. One could neither insure
nor ward off one's fate, because the process by which the next
victims were selected was ultimately so illogical. That seeming randomness, it turned out, was the most powerful scare tac-
tic in the secret state's arsenal, and it too was probably arrived at
randomly.

The war was almost over, and things were starting to look up
(Shostakovich had finally succeeded in moving Nina, the two
children, and himself into a new apartment in Moscow) when
the worst of the unexpected blows fell. And this time it was not
delivered by Stalin. On February 11, 1944, Ivan Sollertinsky died,
quite suddenly, in Novosibirsk.

He had been taking medical advice for a heart condition—
contradictory advice, apparently, with one side advocating exercise,
the other recommending rest—but his death still came as a complete shock. He was only forty-one, after all, and Shostakovich
had seen him just a few months earlier, when Sollertinsky came
to Moscow to hear the recently completed Eighth Symphony.

Sollertinsky's vigorous and rare enthusiasm for the Eighth ("the music is significantly tougher and more astringent than the Fifth or the Seventh and for that reason it is unlikely to become popular," he predicted) was of a piece with the role he had played in Shostakovich's musical life during all the years of their long friendship. And Sollertinsky was to prove right about the Eighth, as he was about so much else. Now that we have all fifteen of them, we can see that it is one of Shostakovich's most gripping and eloquent symphonies, filled with passages of searing intimacy and quiet despair. In that respect it, along with the Fourteenth Symphony, may be the closest in atmosphere to the quartets. To have a friend who could perceive things like this at the symphony's earliest performances was a justly treasured gift, and the loss correspondingly profound. For the rest of his life, whenever he wrote something new, the composer would ask himself, "And what would Ivan Ivanovich have said about this?" He would be answered by a silence.

The two men had become acquainted in late 1926, when Shostakovich was twenty and Sollertinsky just a few years older; that December they were both taking oral exams in Marxism-Leninism to qualify for postgraduate studies at the Leningrad Conservatory. Shostakovich's initial impression was of a terrifyingly erudite student who found it easy to answer questions "about the origin of materialist philosophy in Ancient Greece, Sophocles' poetry as an expression of realist tendencies, the English philosophers of the seventeenth century, and something else" that the young composer couldn't even recall. But he evidently warmed to this paragon, for he was soon telling his younger sister, Zoya, "I have met a wonderful new friend."

"They had an insane friendship," Zoya remembered. "Sollertinsky came to see us every day in the morning and stayed until the evening. They spent the whole day together, laughing and chuckling." Sollertinsky's first wife confirmed this description of the friendship, adding: "When they didn't manage to meet, Shostakovich would usually ring up. They called each other with comic reverence by name and patronymic—Van Vanich, and Dmi Dmitrich—while using the 'thou' form of address. They were simply in love, and didn't conceal their delight in each other. Sollertinsky never tired of repeating: 'Shostakovich is a genius. This will be understood with time.'"

But while he was Shostakovich's greatest admirer and defender, Sollertinsky was also a teacher, a critic, a figure who took the young composer in directions he might not otherwise have gone. It was he, for instance, who strengthened and encouraged Shostakovich's interest in Mahler's music, which turned out to be central to his symphonic development. It was he who enthusiastically introduced an evening of Shostakovich's works—including the First Symphony, selections from *The Bolt*, and an extract from the as-yet-unheard *Lady Macbeth*—on January 17, 1933, when, to judge by the relative size of their names on the poster, it was Sollertinsky rather than Shostakovich who was the major draw. It was he who wrote the key musicological essay in the unusually detailed, pointedly educational program that accompanied the premiere of *Lady Macbeth*. And it was Sollertinsky who, alone in the world, was willing to speak the unadorned truth about his friend's compositions, even when that perception differed from the approved public one. Sollertinsky was like a second self admitted to the nearly private world of Shostakovich's inner life—another wife, almost, but without the inflammatory sexual factor, and with the glorious addition of shared musical knowledge.

There is a wonderful photograph, taken in 1932, of Nina Varzar flanked by Shostakovich on her right and Sollertinsky on her left. All three look out at us with serious, intelligent eyes, though their mouths are just beginning to break into smiles—Nina's with open lips and a definite warmth, the other two tight-lipped, colder and more skeptical. The heads of Shostakovich and his future wife are on exactly the same level, and they veer noticeably toward each other, though a dark space in the photographic background slightly separates them. Sollertinsky seems to tower above them, the large-faced, pale-eyed grown-up next to this pair of fascinating, dark-haired twins. In the way he leans over Nina, his shadowed right cheek perhaps even touching the edge of her wavy hair, one senses his deep, protective affection for them both, but also the keen feeling of twinship, of a different kind, between him and the man on her far side.

Their steady companionship persisted through the 1930s, widening to include other friends (it was Sollertinsky who introduced the composer to Isaak Glikman, for instance) but remaining a unique bond for both of them. When Sollertinsky was evacuated from Leningrad to Novosibirsk, one of the few possessions he took with him was the packet of letters he had received from Shostakovich over the years. There, in Novosibirsk, Sollertinsky continued to function as the musical adviser to the Leningrad Philharmonic—and there, in the absence of printed programs, he would give his remarkable, informative, at times free-associative introductions to the concerts. "My guess is that half the audience came for the introductions, more than the music," said Kurt Sanderling, a German Jewish conductor who, in fleeing the Third Reich, had ended up in the Soviet Union working under Yevgeny Mravinsky. Evacuated to Novosibirsk with the rest of the Leningrad orchestra, Sanderling was brought into close contact with Shostakovich's best friend.

"Sollertinsky is one of the most interesting personalities I ever met in my life," Sanderling recalled nearly seventy years later, at the age of ninety-six. "He was extremely well educated and cultivated in the best sense of the term. He was very erudite in all fields. . . . Once, after a concert, we were walking home and we started talking about the French Revolution. I lacked the more detailed knowledge of what it was about—all I knew was what I had studied in school. We walked back and forth between his place and mine for two hours, and he gave me a whole seminar on the French Revolution, and I understood for the first time what the French Revolution was about. He did this out of the blue."

It was through Sollertinsky that Sanderling first met Shostakovich, on one of the composer's wartime visits to Novosibirsk. This was one of the few times during their prolonged separation

that Shostakovich and Sollertinsky had been able to see each
other. But now, as the war drew to its close, that was soon expected to change. After years of threatening to leave Leningrad
for the capital, the composer had finally agreed to move to Moscow (in part because it was the only way out of Kuibyshev at this
point), and the Soviet authorities had found him a small but
adequate family apartment near the center of the city. To temper
the transition, he was intending to bring his best friend with
him, and at their last meeting, in November of 1943, they talked
over the plan for transferring Sollertinsky to Moscow. Shostakovich was in the midst of making the practical arrangements
when the news of Sollertinsky's fatal heart attack reached him.

One can get a sense of his devastation, though only a distant
sense, from the letter he wrote to Glikman on February 13. For
once, there is no irony or subterfuge in the tone: everything is
flatly, painfully straightforward. If there is a formal quality to the
language, this seems in keeping with the occasion, and that very
formality makes the sudden intrusions of unmediated suffering
all the more noticeable. "Dear Isaak Davidovich," Shostakovich
began:

> I must share with you bitter and most heartfelt condolences on
> the death of our closest and most beloved friend Ivan Ivanovich
> Sollertinsky. He died on 11 February 1944. We shall not see him
> again. I have no words with which to express the pain that wracks
> my entire being. May his memorial be our abiding love for him,
> and our faith in the inspired talent and phenomenal love for the art
> of music to which he devoted his matchless life. Ivan Ivanovich is

no more. It is very hard to bear. My dear friend, do not forget me, and write to me.

Various critics and biographers have suggested that when Shosta-kovich repeats himself, in his music or his letters, it is a sure sign that he is being ironic (as he was, say, with his repetition of the word "joy" in his New Year's letter to Glikman). But there is no Rosetta Stone that allows one universally to decode Shostakovich's meanings, and in this case it is clear that the repetition is, on the contrary, an unwilled indicator of pure feeling. He keeps harp-ing on Sollertinsky's non-being ("the death . . . he died . . . We shall not see him again . . . Ivan Ivanovich is no more") because, like Macduff faced with the news of his family's slaughter, he simply cannot take it in. And yet with Shostakovich there is al-ways another layer. His heart rejects the news ("It is very hard to bear"), but his will insists that he acknowledge it, live with it. That too is what the repetition represents: a drilling-in of the painful circumstance, as if he can only survive by taking the ter-rible truth inside himself, turning it into his own repeating heartbeat.

When Sollertinsky died, Shostakovich had recently begun writ-ing a trio for piano, violin, and cello. It was to become the sec-ond and last piano trio of his career (the first had been written in the summer of 1923, when he was only sixteen), and he was to dedicate it, when he finished it in August of 1944, to the memory of Ivan Sollertinsky. Those who knew Sollertinsky felt that the

second movement of the Piano Trio No. 2 in E Minor, a haunting, lilting Allegro, perfectly mirrored the quicksilver intelligence of the man it honored, and Shostakovich was no doubt
eager to commemorate those years of shared jokes and sardonic
laughter; but there is also a deep sadness to the piece that comes
through most strongly in the Andante and Largo movements, as
well as in the slowed-down, quiet ending.

This is also the first work of Shostakovich's that noticeably alludes to Jewish music, and that too seems linked with Sollertinsky, though in ways that remain obscure. Some people theorize
that Shostakovich and Sollertinsky, though neither was Jewish,
sympathized and even identified with the Jews as a historically
oppressed group. "Sollertinsky and Dmitri Dmitriyevich both
felt that the persecution of *Lady Macbeth* was a 'pogrom'—that
was the word they used in describing it," Shostakovich's widow
told me. She also pointed out that Russian intellectual circles of
the time, and particularly musical circles, were filled with Jews,
so that the composer's connection with them was a relatively
natural one. Others have suggested that Shostakovich's (and, by
extension, Sollertinsky's) allegiance to the Jews was a political
statement, meant to signal a quiet but firm opposition to the
anti-Semitic regime. Still others argue that there was nothing
political about the choice, that Jewish folk music's tendency toward minor-key melodies and bleakly humorous complaint was
simply congenial to Shostakovich's own innate talents and sensi-
bilities, especially as these were encouraged by Sollertinsky. Certainly the two men shared an appreciation of Jewish culture that

was not common in their period and their nation. "Neither Shostakovich nor Sollertinsky was, in the good Russian tradition, an anti-Semite," Kurt Sanderling has drily observed. It is Sanderling who came up with what seems to me the best explanation for the first appearance of Jewish music, out of many such appearances over the course of Shostakovich's career, in the piano trio dedicated to Sollertinsky's memory. "It was not a connection to Sollertinsky, but a connection to tragedy," Sanderling said. "Whenever Shostakovich had to describe tragic experiences, he would use Jewish melodies."

Whatever their source, the Jewish themes were to resurface almost immediately in the Second Quartet, and it seems clear that the Second Piano Trio—a piece which, despite its different instrumentation, comes very close to the mood and spirit of a Shostakovich quartet—provided the impetus Shostakovich needed to return to that medium. The temporal link is at any rate demonstrable, for by September of 1944, barely a month after completing the piano trio, he had finished his next string quartet.

The Quartet No. 2 in A Major is dedicated to Vissarion Shebalin, a very old friend who was not only a respected composer himself, but was also one of the few people who had publicly stood by Shostakovich during the difficult "Muddle Instead of Music" episode. And yet to my ear the piece is really about Sollertinsky. Shostakovich was to manifest this dedication lag more than once in his career—we can hear it again in the Twelfth Quartet, which is dedicated to the Beethovens' first violinist while clearly reflecting on the death of the second violinist, to whom the previous quartet was dedicated—and it is not surprising that it should take one or two compositions for the major losses in his life to sink in. This is not to say that the dedication is not sincerely meant; it's just that the dedicatee is, in each instance, also standing in for someone else. In the case of the Second Quartet, it would be natural for Shostakovich to associate his dead friend with the loyal and musically talented Shebalin.

And just as the living friendship with Shebalin is the mask that Shostakovich puts on in order to cover over the unbearable loss of Sollertinsky, the unemotional titles of the four movements—Overture; Recitative and Romance; Waltz; Theme and Variations—seem designed to lead us away from any psychological or narrative interpretation. But one need hardly invoke the concept of resistance to understand this as a reasonable reaction on Shostakovich's part. If he is to be true to the memory of his strongly rational dead friend, he must not wallow self-pityingly in his grief; and if he is to convey to us the profundity of his loss, he can best do so by not baring his soul too easily. The emotional power of the quartets lies in great part in their inwardness. Something is being given to us freely, on the level where music and intuition converge, and something else is being withheld from us: that is the dynamic that makes the quartets both so moving and so mysterious.

The Second Quartet begins with an emphatic Moderato movement, much more assertive than anything we heard in the fledgling First Quartet. A noticeable melody, bearing klezmerish strains of wailing or shrieking in the highest notes, yet with an essentially sardonic sensibility, appears on the first violin and stays there. This is a voice that is planning to keep us company for a while, indeed to lead us into places that we may find both fearful and enjoyable, seductive and threatening. It is a voice that throbs and scrapes, moving from tenderness to turbulence in the space of a few measures. It is a confident voice, but it invites exchange with the other instruments and finds itself often in harmony with them (though just as often at a dissonant distance from them). Whether it is happy or sad—and it is often both, or neither—it is a strong voice, capable of snappy retorts and enlightening observations. I think it is the voice of Sollertinsky.

Something very strange has happened to this first-violin voice by the time we get to the second movement. Melodically it still dominates the other three—if anything, its plaintive solo is even more prominent now—but the tune it carries in this Adagio movement has become much more self-dramatizing. And though the Recitative clearly comes to us from a first-person perspective, it is a *different* first-person from the one we heard earlier. It is a much less confident voice than the one that carried the Overture, and its song is punctuated on occasion by a complete silence and then a long-drawn-out, two-note refrain on the other three instruments, a mournful phrase that almost seems to hymn the word "Ahhh-mennn." To someone attuned to the recent events in Shostakovich's life, the voice might appear to be talking about intimacy, dependence, and loss; it is professing its own weakness in the face of this death-dealt absence, and also its despair.

Now comes the strangest shift of all in the piece. In the third movement we are back inside the original voice, but that first-violin self is no longer alive. It is being moved by some force outside itself, compelled to do a dance of death, like a skeleton in hell or a puppet on strings. This Mahlerian waltz is an eerie, thoughtful tribute to Sollertinsky (who was the founder of Leningrad's Mahler Society), but it is also a frightening portrait of the emptiness that is death. Shostakovich is attempting to revive his dead friend, to animate the inanimate, by using as his lure the kind of macabre music his friend loved. But the end result is ghoulish and scary, for here the Mahler expert has himself been Mahlerized, made into a thing that is no longer human, and the effort to retrieve him seems all the more hopeless as he disappears into the music.

We get beyond that, though: past the silence that closes this alluring but also terrifying movement, and into the relatively open ground of the Theme and Variations. Rhythmically this movement offers us the most exciting, forward-moving sequence Shostakovich ever put into a quartet, a kind of galloping dance in consecutive sixteenth notes that carries us relentlessly onward. And the way in which the initial theme survives (now on one instrument, now on another, altering its nature yet remaining recognizable) also gives us cause for, if not celebration, then at any rate resignation to the facts of existence. It is as if the central storytelling voice, that reciting figure from the second movement, had by now incorporated into himself some of his dead friend's strength. The feeling of this whole final movement is one of setting off on this road, the only one available to us, and trying to get to the end of it in as good a shape as we can—or, in Samuel Beckett's terms, "I can't go on, I'll go on." That the journey will not necessarily be easy nor the arrival particularly cheerful is signaled by the movement's ending: a series of slow-paced, repeated minor chords, all bowed in unison on the four instruments in a manner that is emphatic yet not fully conclusive. But that first-violin self has at least made the decision to survive, and he has done so not by forgetting his best friend's death, but by taking it into himself.

With the Second Quartet, we have reached true Shostakovich territory. The quartets have found their subject—let's call it death for shorthand, but we could just as easily call it mortal terror, or sorrow, or guilt-ridden survival, or any of the other attributes that surround someone who faces and contemplates death—and they will stick with this subject to the end. As deeper and wider experiences of this "distinguished thing" come their way, they will invent new strategies for expressing it, and they will eventually take the music to places even eerier and more frightening than the third-movement Waltz. But in terms of defining Shostakovich's mastery of the string quartet, we are already there. The medium has become his, completely and irretrievably. He will never again leave so long a space between quartets, and from now on he will always know that this particular mode of expression is waiting for him whenever he has need of it.

The Second Piano Trio and the Second Quartet were premiered at the same Leningrad concert on November 14, 1944. The string players in both pieces were members of the Beethoven Quartet, four men whom Shostakovich had already known by that time for over fifteen years. First violinist Dmitri Tsyganov and cellist Sergei Shirinsky joined the composer himself in the trio, and then the two of them played with second violinist Vasily Shirinsky and violist Vadim Borisovsky in the string quartet. These four musicians were to remain a constant factor in Shostakovich's life—perhaps *the* most constant factor in it—until the mid-1960s, when retirement and death began to alter the personnel of the quartet; and even after that Shostakovich remained true to the Beethovens, offering them the premiere of each string quartet in turn.

He also began quite early in the cycle to tailor specific elements of the quartets to the talents and personalities of these particular string players. Years later, for instance, Dmitri Tsyganov was to comment, while rehearsing with the composer for a performance of the Second Quartet, that he felt the recitative in the second movement had been written just for him. "Yes, indeed it was, Mitya," responded Shostakovich. "I wrote it for you." There is no other musical collaboration in Shostakovich's career to which he returned more frequently or more satisfyingly, and as the years went by, the trust he felt in the Beethovens, both personally and musically, became a rarer and rarer phenomenon in his life. What drew these five men together was friendship, but it was also something more than a friendship: it included unburdensome dependence, intense mutual admiration, and a deep but reserved form of love.

The importance of these performers to the composer was already clear to him by the mid-1940s, for he dedicated his Third Quartet—written in 1946, just a couple of years after the Second—to the Beethoven Quartet. The two years that separated those two quartets were, on the face of it, relatively undisturbed ones in Shostakovich's life. The war had ended, and he and his family were settled in a small Moscow apartment at 21 Kirov Street, in the immediate vicinity of the infamous Lubyanka, the KGB's headquarters and prison. (It is not particularly surprising, by the way, that Shostakovich should have lived at different times on both Kirovsky Prospect and Kirov Street, for the overwhelming presence and then sudden absence of Sergei Kirov's name on boulevards, buildings, and ballet companies is one of the more noticeable features of twentieth-century Russian history. This Communist Party martyr, assassinated in 1934, was one of many Bolshevik figures to receive such treatment, as the Soviets sought to sever themselves from the past by renaming everything in sight, rather in the way the French Revolutionaries had done. Only after the fall of the Soviet Union were these places and institutions allowed to revert to their original titles—at which point Kirovsky Prospect in Leningrad became Kamennoostrovsky Prospect in St. Petersburg, and Shostakovich's first address in Moscow changed from 21 Kirov Street to 21 Myasnitskaya Street.)

The Shostakovich family was not to remain in that small apartment for long. In the spring of 1946 the composer asked for, and eventually received, a much larger Moscow apartment, with two separate entrances and space enough for two pianos. In making this request, he wrote directly to Lavrentiy Beria, the head of the secret police, asking him to intercede on his behalf, and Beria responded with the news that Stalin himself was personally giving Shostakovich not only the new apartment but also a car, a summer dacha in the town of Kellomäki (later renamed Komarovo), and a hundred thousand rubles to fix up the dacha.

It was at this summer retreat on the Finnish border that Shostakovich wrote, between May and August of 1946, the bulk of the Third String Quartet. He had begun it months earlier, but since January had not been able to progress beyond the second movement. His productivity in general had slowed since 1944: the unexpectedly small-scale, apolitical, and emotionally opaque Ninth Symphony (offered in place of an expected tribute to Lenin), which he finished in 1945, and the Third Quartet, completed in August of 1946, were the only two major works he wrote in the two years following the war. Neither earned him much official credit, and both were withdrawn soon after their first performances, as the response to Shostakovich's excessively "formalist" music continued to darken.

But in spite of some sharp criticisms leveled against him by the Central Committee's Directorate for Propaganda and Agitation, Shostakovich was still in reasonably good shape, politically, in late 1946 and early 1947. A three-time Stalin Prize winner, most recently for the Second Piano Trio, he held two simultaneous professorships in music (one at the Moscow Conservatory, the other in Leningrad) and served on at least two official Soviet committees. Yet he was not happy about the way things were going, as his elliptical, sardonic notes to Glikman made clear: "In general all's well with my world and I am in a fabulous mood," he wrote with characteristic irony on February 11, 1946 (not incidentally, the anniversary of Sollertinsky's death). By August of that year, when Andrei Zhdanov, Stalin's hatchet man in the culture department, launched a vicious and career-destroying attack against the writer Mikhail Zoshchenko, the composer had a further reason for sympathetic despair.

That the tide of Zhdanov's pernicious campaign against "bourgeois degeneracy" among Soviet artists was creeping ever closer to Shostakovich himself became clear in early October, when various speakers at the Composers' Plenum openly criticized his Ninth Symphony. Shostakovich could sound coolly detached and even slightly mocking about such developments in his letters to Glikman, but he couldn't afford to stand aloof for long. That he was willing to grovel to preserve his protected status is both understandable and undeniable. In January of 1947 he wrote a thank-you note to Stalin:

> Dear Iosif Vissarionovich,
>   A few days ago I moved with my family to a new apartment. The apartment turned out to be a very good one and it is very pleasant to live in. With all my heart I thank you for your concern

about me. The main thing I very much want now is to justify—if only to a small degree—the attention you have shown me. I will apply all my strength toward that.

I wish you many years of health and energy for the good of our Motherland, our Great People.

Yours,

D. Shostakovich

This stilted, careful, almost childishly simple letter is a long way from the tongue-in-cheek, satiric tone of his patriotic New Year's message to his friend Glikman. It is instead a straightforward belly-to-the-ground crawl, and one cringes for Shostakovich at his need (certainly a *real* need, and not just a perceived one) to humble himself in this way.

But there is no concession of this sort in the String Quartet No. 3 in F Major, which received its premiere on December 16, 1946, about a month before that letter to Stalin was written. A complicated, ambitious, five-movement work, the Third Quartet remains one of Shostakovich's most ambiguous and mysterious chamber pieces. It builds on the terrain he explored in the Second Quartet, but it feels far less specific and personal than that work, as if he were now relying on the quartet to pursue more timeless and universal subjects—or as if the quartet medium itself were the subject, as the dedication to the performing musicians seems to suggest. One dubious but nonetheless persistent story has Shostakovich coming up with and then deleting a series of programmatic titles for the five movements: 1. "Calm unawareness of the future cataclysm," 2. "Rumblings of unrest and anticipation," 3. "The forces of war unleashed," 4. "Homage to the dead," and 5. "The eternal question—Why? and for what?" Though there has never been any solid reason to believe that Shostakovich invented these labels (according to both Laurel Fay and Judith Kuhn, they do not appear anywhere in his autographs or printed scores, nor are they mentioned in rehearsal diaries, interviews, or memoirs of the original players), the rumor that these titles once existed has endured for decades. Perhaps their continuing shadow-life in program notes and elsewhere can be attributed less to their credibility than to a sense, common among players and listeners alike, that there is some kind of capacious, other than merely personal drama behind the Third Quartet.

And yet there must have been something tremendously personal buried there too, because this was the quartet that most visibly moved Shostakovich when he listened to it twenty years later, as the Beethovens were rehearsing the whole cycle for several new performances. Fyodor Druzhinin, the young violist who replaced his own beloved teacher, Vadim Borisovsky, in 1964, gives his account of the episode:

> We were rehearsing his Third Quartet. He'd promised to stop us when he had any remarks to make. Dmitri Dmitriyevich sat in an armchair with the score opened out. But after each movement ended he just waved us on, saying, "Keep playing!" So we performed the whole Quartet. When we finished he sat quite still in silence like a wounded bird, tears streaming down his face. This was the only time that I saw Shostakovich so open and defenseless.

Why was it this quartet, among all the ones he had written by then, that made him weep? Was he remembering how comparatively young the five of them had been when he dedicated this piece to the Beethovens, and was he contrasting that now-distant past to the much-altered present, when one of the players had already died and another had retired? Or was he shedding tears because the five-movement work itself—which can be seen as a forecast about the shape of a human life, from childhood through adult crisis, temporary despair, peaceful death, and beyond—had turned out to be true in ways he could only now appreciate?

Or was he weeping because the music's prophecy had *not* turned out to be true and merely represented the illusions of a younger man? "Life is beautiful. All that is dark and ignominious will disappear. All that is beautiful will triumph" is the message that Alan George, the violist of the Fitzwilliam Quartet, associates with this quartet and attributes to a quotation from the composer himself. It's true that Shostakovich did say these words, but not about the Third Quartet; the remark was part of a public interview he gave in late 1943 about the Eighth Symphony, and in that context it was clearly meant as camouflage for his unexpectedly dark symphonic work. Only someone who cannot adequately hear Shostakovich's intentional distortions and dissonances, I think, would take this simplistic tagline as indicative of the "directness and sincerity" of the "message" in *any* of his serious works, and the statement seems particularly inappropriate to the Third Quartet. By 1946 Dmitri Shostakovich had no reason to believe that light and beauty would triumph,

and I do not hear any such assertion in the complicated shifts
and ambiguities of the Quartet in F Major.

In any case, the gentle tears that Druzhinin describes do not
seem like a sign of disillusionment, but rather an acknowledgment of some very profound kind of truth. So I will stick with
my notion that the Third Quartet meant a great deal to Shostakovich, both at the time he wrote it and twenty years later, and
that this meaning had something to do with the course a life
takes, whether inevitably or by chance. I think those tears were a
response, in part, to the musically induced collapsing of time, so
that for the sixty-year-old composer, the present and the past—
the life as it had actually been lived, and the life as it had been
imagined—were for once brought forcibly together.

The first movement, an Allegretto, seems to be about childhood,
though in a lighter, speedier, more sophisticated form than Shostakovich presented it in Quartet No. 1 (which is not so much
about childhood as it is set within a child's mind). But the composer evidently didn't want it to sound *too* light, as one can
gather from a story told by Valentin Berlinsky, the cellist of the
Borodin Quartet. Preparing a performance of the Third Quartet
some years after its premiere, the Borodins—who had by this
time become quite close to Shostakovich, often giving the second performance of his works—came up with a suggestion about
how the first movement should begin. Instead of having the

cello bow its deep, rhythmic F notes, they thought it would sound livelier or more captivating if the repeated note was plucked. As Berlinsky recalls,

> For some reason we decided that it sounded better played *pizzicato*, while the second violin and viola continue to play *arco*. In our youthful folly, we decided to play it like that for Dmitri Dmitriyevich without any prior warning. This again took place at his home. No sooner had we started, when he stopped us and said, "Excuse me, but you are meant to play *arco* there."
>
> I said, "Dmitri Dmitriyevich, you see, we've given it some thought, and maybe you would like to reconsider. It seems to us that *pizzicato* sounds better here."
>
> "Yes, yes," he hastily interrupted, "*pizzicato* is much *better*, but please play *arco* all the same."

(Shostakovich always knew precisely how his music should sound, and his resistance to other people's revisions was legendary. When, in the dark days of 1936, the internationally famous conductor Otto Klemperer, who was planning to do the first European performance of the new Fourth Symphony, made a practical suggestion about reducing the number of flutes required for it, Shostakovich smilingly but seriously quoted an old Russian proverb: "What the pen has written, even the axe may not cut out." And while first violinist Dmitri Tsyganov would often suggest revisions to the quartets when the Beethovens were rehearsing them, Shostakovich, even if he seemed to agree at the time, would always revert to his own version. "He listened to his own ideas and thoughts, not advice from other people," com-

mented Olga Dombrovskaya, who, as the curator of the Shostakovich Archive, is one of the people most familiar with his hand-
written scores.)

In the case of the Third Quartet, he knew exactly what he
wanted, and he wanted it that way twice, for the full opening is
repeated identically, in a manner that is true to the chief illusion
of childhood: the belief, that is, that things will go on exactly as
they are. Then the melody begins to move into a somewhat
darker, more dissonant, more hesitant and interrupted version of
itself, with a bit of questioning and a bit of anxiety. Yet there are
constant returns to the initial tune, as if to reassert the cheer, and
the movement's ending is playful: not the death-haunted
morendo that is already so common in this composer's work, nor
any kind of harshness, but a high-pitched note accompanied by
a jolly pizzicato that is the closest Shostakovich ever comes to
optimism or hopefulness.

The apparent jollity is quickly modified in the second movement, though, where the opening waltz tune is more complicated, more knowledgeable, and much leerier than anything we
heard in the previous movement. And even that melody never
lasts long: it keeps being interrupted by the sudden rat-a-tat of
percussive triplets, as if to suggest the sound of distant gunfire
gradually approaching the previously oblivious waltzer. Only in
the very moving Adagio that ends the movement—a series of
long, slow, mournful notes on all the instruments, and then a
dying out—do we achieve a kind of peace at last; but it is a peace
that contains within itself an awareness of loss and possible death.

In sharp contrast, the third movement begins at full blast, with a first violin that is frantic from the start, sounding its wailing notes against the strong, unmelodic rhythm of the lower instruments. If the second movement was young adulthood reaching a crisis point, then this is the heart of the crisis; and if the second movement contained the intimations of war, then this is war itself, or even its aftermath. The fourth or fifth time I heard this music, it occurred to me that, even if we credit the presence of war behind this quartet, the third-movement crisis might not be the field of battle itself, but the supposed return to normalcy that followed the war. There can be no return to normal, however—one is constantly being tripped up by the unsettling meter, which changes every measure or two from 2/4 to 3/4 and then back again. Anxiety is the overwhelming emotion of this section of the quartet. All four musicians are playing all the time, but they do not support each other as they did in the first movement. Instead, there is more the sense of either desperation in unison or else anxiety responding to anxiety, a contagious nervousness that flickers from one instrument to another in turn. The end of the movement is harsh and fast, punctuated by a few abrupt bow strokes that are then cut off suddenly, almost in midstream.

In the Adagio fourth movement, we are dead. Death, in this form, is pleasurable—it is a cessation of the anxieties and tensions of the previous movement, and therefore relaxing, a relief. (There is a story, which dates from a slightly later period than this quartet, of Shostakovich's consolatory visit to a friend whose

father had just died, a visit that took place on the very day
Shostakovich was censured by the Central Committee. "Silently
he embraced me and my husband, the composer Moisei Weinberg," reports the bereaved friend, Natalya Mikhoels; "then he
went over to the bookcase and, with his back to everybody in the
room, pronounced quietly but distinctly and with uncharacteristic deliberation, 'I envy him . . .'" That emotion—Shostakovich's envy of the dead man—is what we hear in the fourth movement of the Third Quartet.) The mood of the whole movement
is pensive, with room for a thoughtful solo melody on the first
violin and for conversation among the instruments. The tune
here is more openly melodious than in any other movement of
the piece, and because the dynamics shift suddenly, going
from *fortissimo* to *pianissimo* in a relatively brief period, one
has to listen very closely to catch the beautiful, quietly searing
notes. Throughout, there is a strong sense of silence in the background—that new but soon to be characteristic Shostakovichian
silence, from which the solo voices and rhythmic punctuation
emerge, and into which they ultimately disappear.

The last note of the fourth movement is actually the setup, the
beginning, for the final movement that follows: a sudden coming back to life even in the midst of death. This last cello note is
not loud, but it is noticeable (marked *arco*, it breaks the pizzicato
pattern of the ending); and it becomes the only voice in the first
part of the fifth movement, where the higher instruments and
especially the first and second violins remain silent for quite a
while. This Moderato movement combines many of the things

we've heard before—the rhythmic pizzicato, the waltzlike triplets, the frequent and extreme dynamic changes from *pianissimo*
to *fortissimo* and back, the occasional rushes of sixteenth notes.
The music is trying out life again, after having been dead. But
instead of the sad but willfully enduring feeling that informs the
last movement of the Second Quartet, the feeling that life must
be gotten through somehow, *this* final movement conveys the
sense that life is already over.

There is a very otherworldly atmosphere here, though not
necessarily in a religious, redemptive, life-after-death sense.
Shostakovich was a self-described unbeliever—a man who reportedly said (on the occasion of the first performance of his
elegiac Fourteenth Symphony), "Death is terrifying, there is
nothing beyond it. I don't believe in a life beyond the grave"—
and this is utterly consistent with the feeling conveyed by the
string quartets, individually and as a whole. Yet there is something about the last movement of the Third Quartet that makes
one want to interrogate him a little further, to ask exactly how he
feels about the nonexistent afterlife. Perhaps in this quartet he
was using a musical evocation of life after death not in a religious
way at all, but as a means of commenting on human existence
from a metaphorical distance (a strategy comparable, for instance, to Thornton Wilder's in *Our Town* or Michael Powell's in
Stairway to Heaven, neither of which is in any way a "pious"
work). Or perhaps Shostakovich, in this final movement of the
Quartet No. 3, was simply referring to the way memory, with its
hauntings, can produce a kind of afterlife.

This feeling of otherworldliness comes through most strongly at the very end of the quartet, in the first violin's high-pitched harmonics and melodious pizzicato, played against the long-drawn-out *morendo* notes of the lower three instruments. Once again Shostakovich has given us an Adagio ending to a Moderato movement, but here he really means it—there will be no temporary return to attempted normalcy, as there was after the brief Adagio that ended the second movement. This final Adagio is eerie and a bit frightening, as if everything really were over and nothing could ever come afterward. *We think we are alive, but we are actually already dead*: that is what the whole fifth movement seems to be saying, as if we had awoken from a nightmare only to find ourselves in a worse, waking nightmare.

And yet there is something very sweet about that ending too, very moving and appealing; the sweetness is creepy here, and the creepiness sweet. The runs of spooky pizzicato notes have something to do with this, and so do the haunting patterns in the melody. Melodically, this movement recapitulates what the middle movement did rhythmically, constantly tripping us up, forcing us to shift gear. And there is also a great deal of starting over here, just as there was in the first movement, but this time the repetition evokes experience, sadness, and the knowledge of endings rather than a sense of innocence.

More than any quartet Shostakovich had written to date, possibly more than any he was ever to write, the Third Quartet is filled with extreme contrasts: between fast-plucked pizzicato and strongly bowed arco, between loudness and near-silence, between

legato smoothness and staccato abruptness, between slowness
and speed, between very high notes and very low ones, between
harsh rhythm and sweet melodiousness, between sections where
all the players are playing at once and those where one or more
sit motionless for long periods. It is as if the quartet is about
the whole range of experience—life, from beginning to end, and
from top to bottom. No wonder it made the aging composer
weep.

And, maybe because of this unusual depth and variety, the
Third Quartet sounds different every time it is played. You can
never pin it down, in regard to subject matter or meaning or
tone. Perhaps more than any other quartet of Shostakovich's,
this one seems to depend on the interpretation given to it by its
players. The opening movement can sound either lightly, self-
consciously comic, as it does when the St. Lawrence Quartet
plays it, or slower, heavier, and less childlike, as it does in the
Philharmonia Quartett Berlin's version. The Fitzwilliam Quartet
plays the third movement with the most military force, the fourth
movement with the least creepiness, and the fifth with the greatest tone of redemption, as if following to the letter the line about
all that is dark and ignominious disappearing. In the Fine Arts
Quartet version, the fourth movement is by far the saddest and
the sweetest, while the fifth is quieter and darker than usual.
When I listen to the recordings by the Emersons and the Borodins, the two groups that have most strongly shaped my
conception of the Third Quartet, I hear pure childhood in the
beginning; and in their versions of the ending, the final Adagio

seems poised in the balance between sorrow and sweetness, consolation and despair. And yet, when I listen to those same recordings again, I always hear something else as well, as if the Third Quartet were an infinitely refillable vessel that could pour out new meanings each time and still never run short.

But "meanings," in a precise verbal sense, are exactly what the quartets in general and this quartet in particular are avoiding. Much as it may suggest fragmentary plots and related human emotions, Shostakovich's Third Quartet strongly conveys the composer's effort to move as far away as possible from verbal significance—the kind of verbal significance that could be found (and condemned) in operas, for instance. As the composer Karen Khachaturian was to point out some years later, "Shostakovich hated being asked questions about his music and whether this or that theme represented something or had any particular meaning. When asked, 'What did you want to say in this work?' he would answer, 'I've said what I've said.'" Any composer might say the same, but only one who had been severely persecuted for his musical "messages" (or lack thereof) would be likely to say it with such vehemence.

"There is no necessary connection between the Third Quartet and war," Kurt Sanderling told me. "War was simply a symbol for the horrors in the world." And then, as if to correct himself for his own symbol-mongering, Sanderling interjected, "But these are all speculations. He didn't like to talk about his work at all. For example, when Mravinsky was working on the Eighth Symphony, he would ask Shostakovich to explain the meaning of this or that passage, and finally Shostakovich said: 'The scherzo in the second movement represents the functionary who has received his exit visa to the West.' He made this joke to Mravinsky. But Shostakovich never told everything to one person. To this person he told one thing, to others he told other things."

Intermezzo

Somehow the music seemed to have helped him to understand
time. Time is a transparent medium. People and cities arise out
of it, move through it and disappear back into it. It is time
that brings them and time that takes them away.
But the understanding that had just come to Krymov was a very
different one: the understanding that says, "This is my time," or, "No,
this is no longer our time." Time flows into a man or State, makes its
home there and then flows away; the man and the State remain, but
their time has passed. Where has their time gone? The man still
thinks, breathes and cries, but his time, the time that belonged to him
and to him alone, has disappeared.
There is nothing more difficult than to be a stepson of the time; there
is no heavier fate than to live in an age that is not your own.

—VASILY GROSSMAN, *Life and Fate*

In considering the vile public interrogation to which Shostakovich was subjected by Andrei Zhdanov and the Central
Committee of the Communist Party in early 1948, I cannot
help feeling that there is an unfortunate analogy between the
work of an artist's biographer and that of his political persecutor.

That is, there is something slightly Zhdanov-like in my desire to root around in Shostakovich's mind, seeking out the private meanings behind the compositions and performances. Yet the impulse to unmask his music is hardly unusual. On the contrary, there seems to be something in the work that repeatedly elicits such attempts, as if Shostakovich were both giving meaning and withholding it at the same time.

Even those who were most sympathetic to his political position and most attuned to his musical techniques could find themselves unwittingly falling into the search-for-meaning trap. Take, for instance, the Beethoven Quartet's latter-day violist, Fyodor Druzhinin, the cherished youngster for whom Shostakovich composed the last piece he ever wrote. Here is Druzhinin commenting on the effects of the infamous Zhdanov Decree:

> While still a schoolboy, I was present at the famous meeting at the Grand Hall of the Conservatoire in 1948, the most shameful moment of our cultural history. The civic punishment of such artists as Shostakovich, Shebalin, Prokofiev, Akhmatova, and Zoshchenko, with ignorant nonentities cast as their executioners, had been prophesied in Shostakovich's music. It is our good fortune that, thanks to the abstract nature of music, they were unable to put the composer before a firing squad.

Like Shostakovich's music itself, this account seems to have it both ways: the "abstract" nature of music set against its clear ability to "prophesy," and both affirmed. Druzhinin was speaking many years later, long after Shostakovich had emerged from this dark moment and been restored to his high position in Soviet society—long after that society had itself disintegrated, for that matter. But in February of 1948, when the decree against him was first issued, Shostakovich must have been far from sure that he would escape the firing squad.

There were actually multiple phases to the Zhdanov disaster. The first took place in mid-January of 1948, when Shostakovich was summoned to a conference of composers convened by Andrei Zhdanov and was told in no uncertain terms that he was still guilty of the bourgeois, decadent, formalist tendencies that had plagued him in *Lady Macbeth of the Mtsensk District.* Zhdanov himself compared Shostakovich's music to "a piercing road-drill, or a musical gas-chamber"; then various hack musicians chimed in with their specific critiques of the Eighth and Ninth Symphonies, while the soon-to-be head of the Composers' Union, Tikhon Khrennikov (not a hack, but definitely an opportunist), criticized Shostakovich in order to raise his own political profile. On January 13 Shostakovich, who was by far the best known of the composers under attack at the conference, addressed the assembly for the second time, confessing that his work had suffered from "many failures and serious setbacks," but that he had always tried "to make my music accessible to the people" and "to work harder and better. I am listening now, too, and will listen in the future. I will accept critical instruction." Thus humbled, he went home in a terrible state, stopping on the way to console his friend Natalya for the death of her father, Solomon Mikhoels. (It was suspected, and later confirmed, that this well-known Jewish actor had been murdered in an act of politically motivated anti-Semitism; in fact, it is now known that the killing was carried out on Stalin's orders, in an early manifestation of what was to become his explicit campaign against "rootless cosmopolitans.")

And then, on February 10, the Central Committee issued its resolution, formally called "On V. Muradeli's Opera *The Great Friendship*," but informally known forever after as the Zhdanov Decree. (The decree was permanent, in the sense that it was never officially rescinded; even much later, under Khrushchev, its principles were simply described as having been misapplied at the time.) In the resolution, not only Shostakovich's works but also those of Prokofiev, Khachaturian, Myaskovsky, Shebalin, and others were condemned for manifesting "formalist distortions and anti-democratic tendencies." But Shostakovich was the one who attracted the most attention, and his fall, coming as it did from the highest height, was certainly the most precipitous.

Still, he seemed to embrace his abasement beyond the strictly necessary. For instance, he was the only one from his group of composers to speak before the committee and publicly accept the criticism. Once again the false note—that same studiously accurate imitation of Soviet-speak, which could be satiric in his letters but was clearly not meant to be here—was sounded: "When, today, through the pronouncements of the Central Committee resolution, the Party and all of our country condemn this direction in my creative work, I know that the Party is right," he intoned. "I know that the Party is showing concern for Soviet art and for me, a Soviet composer." There is anecdotal evidence from a similar occasion suggesting that Shostakovich did not write his contrite remarks himself, but was handed them by a Party official as he stepped up to speak. Even if this were true, it would still be fair to say that he *delivered* such a speech, whereas the other composers, who silently avoided him afterward, did not. Was this response an act of extreme political intelligence on his part, or did it stem from some kind of self-punishing masochism? Perhaps at that point in time, and in that particular personality, the two were not separable.

His concessions did him no good in the short run. Much of his music was explicitly banned from public performance, and even the works that weren't on the prohibited list (including the quartets) remained unplayed for years. He lost both of his professorships and all of his regular income. Eventually he was able to eke out a living writing film music, but in the immediate aftermath of the decree, Shostakovich's family ran so short of money that they had to borrow from their longtime servant, Fenya Kozhunova, to survive. As a ten-year-old, Maxim was briefly made to participate in a public condemnation of his father's music at school. (His sister, Galina, was later to recall this incident from a child's point of view: "At that time Maxim was at music school, where they were studying the 'Historic Decree.' In view of this our parents decided he had better not go to school for a while, which made me jealous of him.") The Shostakovich household, previously an unusually social and open place, was now forced back on itself. And though many in his intimate circle remained close and supportive during this time, others stayed away, either because they feared his misfortune might prove contagious (a not unreasonable theory, in that climate) or because they were disappointed by his public embrace of Zhdanov's criticism.

Those who avoided him were "not his friends," according to Kurt Sanderling, "but people who thought of themselves as closely connected—they distanced themselves." But Sanderling was certain that Shostakovich wouldn't have condemned these people; on the contrary, the composer understood their situation all too well, and to a certain extent sympathized with it. Sanderling (who, by the time he was speaking of this long-past era, had lived in Berlin for nearly fifty years, but who had endured the postwar Stalin period in Moscow) was anxious to clarify the terms of Shostakovich's isolation:

> We have a somewhat wrong notion about how things worked. There wasn't a moment when someone was told by Stalin that Shostakovich should be suppressed; they just sensed that if Stalin was making these remarks, they should draw these conclusions. It's part of the absurdity of the regime that Stalin personally supported Shostakovich by telling people to give Shostakovich work writing for the movies. Stalin had a very ambivalent attitude toward Shostakovich. He never understood anything about Shostakovich (not to mention music in general), but he understood that Shostakovich was a great personality. And as a musician he could not be dangerous to Stalin, as an author would have been. Stalin wanted to use Shostakovich for prestige—for the Party and the country.

Whether Shostakovich was in turn ambivalent about Stalin is something we will never know for sure. The very absence of resistance in his official speeches can be, and has been, marshaled as a sign of his secret disagreement with the regime: in contrast to Prokofiev, for instance, who earnestly (if uselessly) attempted to justify his compositional choices to the Zhdanov committee by explaining how his methods actually fit in with Soviet aims, Shostakovich hid himself completely behind a mask of self-critical jargon. What we *can* say, though, is that when he witnessed the same thing from the outside, after Zhdanov had condemned the work of Anna Akhmatova and Mikhail Zoshchenko in 1946, the composer was sympathetic and helpful to those who had been criticized. Natalya Mikhoels reported that, shortly after that earlier decree, "Shostakovich told us that he had met Zoshchenko, and that he was in a dreadful state and completely destitute. In his quick patter, so familiar to us, he kept repeating: 'One must help him. It's essential that he gets help.' And Dmitri Dmitriyevich himself did help, in the most discreet and tactful way."

Nor can we judge whether, in his way of responding on his own behalf to the Zhdanov Decree of 1948, Shostakovich actually did the right thing in strategic terms. Certainly no one, himself included, would have argued that total capitulation was the right thing in moral terms. But then, moral triumphs in such situations can be Pyrrhic victories, as can merely strategic triumphs; there is no way of emerging unscathed from times like those. As Sanderling said about Shostakovich's political compromises, "How could it be otherwise? You would have acted the same way." But there was clearly something unusual about Shostakovich's relationship to power in general and Stalin's power in particular. No other Soviet artist that I know of managed to survive with equal success the kind of degradation he went through— and he went through it *twice*, only to emerge each time in a stronger position than ever. The reasons for this (if one can ever find reasons in such irrational circumstances) may have something to do with the essential contradictions in Shostakovich's situation, and in his character: his astonishingly original talent, his unusual fame, and his worldwide popularity paradoxically helped account for both his downfall and his restoration. And the "ambivalence" Stalin felt about him, obviously a primary factor in Shostakovich's unusual fate, might well have been reinforced by the composer's reactions to that fate. In other words, Shostakovich's apparent weakness in the face of condemnation may actually have been a hidden strength. It kept him alive, at any rate, though just barely: suicide, according to those who knew him well, was often in his thoughts in 1948.

Things continued in this same difficult state for a whole year, through the beginning of 1949. Shostakovich's only serious new project undertaken during this time was the ill-fated song cycle *From Jewish Folk Poetry*. It was ill-fated because, although Shostakovich was ostensibly obeying official criticism by seeking out the kind of captivating melodies to be found in folk music, the "folk" he chose were not at all the ones Zhdanov and Stalin had in mind. Could he actually have been unaware throughout 1948 of the growing campaign against the Jews? Given the number and closeness of his Jewish friendships, this seems unlikely. On the other hand, one can't be sure that his choice of Jewish sources, when he had been instructed to learn from ethnic music, was a conscious act of resistance. "Half-conscious," Kurt Sanderling argues. "Not a conscious protest, but half-conscious. No composer, not least Shostakovich, sits down consciously to write about the individual versus society. But the composer sits down and then the conflict finds its expression." Not everyone agrees with even this degree of political analysis. According to Shostakovich's widow, his use of Jewish melodies was not a politically motivated choice at all; it was simply the private pursuit of a long-held personal interest. It became that, anyway—a completely private pursuit—for at the end of January 1949 he decided not to submit his "Jewish songs," as he called them, to the Composers' Union for approval. Instead, they were put quietly away and were not played publicly until 1955. (A similar fate afflicted the wonderful Violin Concerto No. 1, which Shostakovich was completing during the very months when the Zhdanov Decree came into being. This piece remained underground—shown only to his fellow musicians, including the violinist David Oistrakh—until October of 1955, when Oistrakh at last performed it.)

In the midst of all this misery, Shostakovich suddenly received an invitation to accompany an official delegation of artists and officials on their March 1949 visit to the United States. No doubt his name had been brought up by the host country; certainly it would have seemed odd to the Americans if the most famous artist in the Soviet Union, the hero of the Seventh Symphony, had not been among the visiting delegates. That he was being so poorly treated by his own government would have been only part of Shostakovich's motive for refusing, when he first received the invitation in February. His general gloom and consequent ill health made the prospect of travel—especially as a hollowed-out Soviet mouthpiece, "a cut-out paper doll on a string," as he reportedly described himself to a friend—seem especially unenticing. But apparently he was not going to be allowed even this measure of resistance.

On March 16 (though the reported date can vary, depending on who is telling the story), Shostakovich received a telephone call from Stalin himself. Here's how Yuri Abramovich Levitin, a former student and close friend of the composer's, recounts the incident:

> At the end of February or the beginning of March of 1949, I was visiting the Shostakoviches during the daytime. Dmitri Dmitriyevich wasn't feeling very well. I sat talking with him and Nina Vasilyevna. The telephone rang, and Dmitri Dmitriyevich picked up the receiver. A second later he said helplessly, "Stalin is about to come on the line . . ."
>
> Nina Vasilyevna, a woman of determination and energy, immediately jumped up and went to the next room and picked up the other receiver. I froze in position on the sofa. For the next moments, naturally all I heard were Dmitri Dmitriyevich's answers, but from them I could clearly deduce the nature of the talk. Stalin was evidently enquiring after Shostakovich's health. Dmitri Dmitriyevich answered disconsolately: "Thank you, everything is fine. I am only suffering somewhat from stomach-ache."

Stalin asked if he needed a doctor or any medicine.

"No, thank you, I don't need anything. I have everything I need."

Then there was a long pause while Stalin spoke. It transpired that he was asking Shostakovich to travel to the USA for the Congress of Peace and Culture.

". . . Of course I will go, if it is really necessary, but I am in a fairly difficult position. Over there, almost all my symphonies are played, whereas over here they are forbidden. How am I to behave in this situation?"

And then, as has been recounted many times since, Stalin said with his strong Georgian accent, "How do you mean forbidden? Forbidden by whom?"

"By the State Committee for Repertoire (Glavrepertkom)," answered Dmitri Dmitriyevich.

Stalin assured Shostakovich that this was a mistake, which would be corrected; none of Dmitri Dmitriyevich's works had been forbidden; they could be freely performed.

And in fact on March 16, as a result of Stalin's direct order, the official ban on the performance of Shostakovich's works was lifted (though, as Sanderling's remarks make clear, it was the *un-official* position that mattered, and Shostakovich's compositions were to remain largely unperformed for the rest of Stalin's life).

Laurel Fay, in her masterful biography of the composer, gives us Shostakovich's own remembrance of this event, as taken from his 1973 reminiscences:

At the appointed time, Nina Vasilyevna and Anusya Vilyams took up their posts at extensions, just in case. When I was told that Comrade Stalin would speak with me, I took fright. I don't remem-ber the conversation exactly, but Stalin proposed that I travel to the

United States with a delegation. I imagined with horror how I would be pestered there with questions about the recent resolution and blurted out that I was sick, that I couldn't go, and that the music of Prokofiev, Myaskovsky, Khachaturyan, and myself was not being performed.

The next day a brigade of doctors arrived, examined me, and really did pronounce me sick, but Poskrebishev said he would not relay that to Comrade Stalin.

The medical issues come up again in Galina Shostakovich's reminiscences, though in a slightly different form:

And then something unprecedented happened—on 16th March Father received a telephone call from Stalin himself. Shostakovich tried to excuse himself from going to the United States, saying he was embarrassed as his music was banned at home. Stalin lifted the ban at once. But the conversation didn't end there. Still trying to avoid going on the trip to America, Father said: "I'm not feeling well . . . I'm ill . . ."

Then Stalin asked: "Where do you receive medical care?"

The answer was: "At my local polyclinic . . ."

The conversation carried on, but this exchange was not without consequence. As I already mentioned, one of the results of the Historic Decree of 1948 was that our family had lost the privilege of using the "Kremliovka" [the clinic attended by the Soviet elite]. And the very day Stalin rang my father, we started getting telephone calls from this polyclinic, requesting us to fill in forms, submit our photographs, and, most importantly, come at once to see them—the whole family—to have a full check-up.

What all these accounts stress is the surprising and somewhat terrifying nature of Stalin's personal intervention, and also its immediate effectiveness. What they do not mention is the terribly double-edged nature of such help—the uncomfortable, disorienting, and ultimately self-eroding effect on the recipient of such unasked-for assistance. Despite his humiliating capitulations in public, Shostakovich had managed to retain a kind of innocent martyr's dignity during the period when he was left completely out in the cold. But now, with Stalin's overt intervention in his case, even that moral high ground was taken from him.

It would take a novelist's skill to portray the complexity of this situation; luckily, a very good novelist has done so. Vasily Grossman's *Life and Fate* is a massive, ambitious attempt to do for the Second World War what Tolstoy had done for the Napoleonic Wars, and if it does not quite achieve that unreachable height, it is nonetheless a remarkable piece of fiction. Completed in 1960 but only published posthumously in 1980 (and even then only outside the Soviet Union, in smuggled-out versions), the novel is set in the Russia of the 1940s, both during and after the war. One of its main characters is a Jewish physicist named Viktor Shtrum, a brilliant scientist whose postwar work life has essentially been destroyed by anti-Semitism. One day in about 1946 he receives an unexpected phone call at home:

> A voice unbelievably similar to the voice that had addressed the nation, the army, the entire world on 3 July, 1941, now addressed a solitary individual holding a telephone receiver.
> "Good day, comrade Shtrum."
> At that moment everything came together in a jumble of half-formed thoughts and feelings—triumph, a sense of weakness,

fear that all of this might just be some maniac playing a trick on him, pages of closely written manuscript, that endless questionnaire, the Lubyanka . . .

Viktor knew that his fate was now being settled. He also had a vague sense of loss, as though he had lost something peculiarly dear to him, something good and touching.

"Good day, Iosif Vissarionovich," he said, astonished to hear himself pronouncing such unimaginable words on the telephone.

The conversation that follows takes very much the form of Shostakovich's reported conversation with Stalin, though the subject is of course science rather than music; and by the close of it Shtrum has his laboratory back, just as Shostakovich ended up with the ban on his performances lifted. In fact, the parallel is so close that I would not be surprised to learn that Grossman had based this fictional interview on the famous composer's widely reported experience. (Shostakovich and his music are explicitly mentioned elsewhere in the novel, and one of the central characters even spends most of the war years in Kuibyshev, the town to which the Shostakoviches were evacuated.) On the other hand, Stalin made many such phone calls, and they were all heavily publicized. As Laurel Fay has commented, it was "one of his more gruesome mechanisms: hope."

Though I had read many accounts of Stalin's phone call to Shostakovich, it was not until I read *Life and Fate* that I realized how the anguished man's sense of relief must have been mingled with something much darker and more disturbing—disturbing in part because it was confusing, since even the man to whom it was happening could barely comprehend his own complex mixture of emotions. "There was just one thing he didn't understand," Grossman says of Shtrum. "Mixed with his joy and his feeling of triumph was a sadness that seemed to well up from somewhere deep underground, a sense of regret for something sacred and cherished that seemed to be slipping away from him. For some reason he felt guilty, but he had no idea what of or before whom." I am as morally certain as one can be of such things (though that, from this distance, is not very sure at all) that Shostakovich felt something very much like this on that March day in 1949.

He went, at any rate, to America—as a delegate to the so-called Cultural and Scientific Conference for World Peace, held at the Waldorf-Astoria Hotel in New York—and he suffered there as badly as he expected to. Not only did he have to sit in uncomfortable silence as his translator delivered a 5,000-word speech attacking Igor Stravinsky and modern music; he also had to weather a public cross-examination by a hostile (and, as it turned out, CIA-funded) émigré, Nicolas Nabokov, who kept asking Shostakovich to critique Zhdanov's pronouncements about music. Twisting and drumming his fingers in his characteristic manner, and radiating unease with his whole face and body, Shostakovich was eventually forced out of his silence and into a single comment: "I fully agree with the statements made in *Pravda*." If this flat statement was meant to carry an undertone of the intentional false note, there was no one present at the conference who could hear it. Later he apparently told Yevgeny Mravinsky that being forced to agree publicly with Zhdanov's condemnation of Stravinsky was "the worst moment of his life."

Still, he gained something on this American trip as well. At a concert in New York he heard the Juilliard Quartet perform Béla Bartók's First, Fourth, and Sixth Quartets, and though he professed to dislike the Fourth, he expressed substantial enthusiasm for the Sixth. One cannot necessarily say that the experience of hearing Bartók's music was a direct cause, any more than the phone call from Stalin or all the miseries of the preceding year were. But it is demonstrably the case that soon after he got back from America, Shostakovich began work on his own Fourth Quartet.

What one hears in Shostakovich's Quartet No. 4 in D Major, animating the lyrical solos and braided sonorities of the stringed instruments, is the suggestion of a singing voice. Sometimes the singer is humming to himself, but more often he is singing out loud, trying to get through to us, begging to be understood. The song may be wordless and indeed, in a literal sense, voiceless, but it is laden with feeling and hence with meaning; in this version of song, the words have been transmuted into the melody itself. If Shostakovich borrowed from his "Jewish songs" to create this quartet, the reused element is not so much the Jewishness— though that is what everyone, including the Soviet watchdogs, focused on—as the idea of song.

For me, the way into the Fourth Quartet has not been through the somewhat overbearing fourth movement, with its explicitly klezmerish solos and its self-mockingly jocular reliance on pizzicato, but through the singularly beautiful and moving second movement, the Andantino. I am not the first to feel this way. Alan George, the Fitzwilliams' violist, has said in his program notes that "if the finale is the focal point of the quartet, then its heart lies in the Andantino." This seems to me exactly right. And yet the more self-effacing Andantino (at six and a half minutes, it is only two-thirds the length of the final Allegretto, and it is the only slow movement of the four) did not really call itself to my attention until I heard the Beethoven Quartet's recording. Something about the way the Beethovens played this second movement, in a performance pitched exactly between eloquence and restraint, made me understand for the first time how much Shostakovich was relying on the notion of song.

In this movement, that song belongs to the first violin, which carries the melody at almost every point—sometimes on its own amid the complete silence of the other three, more often against a soft, sweet, gently rhythmic background provided by the viola and the second violin. The cello sits out the first minute and more; when it does finally enter, it carries a melody that echoes, in a slightly depressed, low-register way, the much higher tune of the violin, lending an added depth of feeling to this already very moving piece of music. But the emotion, though it borders on the kind of pure, enjoyable sadness that certain folk melodies evoke, is not easy or comfortable: this sadness is also anxiety-ridden and painful in the usual Shostakovich way.

For the Andantino to work as it should, the players need to strike a careful balance between conveying the privacy of an inner life and communicating through song. The Beethovens, in particular, seem to me to render it perfectly, avoiding either breast-beating display, on the one hand, or cerebral interiority, on the other. But all the recordings I've listened to capture something of what is at work in the beautiful Andantino movement, a quality of direct and pensive tenderness that gives way, in the subsequent Allegretto, to an utterly different Shostakovich mode.

If the second movement is song, then the third—fast-paced, rhythmically regular, and thrumming with repeated eighth notes—is dance. In Shostakovich, dance is always allied to something slightly manic: a forced cheerfulness, a leaning toward the macabre or the grotesque or the satiric. It seems to have a connection to sex (in his youth, Shostakovich apparently loved the ballet not just as an art form he could write for, but because of the beautiful girls), and also to a kind of life-infused version of death. From Bach to Mahler, the composers who mattered to Shostakovich had drawn on dance forms to create their most purely musical pieces, and he did too: hence the profusion of waltzes, polkas, marches, and so forth in his works. But dance was also linked, for him, to the homey and the mundane, to having fun with friends and family in the privacy of one's living room, as we can see from the numerous stories about his playing the piano, from his teenage years onward, while others danced.

There is one such account which actually brings together the homey and the grotesque, the joy of dancing and the macabre being-made-to-dance. Recounted by his daughter, Galina, the story refers to a birthday party of hers that took place sometime between 1947, when the family moved to the new apartment, and 1954, when Galya turned eighteen—probably in the early 1950s, when she was in her mid-teens. On this occasion, she had invited over a few of her school friends to share celebratory refreshments with her parents and brother. "But they were tense, and no one said a word," Galya recalls. "These girls were living in terrible Soviet communal flats, and our separate apartment with two pianos and beautiful old furniture must have seemed like a fairy-tale palace to them." Reacting to the uncomfortable silence at the dining table, her father decided to "lighten the atmosphere" by playing some dance music:

> He invited us into his study, sat down at the piano, and began playing foxtrots and tangos, but he still couldn't get my school-friends to relax. Even today I can still hear his voice:
> "Well, let's dance, let's dance."

As Galina remembers it, "Two or three of my friends started to move hesitantly, but even then the ice didn't break." The attempt to cheer things up had not succeeded; if anything, it had made things worse by adding a new level of strain and embarrassment.

If dance is something that could turn compulsive and uncomfortable in Shostakovich's hands, song was something much more likely to be heartfelt. (Except, that is, when it was just the reverse: nothing could sound less emotionally authentic than Shostakovich's 1949 *Song of the Forests*, a patriotic oratorio composed explicitly to please his Soviet critics, unless perhaps it was his 1952 cantata, *The Sun Shines over Our Motherland*, written for the same purpose.) Expressive song had repeatedly gotten him into trouble, first in his opera *Lady Macbeth*, later in his cycle *From Jewish Poetry*, but he apparently could not stay away from the idea of a text-based composition, and he was to return to it, complete with its attendant troubles, in his Thirteenth and Fourteenth Symphonies. There was no place for the human voice as such in a quartet, but in the Fourth Quartet Shostakovich appeared to be working hard to incorporate that voice into the music, trying to achieve the kind of direct access to emotion that is normally expressed in song. And yet it's not really accurate to describe anything in a Shostakovich string quartet as "direct," for in these highly ambiguous works, every feeling also seems to contain its opposite, every gesture to imply a possible counter-gesture.

The Quartet No. 4 is dedicated to the memory of Pyotr Vilyams, a close friend of Shostakovich's who died in late 1947 at the relatively young age of forty-five. (His widow was the "Anusya" who, with Nina, stood by for moral support during Stalin's phone call.) Vilyams, a prominent painter and set designer, worked during the 1940s mainly as chief designer at the Bolshoi Theater, where he earned three Stalin Prizes, the first of them for his 1942 production of Rossini's *William Tell*. So the song and dance elements in the Fourth Quartet may well allude partly to the dedicatee's career in opera and ballet, just as the galloping rhythm that arises midway through the fast-paced third movement might be heard as a suppressed reference to the *William Tell* overture.

Vilyams's father, Robert Williams, was an American scientist who had moved to Moscow and taken Russian citizenship in 1896—a real-life version, as it were, of the Anglo-Russian characters in Penelope Fitzgerald's novel *The Beginning of Spring*. Pyotr, born in 1902, entered art school in 1919, studied painting under Wassily Kandinsky, and within a few years became a founding member of one of the Soviet Union's early avant-garde art movements. Like Shostakovich, he was a very young man when the revolution itself was young, and like the composer, he reveled in the artistic and social ferment of the 1920s, a period that, from the perspective of the 1940s, seemed unimaginably free and hopeful. In 1934—the same year Shostakovich premiered *Lady Macbeth*, practically the last year of that pre-Terror brave new world—Vilyams painted his *Nana*, a portrait that Shostakovich acquired and hung in his study, where it remained for the rest of his life.

Vilyams's *Nana*, like Manet's 1877 painting of the same name, is obviously based on the Zola character from the novels *L'Assommoir* and *Nana*, a precociously attractive, earthily money-grubbing, somewhat heartless, ultimately pitiable prostitute. It's also clear that Vilyams had seen the Manet, or at least a reproduction of it: he openly steals the top-hatted gent who edges into the picture's right-hand frame, and he also copies exactly the revealing style of Nana's bodice (though, in the process, he changes Manet's cool, girlish blue to a hot orange-pink). But the feel of the two paintings is completely different. If Manet's young woman is essentially a figure of the nineteenth century—still capable of emitting, and attracting, a measure of true feeling—

Vilyams's somewhat older Nana seems like a cross between a Weimar moll and a de Kooning Woman. She is voracious, comic, and a little bit frightening, her allure acknowledged but also viewed with a satiric edge. The difference between them is, in a way, the difference between the second movement of Quartet No. 4 and its final movement. What begins as a delicate expression of a tender emotion becomes exaggerated and slightly monstrous, self-dramatizing and therefore self-mocking, even about its own despair. There is great vitality to the Vilyams, but there is also a degree of feverish anxiety—a sense of running out of time, racing to get the most out of life before it is all used up—that is utterly absent from the calmly appealing Manet, and that makes the picture desperately sad as well as blowsily amusing. The portrait contains, and evokes, a complicated mixture of emotions; and Shostakovich, looking at *Nana* every day as he sat down to work, recalling the world she had come from in 1934 and contemplating the one he had arrived at in 1949, somehow managed to get them into the Fourth Quartet.

Or so it seems to me. But whatever the private references behind the quartet may have been, the music itself was not intended for merely private consumption: it was written to be heard. That Shostakovich never ceased in his efforts to have his new work played, even during the period when almost all his music was informally banned, comes through in a story told by Valentin Berlinsky, the Borodin Quartet's cellist. Apparently the Borodins, with Shostakovich's assistance, had prepared the Fourth Quartet for an "audition" in front of the official who headed the music section of the Ministry of Culture; their aim was to get the already finished quartet commissioned by the Ministry, so that Shostakovich could at least be paid something during this dark time. According to Berlinsky, this official

> came from Leningrad and was a cultured, intelligent man, with progressive attitudes. He tried to help Shostakovich. The audition succeeded in its purpose, and the Ministry bought the quartet and paid Shostakovich a fee. However, it was only performed in public after Stalin's death. There is a story in circulation that we had to play the quartet twice on this occasion, once in our genuine interpretation, and a second time "optimistically," to convince the authorities of its "socialist" content. It's a pretty invention, but it's not true: you cannot lie in music.

Whether you can lie or indeed tell the truth in music is a question that is not, I think, as open-and-shut as Berlinsky makes it here. But this is a complicated matter that I hope to revisit later. For the moment, the important point is that two of the most significant works Shostakovich wrote between the Zhdanov Decree of 1948 and Stalin's death in 1953, the Fourth and Fifth Quartets, were never performed in public during that time, though they were repeatedly heard at "rehearsals" attended by a small number of colleagues, students, and friends.

Very little had changed in Shostakovich's external life between the composition of the Fourth Quartet in 1949 and the writing of the Fifth in 1952. Despite Stalin's having rescinded the official ban on his music, hardly any of it was played in public during those years, and his reputation remained under a heavy cloud. He survived on movie scores and other commissions—survived comparatively well, as Galya's story about the impressive apartment suggests, with enough income to pay for a chauffeur and to subsidize his mother's expenses in Leningrad. But money was still tight, and hard-earned. He remained available to those students who sought him out, but he had not been restored to either of his teaching posts. Nonetheless, in what was perhaps simply a refinement of the torture, he continued to receive political appointments throughout this period: in 1950, for instance, he was one of the musicians elected to the Soviet Committee for the Defense of Peace, and in 1951 he was re-elected as a deputy to the Supreme Soviet from Leningrad's Dzerzhinsky District. Over the years he was also obliged to attend a number of international and national congresses, often delivering speeches in support of the Party and the USSR which would then be published and distributed under his name. The sense of oppression was still ever-present. If the sense of immediate fear had dissipated somewhat, it was only because that particular emotion, like any other intense emotion, cannot be maintained at fever pitch for long.

Shostakovich did manage, during this period, to produce one solo work that had at least a half-presence in the wider world, and that was the *Twenty-four Preludes and Fugues* for piano. Though they were completed in early 1951, the fugues provoked violent criticism when Shostakovich first attempted to play them to the Composers' Union; it wasn't until another pianist, Tatiana Nikolayeva, performed them before the Committee for Artistic Affairs in the summer of 1952 that the work was approved for publication. But even before the official approval, bits and pieces of the cycle had been publicly played in 1950 and 1951 by various performers (including Shostakovich himself) in Moscow, Minsk, Helsinki, and Baku.

Whether it was due to the experience of writing *Twenty-four Preludes* or the prior experience that apparently gave rise to them—that is, Shostakovich's 1950 visit to Leipzig during the two hundredth anniversary of Bach's death, and his consequent reimmersion in the forty-eight preludes and fugues of *The Well-Tempered Clavier*—something of Bach's complicated and profound influence can be felt in the Fifth Quartet. And once again, as he had in the relatively recent Third Quartet, Shostakovich chose to dedicate this musically complex work to his players, the members of the Beethoven Quartet. He inscribed the autograph score he gave to them as follows: "This Quartet has been composed to mark the 30th anniversary of the Beethoven String Quartet and is dedicated to the artists, its members. Dear friends, please accept this modest gift as a testimony of my admiration of your wonderful art, of my deep gratitude for your splendid performance of my works, and of my great love for you. D. Shostakovich, November 13, 1953." (The inscription bears the date of the first performance, which took place at the Small Hall of the

Moscow Conservatory almost exactly a year after the completion of the quartet and, not coincidentally, eight months after the death of Stalin.)

The Quartet No. 5 in B-flat Major has no plot, no characters, no obvious personal agenda of any kind. It is one long, continuous sweep of music. Though its thirty minutes have been formally divided into three movements (an initial Allegro, a middle Andante, and a final Moderato), you cannot actually hear the breaks between them, try as you might. The quartet itself seems to ask you to try: it so often moves into near-silence that, as you listen, you find yourself leaning into the music, straining to catch the moment at which one sound breaks off and another starts. Despite the illusion of silence—a silence that seems to be the quartet's deepest and most prominent element—there is no passage, except at the very end, where all four instruments cease playing at once. And though we often have the sense of a small solo voice eking out its little tune against nothingness, this background "nothingness" is actually created by a series of very high (or, occasionally, very low) simultaneous *pianissimo* notes played on the three other instruments.

The whole feel of the piece is at once vast in its scope and tiny in its focus. The visual equivalent might be a Poussin landscape, with its distant sunlit mountains in the background and, in the shadowy space up front, the smallest human gesture closely examined. But there can be no visual equivalent, nor any literary or theatrical equivalent, because the Fifth Quartet is utterly abstract and irreducible in the way only music can be; it *is* its patterns and repetitions and chords and silences, which do not stand for anything other than themselves. In this quartet Shostakovich seems to have taken the freedom that was forced on him by the Soviet censors—those listeners who found even his earlier works too abstract or formalist or individualist to be performed in public—and used it to produce something that went as far as he could go in that direction. He could not have known when he wrote the Quartet in B-flat Major whether he would ever be allowed to hear it in public, and though he certainly did not write it in order to hide it away (as we can see from the fact that he got it played at the first opportunity), the knowledge that in the short run it would probably remain private might have made it easier for him to venture into this implicitly forbidden territory. Musically and politically, this move toward abstraction was a very brave gesture, and it represented a kind of implied resistance, even if of a determinedly apolitical sort. But whether it sprang from courage, or stubbornness, or self-indulgence, or sheer obliviousness to the consequences, is impossible to say. Perhaps, in Shostakovich, all those elements were too closely bound up to be separable.

If the music of the Fifth Quartet is highly abstract, in the manner of a Bach fugue—that is, with a focus on brief repeated themes that alter slightly each time they are played, appearing and disappearing with profuse inventiveness, recalling each other only to depart from each other—the feelings it conveys are

nonetheless intense. The repetitions are both obsessive and prob-
ing, not reassuring, as they are in Bach; and those nearly unde-
tectable background chords create an eerie, almost frightening
sensation of extreme depth beneath the etched surface. "There's
a sense in Shostakovich of a suspension of time," observes the
Emerson Quartet violinist Philip Setzer, and he connects this
with the fact that "a lot of Shostakovich's suffering, his form of
'imprisonment,' was waiting." That particular sense of dread—
that waiting for the knock on the door in the middle of the
night, or for the arbitrary committee decision that will bury
a life's work, or for the next public demand that will require
painful self-abasement and induce extreme self-disgust—is what
Setzer and other performers hear in the quartets, and perhaps
especially in the Fifth Quartet. This anxiety may well be the
strongest feeling his music conveys, and it communicates itself
even to nonmusicians, both those who never knew Shostakovich
and those who knew him well. "When I listen to my father's
work, it evokes in me some kind of nervousness," said his daughter Galina, speaking a half-century after this quartet was composed. "I can't say I picture my father, but I can sense his nervousness."

Shostakovich's ever-present feeling of anxious melancholy, or
melancholic anxiety, may pervade the Fifth Quartet, but at the
same time there is an almost comical aspect to the musical line's
willful changeability. Paul Epstein hints at this slapstick quality
when, in his program notes, he describes how "the opening
theme seems to stroll out of the front door, walk twelve bars

down the street and then get hit in the face with the full force of violent events." (And one might also think, in this context, of Shostakovich's passion for watching professional soccer, a game where the direction of play, the movement of the ball, can and does shift with surprising suddenness.) Still, as always in the quartets, the presence of humor doesn't undercut the feeling of anxiety; on the contrary, the willed attempt to lighten the mood only points out how very dark it is.

Simultaneously melodic and unmelodic, constant and yet changeable, amorphous-seeming though discernibly structured, the Fifth Quartet "contains multitudes," to borrow Walt Whitman's description of his own self-contradictions. This is part of what makes it feel so large. Then there is also the curious way it seems to draw into itself all those moments of time in which the music is not playing, the moments that lie behind and between and outside the particular notes we hear. Listening to this quartet, we seem to be listening for silence itself, waiting for the music to emerge out of silence. And this means that when it finally disappears back into that realm—when, at the very end, all four instruments fall silent together—there is a powerful sense of resolution. To the usual feeling of his *morendo* endings, with their sad, gradual dying away, Shostakovich has added something new, as if to say: ah, yes, *this* is how silence sounds; *this* is the thing itself, the one we've been searching for all along.

The Quartet No. 5 is, in its own way, a triumph over T. S. Eliot's dissociation of sensibility, that post-seventeenth-century malaise whereby thought allegedly became separated from emotion. The music is cerebral and controlled, filled with patterns that point to themselves as such, and yet it is also touchingly human, profoundly moving. This, too, the composer might have derived from his recent immersion in Bach. Shostakovich had found a way to be expressive, as he was in all his quartets, but what was being expressed here was nothing more nor less than the music itself.

To seek out coded private meanings in a work as grand and abstract as the Quartet in B-flat Major seems particularly pointless. And yet this is the first quartet in which Shostakovich explicitly inserted such a code. It's there in the second movement: a repeated, direct quotation from the 1949 trio for clarinet, violin, and piano by Galina Ustvolskaya, a student of his who had become an excellent composer in her own right and who was also, at the time he wrote the Fifth Quartet, his lover. What this suggests to me is that we need to handle such codes with all the care we use in handling Shostakovich's written and reported statements. That is, they cannot be taken at face value. More importantly, they cannot be taken to stand in for the "meaning" of the musical piece. If Shostakovich wants to base a particular musical passage on his girlfriend's clarinet trio—or his own initials, or somebody else's first name, as he was to do in the Tenth Symphony, which came right after the Fifth Quartet—that does not mean he has handed us the key to the whole work. He is playing with us; or maybe he is just playing.

Galina Ustvolskaya was not the first of Shostakovich's extramarital infatuations, nor was she to be the last. His obsession with Elmira Nazirova, a young pianist who had also been a student of his, came so soon upon the heels of the Ustvolskaya affair that by 1953, when he was composing the Tenth Symphony, it was Elmira's name that he wove into the texture of the music, along with his own signature initials in their first distinct appearance. (Some readers might reasonably wonder how either "Elmira" or "D. Sch." could possibly be turned into scored passages on an A-through-G staff. When I get to the Eighth Quartet, the piece in which he used his D–S–C–H monogram most intensely, I'll go into his method for converting letters of the alphabet to musical pitches; for now let me just say that Elmira's name can be rendered as the notes E, A, E, D, A, and Shostakovich's as D, E-flat, C, B. This too, like so much else during that period, is a strategy Shostakovich doubtless borrowed from Bach, who inserted his own B–A–C–H signature into his final series of fugues.)

The relationship with Nazirova was probably largely if not entirely epistolary—she lived in faraway Baku, and he was spending that summer at his dacha in Komarovo—but Shostakovich clearly treated her as his "muse" in the thirty-four letters he sent to her outlining the progress of the Tenth Symphony. It must have helped, at least in his decision to keep the allusion if not in his initial invention of it, that the coding of her name produced the same sequence of notes as a recognizable passage from Mahler's *Das Lied von der Erde*, one of Shostakovich's favorite pieces of music.

The muse tradition, or at least the habit of being constantly in love, goes back to his earliest years as a composer. Like his friend Sollertinsky, Shostakovich had been a notorious ladies' man in his (and the century's) twenties. When he first met Nina Varzar in 1927—the year he turned twenty-one—he had already been deeply in love with Tatiana Glivenko for four years, and that affair persisted through Tatiana's marriage to someone else. (According to Glivenko's rather self-serving account, Shostakovich's sudden marriage to Nina in 1932 was merely a reaction to the birth of her own first child, the final sign that she would never leave her husband for him.) A couple of years after he married Nina, he fell madly in love again, this time with the young interpreter Yelena Konstantinovskaya, whom he met at an international music festival in Leningrad in 1934. This relationship proved so intense that it broke up the marriage for a while: Nina left him in 1934, and though Shostakovich briefly tried for a reconciliation, he later divorced her for Yelena, only to return to Nina for good in the fall of 1935. Whether the final reconciliation with Nina predated or followed his discovery that she was pregnant with their first child cannot be determined with any certainty. All we know is that he wrote to Sollertinsky in the early fall with the words "There can be no question of a divorce from Nina. I have only now realized and fathomed what a remarkable woman she is, and how precious to me." To his friend Levon Atovmyan, he then telegraphed: "Remaining in Leningrad. Nina pregnant. Remarried. Mitya."

Atovmyan's take on the marriage, and on Nina's role in Shostakovich's life, echoes the view presented by a number of their friends from that era. "I have to say that Nina Vasilyevna not only had a marvelous mind, but was spiritually a person of great beauty," Atovmyan noted,

> and she proved to be a unique friend to Dmitri Dmitriyevich, a wonderful companion who under all kinds of circumstances never lost spirit. During the most difficult times, she exercised great tact in maintaining a cheerful atmosphere in the house, and she knew how to transmit a firm confidence to Shostakovich. I was never to see another such true and steadfast friend in the Shostakovich circles.

Flora Litvinova, who met the Shostakoviches together during their wartime evacuation to Kuibyshev, was equally impressed: "I was full of delighted admiration for Nina, her exceptional and independent mind, her decisive yet calm character." She felt Nina made Shostakovich's composing life possible, in part by fending off people who would otherwise have destroyed his peace. One such character, for example, was a powerful and pushy playwright who wanted Shostakovich to compose an opera based on his new libretto—an assignment the composer had no intention of taking on, though he didn't know how to say no directly. (With frightening self-awareness and eerie pre-science, Shostakovich apparently told Litvinova, "When somebody starts pestering me, I have only one thought in mind—get rid of him as quickly as possible, and to achieve that I am prepared to sign anything.") But Nina assured her husband she would handle the problem while he was away in Moscow. As

Litvinova remembers it, "Nina laughingly showed me the note that Shostakovich had left, listing chores for her to do in his absence; it included 'Tell the librettist to f—— off.'" This nay-saying role was repeatedly assigned to Nina within the family economy, and as a result there were many acquaintances and petitioners who disliked her, attributing every harsh or disap-pointing element in Shostakovich's behavior to her influence. But she seems to have been very much loved by most of the people close to him.

With the distinct exception of his mother. Wives and mothers of male geniuses are not expected to get along: the spouse, who is in any case cruelly depriving the mother of sole possession, can never live up to the unrealistic expectations of the proud parent; and the mother-in-law, even if she could stop interfering— which she can't—will naturally receive all the daughter-in-law's blame for the impossible temperament of her spoiled husband. But in Shostakovich's case the clash was even worse than usual. His mother, Sofia Vasilyevna, actively opposed the marriage to Nina Varzar, and the Varzars actively opposed Sofia Vasilyevna— in particular, they objected to the fact that she planned to live with the young couple indefinitely. Whether because of his mother's influence or his own fear of marriage (they were prob-ably connected, in any case), Shostakovich simply failed to show up at one of his scheduled weddings to Nina, and Sofia Vasil-yevna believed he had broken off the engagement for good. Her shock was therefore intense when he returned home from a trip in 1932 with Nina in tow, having married her suddenly while he was away. Nina's feelings cannot have been much more sanguine, since she now found that they were to live with his mother in the overcrowded flat at 9 Marat Street, within those same three rooms where Shostakovich had grown up. Indeed, these psychologically volatile living arrangements may have been part of the reason—on top of the affair with Konstantinovskaya, of course—that the marriage broke up in 1934. Certainly when they got back together, the young couple did not return to Sofia Vasilyevna's household (which had by this time moved to 5 Dmitrovsky Pereulok, a couple of streets west of Marat). Instead, for the duration of their Leningrad life they had their own flat in the area north of the Neva—first in a rather plain but solid apartment house at 14 Kirovsky Prospect, and later in an even plainer, distinctly unattractive building at 23 Bolshaya Pushkarskaya.

From the account Sofia Vasilyevna later gave to Victor Seroff, Shostakovich's wartime biographer, it would appear that Nina's ultimate victory was never forgiven. Seroff is so in thrall to this powerful mother than he essentially speaks in her voice, describing the young Sofia as "a brilliant student" and "a young lady of beauty" who also possessed "a keen intuitive judgment." Nina, in contrast, is presented as one of three sisters "who were not great beauties," a quiet girl "whose interests lay only in her academic studies." (Let it be said, for the record, that the photographs of each young woman in her prime do not bear out this relative assessment.)

At any rate, Shostakovich proved to have his own keen intuitive judgment about what he needed in a domestic partner. Years earlier, when he was sixteen years old and spending the summer in the Crimea, recovering from his recent operation for tuberculosis of the lymph glands, he had written his mother a letter that rather amazingly predicted the shape of his future married life:

> Of course the best thing imaginable would be a total abolition of *marriage*, of all fetters and duties in the face of love. But that is utopian, of course. Without marriage there can be no family, and that really does spell disaster. And Mother dear, I want to warn you that if I ever fall in love, maybe I won't want to marry. But if I did get married, and if my wife ever fell in love with another man, I wouldn't say a word; and if she wanted a divorce I would give her one and I would blame only myself. (If that didn't seem right, for example, if the man she loved was married and his wife had prejudices, then I would handle the situation differently; and if she was afraid of social prejudice she would have to keep living at my address.) But at the same time there exists the sacred calling of a mother and father. So you see, when I really start thinking about it my head starts spinning. Anyhow, love is free!

The astonishing thing is that the mature Shostakovich was able to act so consistently on this romantic, idealistic, early-Soviet, late-adolescent fantasy—so consistently, and so fairly, for the husband in this marriage got as good as he gave. Nina was no Penelope, waiting chastely at home for her wandering Ulysses to return. She too took lovers, had adventures, threw herself passionately into life and work.

After the war Nina had finally been able to return to her career as a physicist, and by the early 1950s—the same period as Shostakovich's dalliance with Ustvolskaya—she was working closely with an old friend and eminent colleague, Artyom Alikhanyan, who was also widely known to be her lover. Each fall she went to Armenia to work with him on cosmic radiation at the Mount Alagez facility, leaving the two teenaged children in Shostakovich's care. That Alikhanyan was also a family friend, and that Shostakovich kept his youthful promise not to "say a word" about this longstanding relationship, is only part of what made the marriage bond remarkable and enduring. Evidently, despite its oddities and difficulties (difficulties that were exacerbated by the repeated political blows Shostakovich had suffered, through all of which Nina stood by him and protected him), the marriage really worked—and, even more unusually, worked equally well for both of them.

In the fall of 1954, Nina was in Armenia as usual. Shostakovich, meanwhile, was at home in Moscow, supervising the performances of several new pieces. Since the death of Stalin on March 5, 1953 (the same day, sadly, that brought the death of Prokofiev, who thus never knew the terror had ended), Shostakovich's music had been restored to the concert halls. In this atmosphere of "thaw," as it was called, he was once again a favored composer. In quick succession, he was able to premiere the String Quartet No. 5 (on November 13, 1953), the String Quartet No. 4 (on December 3 of the same year), and the long-awaited Tenth Symphony (on December 17, with the Leningrad Philharmonic performing under the baton of Yevgeny Mravinsky). The following November brought the first performances of the *Festive Overture* and, two days later, the Concertino for Two Pianos, which featured Shostakovich's sixteen-year-old son, Maxim, as one of the pianists.

On December 3, 1954, Shostakovich was sitting in the audience of a Moscow concert hall when he was reached with news of a family emergency. Nina, he was told, was in the hospital in Yerevan. He and eighteen-year-old Galya flew to Armenia immediately, but by the time they got there the next day, Nina had already undergone surgery for a cancerous colon and had lapsed into a coma. "Our first impulse," Galya said many years later, reporting on the events of that evening as if she were still in the midst of them, "is to resolve immediate problems: how to organize a 24-hour watch by her bedside; who will stay with her that first night. And at that moment someone in a white gown comes in and informs us that Mother has died."

That night Shostakovich called Natalya Mikhoels and Moisei Weinberg, who had been among his and Nina's closest family friends, and asked them to go to his apartment so that Maxim would not be alone when his father telephoned him with the news. "When we got to the flat we found his son Maxim on the phone," Natalya reports. "When he put down the receiver he said, 'Now they'll devour him,' and burst into tears." And Maxim, too, in his own recollection of that terrible night, describes it mainly in terms of the devastating effect on his father:

> I remember sitting and waiting for the telephone call. My slippers were torn and I was trying to sew them up myself. Then the call came from Yerevan.
> Papa said: "Mama has died."

I realized that I must support him somehow. And I tried to say something to comfort him.

The body was brought back to Moscow by train, and the funeral took place on December 10. "It was during those days," Galya recalls, "that I saw my father weeping for the first time." Maxim's memory is of visiting the graveyard with his father: "When he was shown the place of mother's grave at the cemetery, Father kept saying, 'Here's a place for me too, here's a place for me too. . . .'" Before the body was taken to the cemetery, it lay at the Shostakovich apartment, visited by friends and family. "I only remember that when I walked into the flat, I saw Nina lying in the open coffin on the table; she looked tranquil, beautiful, and appeared to be only asleep," Flora Litvinova says. "Dmitri Dmitriyevich stood next to her. We kissed and both burst into tears." Isaak Glikman remembers the events of that day in more detail:

> In the grief-laden hours before the funeral, Shostakovich told me of Nina Vasilyevna's last minutes, his haggard features twitching and the tears starting from his eyes. However, with an effort of will he brought his emotions under control and we abruptly turned to other, unimportant topics.
>
> A long line of people wishing to pay their last respects filed through Shostakovich's study. Lev Atovmyan had got hold of a tape recorder, and the music of the Eighth Symphony filled the room. I sat on the sofa next to Shostakovich, who wept silently.

This is the account given in Glikman's own notes, in his published book of letters from Shostakovich. But a slightly different version appears in Michael Ardov's book, where he quotes Glikman as saying: "The music of Shostakovich's Quartets and the Eighth Symphony was played on a tape recorder set up by Levon Atovmyan." Which is the error and which the true account? Perhaps it doesn't matter. The point is that the mournful music coming from the tape recorder during Nina's wake *felt* like Shostakovich's string quartets, even if it wasn't.

For a long time after Nina died, Shostakovich barely wrote anything at all, except some commissioned film music and one or two occasional pieces. It was the longest fallow period of his life, longer even than the gap after the Fifth Symphony, and he began to worry that it might become permanent. "I have very little news. And even less good news," he wrote to a friend in March of 1956. "The saddest thing is that after the Tenth Symphony I have hardly composed anything. If this continues I'll soon be like Rossini, who, as is well known, wrote his last work at the age of forty. He then went on to live till seventy without writing another note. This is small comfort to me."

But he finally broke his long silence, just as he had done in 1938, by writing a string quartet. The Quartet No. 6 in G Major, composed in the summer of 1956 and first performed in October of that year, shortly after Shostakovich's very public fiftieth-birthday celebration, is perhaps the hardest to read of all the quartets. This is not because it is especially difficult or dissonant or clouded with sorrow. On the contrary, what obscures our view of this quartet is its apparent—I would say its actual— lightness. Here, at what might be seen as the darkest period in Shostakovich's personal life, we get something that occasionally approaches cheer.

Well, not cheer as such: not cheer as it would be in, say, Rossini's hands. But for Shostakovich, the overall tone of the Sixth Quartet is surprisingly hopeful. Like the First Quartet, it begins with a limpid, almost happy tune, this time played confidently on the first and second violins. We are back in that forest where we met that adventurous little boy, that solitary traveler—only now he is much less hesitant, much more sure of himself and his strengths. He has been through dark times and survived them; he knows how badly life can treat him, and he is grateful for the occasional if always brief moments of respite. He is surprised to discover in himself, at this late date, some small possibility of happiness, and he wishes to grab hold of that feeling if he can. On the other hand, he understands himself—and the world— too well to believe that the good mood can last. Whether because of his own deeply melancholic nature or the sudden turn of external events (most likely a combination of both), his apparent rescue will only be temporary. So it is an uneasy cheer, a disquieted sense of hope, that we feel in this quartet.

We can hear the anxiety surfacing in the high-pitched notes and slithery arpeggios of the second movement, which introduce into this hesitantly playful waltz a note of spooky otherworldliness. The skating-on-thin-ice waltz tune becomes, in these moments, something akin to a Mahlerian dance of death (as manifested, for instance, in Mahler's Fourth Symphony Scherzo and his Ninth Symphony Ländler, both of which rely on the frightening yet seductive sound of a distortedly shrill violin playing in 3/4 time). We can also hear the nervousness in the quartet's final movement, where cheer modulates briefly into hysteria, as if even the briefest happiness cannot help becoming manic, or anxiety-ridden, or at any rate harsh and piercing in the manner of those loud, fast, rough bow strokes. And we can hear it, of course, in the strangely unexpected dissonances that are, as in any Shostakovich quartet, sprinkled over all four movements, drawing on and then disrupting the ear's expectations of harmony. But the strongest melancholy tone, the deepest sense of an underlying sorrow, comes through in the Lento third movement, where we at last get something like the recognizable, essential Shostakovich, once again in communion with himself. Yes, I am still here, he is saying, the same mournful person I've always been, and while that is sad, it is also deeply reassuring, because it is something familiar, not shocking or strange the way happiness would be.

Astute listeners like David Fanning and Judith Kuhn have sensed a "problem of tone" or an "emotional ambivalence" in this quartet, and have variously attributed this "deceptive cheer" to politically inspired hypocrisy, satiric mockery, ironic grotesquerie, willed naïveté—something self-imposed, at any rate, that mars the coherence of feeling. But to my ear the cheerfulness does not sound willed from within. There is no overt sardonicism here, no purposeful irony, no mockery at either the personal or political level, except insofar as any distance from the self counts as self-mockery. (And Shostakovich was never entirely without that kind of distance: consider, for instance, the wry tone in his epistolary comment about Rossini's fate—"This is small comfort to me"—which simultaneously expresses his true feelings and pokes minor fun at his own dolefulness.) If anything, it seems to me that the Sixth Quartet's cheer or lightness or call-it-what-you-will has been forced on the composer by unexpected and probably temporary circumstances. He has been surprised by joy, and he feels guilty about it.

Politically, 1956 was an unusual year in Soviet history. Nikita Khrushchev, speaking at the Twentieth Party Congress in February, had gone so far as to denounce Stalin and his "cult of personality," and this rather astonishing gesture by the Party leader had rapidly filtered down into all aspects of Soviet life. In Shostakovich's own realm of music and the arts, enlightened change was suddenly called for. The composer himself was summoned, in early 1956, to a meeting with a high Soviet official to discuss how the artists whose reputations had been destroyed under Stalin could now be "rehabilitated." The fact that some of these people (including Meyerhold, Prokofiev, Myaskovsky, and Mikhoels, to name but a few) had died or been murdered during the Great Terror and were no longer around to savor their rehabilitation would have accounted for at least part of his mixed feelings. Unadulterated cheer was neither appropriate nor possible in the circumstances, despite the obvious feeling of relief; irony, in that sense, was built into the times, not imposed by Shostakovich or any other interpreter.

To the complex reactions that everyone felt during the thaw, Shostakovich, with his propensity for guilt, would have brought his own particular twist. If he felt angry on behalf of himself and his fellow sufferers about all those lost, miserable years, he also felt ashamed at having survived them. The unfortunate victims were vindicated but dead; he, the lucky one, was still alive and therefore somehow less vindicated. The very reason for his present happiness—that he had lived long enough to see Stalin's crimes unmasked—also became the root of his unhappiness, when he focused on how many of his loved ones had not. And his own restoration to a position of power and influence, not only within the musical community but in the culture at large, would have exacerbated this tension.

But 1956 was also a significant year in Shostakovich's personal life, for early that summer, at a Komsomol-sponsored song contest, he met a young Party activist named Margarita Kainova, and by July he had married her. Like his first marriage, this one took place suddenly and nearly secretly (though not, this time, in order to avoid the interference of his mother: Sofia Vasilyevna had died the previous November, leaving Shostakovich orphaned as well as widowed, and hence doubly alone). Unlike Nina, however, Margarita was not popular with Shostakovich's friends. To judge by the after-the-fact commentary, not a single soul approved of the marriage, and no one could understand what he saw in her. Flora Litvinova reports that, even before the marriage, she learned from Anusya Vilyams "some frightening rumors about Dmitri Dmitriyevich's intended: that she worked for the Central Committee of the Komsomol, was a Party member, that she was unattractive and uncharming, and knew nothing about art." When she finally met the new bride, Flora recorded the event in her diary:

> Yesterday we went to see Shostakovich. Since Nina's death, we had only been around a few times. There is always an unpleasant feeling, a loss for words, a sense of awkwardness. Besides the absence of Nina and my own sadness at the loss of a genuine friend, I also miss that simplicity in my relations with Dmitri Dmitriyevich. . . . But on this occasion, Misha and I were just paying a visit. And there was no Nina, but an alien and unattractive woman, who, thank God, left the room after greeting us. . . . At supper time, Madame came to sit at table. She is terribly uninteresting, and there is something horse-like about her. She tries terribly hard to please everybody, from the guests to the children, and to adopt the right tone. But goodness, how vapid and unpleasant she is— particularly after Nina.

Shostakovich's whole circle was aware that he had felt in urgent need of a wife—shortly after Nina's death, he had pleaded with Galina Ustvolskaya to marry him, but she had firmly refused—and people may have assumed that when he chose Margarita, he was just looking for someone to take care of his children, his household, and himself. Her Communist Party membership, though it alienated his friends, might have struck him as an important element in this caretaking function: per-

haps he hoped that she could function as a shield against political pressure, and while such a hope would have been naive, it
would not have been uncharacteristic. That his children disliked
their stepmother intensely would not have prevented him from
marrying her. Part of her intended function was to quell their
wild ways, and he purposely didn't introduce her to them until
after the wedding. In any case, like Flora Litvinova, they would
probably have disliked anyone who proposed to take Nina's
place.

   But the degree of ire induced by Margarita among Shostakovich's friends and family cannot be solely attributed to their cherished memories of his first wife. Something about this marriage
troubled everyone. Even people who never *met* Kainova have
been anxious to banish her from the Shostakovich household.
Olga Dombrovskaya—who, as the curator of the Shostakovich
Archive, feels closely connected to the composer, though she is
too young to have known him personally—responded with a
shrug to questions about the current whereabouts of Margarita
Kainova. Was she alive or dead? What ever happened to her?
"Nothing special," asserted Dombrovskaya. "She was an occasional person, just on his way. . . . She was a person of a different
circle, of different interests. There was much more influence on
his life by women he was not married to—Konstantinova, Ustvolskaya. She was just flying over, and afterwards there were no
memories of her." And in the massive photograph album that
Dombrovskaya put together to commemorate the Shostakovich
centennial in 2006, there are indeed no memories of this second

wife—not a single picture of her, not even a brief mention. It is as if she never existed.

But she did exist; and Laurel Fay, in her scrupulously fair and accurate biography of the composer, has included a photograph of Shostakovich and Margarita that was taken in Paris in 1958. Because there is virtually no information about Kainova other than the catty remarks left to us by Shostakovich's associates, Fay hazards no theories about the marriage and its successes or failures: she is not the kind of writer who allows herself to indulge in guesswork or half-truths. But the picture tells its own story. In it, we can see that Margarita is rather pretty, and that Shostakovich is smiling. I do not know him well enough to read his often-masked face—I will never know him well enough for that, and the mask is particularly heavy during this period of his life—but if I were simply to look at this as a photo of two strangers, I would say that the graying, somewhat portly middle-aged gentleman standing on the bridge in Paris, glancing back at us over his right shoulder and smiling broadly, was very much enjoying the company of his significantly younger wife.

The Sixth Quartet was finished (and mostly written) in August of 1956—one month after the marriage to Margarita, less than two years after Nina's death, and almost four years after the completion of the previous string quartet. It came at the end of the three-year-long dry period that had followed the composition of the Tenth Symphony in 1953, and it was this dry period, rather than any lasting pain over the 1954 death of his much-loved wife or the 1955 death of his devoted mother, that Shostakovich called the "saddest thing" in his letter of March 1956. Of course, he was purposely avoiding the aura of self-pity even as he was being overtly self-pitying, and he was also writing to a former student rather than an old friend, so he would not necessarily have revealed his deepest or darkest feelings. Still, the expressed anxiety was real, and, given his fears of a permanent blockage, the arrival of a new quartet in the summer of 1956 would have been cause for celebration.

But what if the new string quartet had itself been brought about by the happiness, however fragile and unpredictable, of his second marriage? In this case, the unavoidable feelings of triumph and cheer could only have compounded Shostakovich's sense of guilt. The Quartet No. 6 was his first substantial piece undertaken after Nina's death, the only quartet he had ever written without her presence: it should, by rights, have been a work of mourning, acknowledging this severe loss in the way he had done in the Second Piano Trio for Sollertinsky, or in the Fourth Quartet for Vilyams. And instead it celebrated—uneasily, shamefacedly, with tremendous anxiety and trepidation and, yes, sadness, but nonetheless celebrated—the odd and amazing lightness he felt in his new marriage. It turned out that it was not only possible to survive the deaths of those he loved; it was also, at times, pleasurable. The shock to his system, to his whole sense of self, must have been immense. No wonder the Sixth Quartet (in this, too, like the First, and unlike any other until the last) bore no dedication of any kind. And no wonder it contained, and conveyed, such an odd mixture of tones—not deceptive cheer, not willed naïveté, but a true and disturbing acknowledgment of guilt-ridden happiness and doubtful hope.

The late 1950s, as they wore on, were not easy years for Shostakovich. For one thing, his health began to deteriorate. He was having severe troubles with his right hand—a very bad thing for a right-handed composer, and a disaster for a performing pianist. He was hospitalized twice in two years for the condition, once in the fall of 1958 and again in the early months of 1960, and though injections and massages proved temporarily helpful, he was ultimately forced to give up his performing career. (What this sacrifice might have meant to him is suggested, though only obliquely, by a private letter from the philosopher Isaiah Berlin, written about a visit Shostakovich paid to Oxford in 1958. After observing and sympathizing with the composer's trembling diffidence at the various public events connected with his honorary degree, the Russian-speaking Berlin suggested to Shostakovich that the guests at one soirée would be delighted to hear him play something on the piano: "Without a word he went to the piano and played a prelude and fugue—one of the twenty-four he has composed like Bach—with such magnificence, such depth and passion." And, Berlin added, "While playing S.'s face really had become transformed, the shyness and the terror had gone, and a look of tremendous intensity and indeed inspiration appeared; I imagine that this is how nineteenth-century composers may have looked when they played." It was precisely this form of escape, one of the very few remaining to him, that was closed off when he could no longer perform on the piano.)

Aside from the physical problems, which provoked in him a combination of gallows humor and real despair, there was his increasing irritation with the way the country's cultural and political life was being run. The early years of the Khrushchev Thaw had perhaps raised hopes unrealistically, causing Shostakovich and his fellow artists to imagine that things might somehow return to the salad days of the 1920s. But even granting the fact that one never gets one's youth back—one cannot, in that sense, recapture the salad days—the late 1950s demonstrated a disturbing continuity with the early 1950s, at least in structural terms. The Terror may have been over and the cult of personality denounced, but massive portraits of Party leaders still adorned the city streets on public holidays, *Pravda* kept on publishing its mind-numbing pap, and the same petty bureaucrats who had strangled the arts under Stalin continued in their posts throughout the decade.

In December of 1957, Shostakovich sent two letters to Glikman that wryly hinted at his attitude toward these developments. One described the fortieth-anniversary festivities marking the founding of the Soviet Ukraine, as celebrated in Odessa, where he happened to be on tour:

> Everywhere were portraits of Marx, Engels, Lenin, Stalin, and also Comrades A. I. Belyayev, L. I. Brezhnev, N. A. Bulganin, K. Ye. Voroshilov, N. G. Ignatov, A. I. Kirilenko, F. P. Kozlov, O. V. Kuusinen, A. I. Mikogan, N. A. Mukhitdinov, M. A. Suslov. . . .

On every side can be heard joyful exclamations hailing the great names of Marx, Engels, Lenin, Stalin, and also those of Comrades A. I. Belyayev, L. I. Brezhnev, N. A. Bulganin, K. Ye. Voroshilov, N. G. Ignatov . . .

and so on through the rest of the alphabet, with made-up names mingled slyly among the real ones. At the end Shostakovich says, "I myself walked the streets until, no longer able to contain my joy, I returned home and resolved to describe to you, as best I might, Odessa's National Day of Celebration." To a Soviet-trained ear, the imitation of official-speak was unmistakable, and dourly hilarious.

But a more personal note enters an equally veiled letter that he wrote to Glikman about their shared passion, soccer. Enclosing a clipping from *Soviet Sport* about the recent death of a once famous player, Shostakovich contrasts this forgotten athletic star, who only knew how to score goals, with a politically devious survivor: "The deceased was admired throughout the world of sport, more so than many of his peers, but unfortunately, unlike the happily still with us V. Bobrov, he suffered from being apolitical." The letter goes on to point out that this Bobrov, who had apparently accused a fellow player of being "Tito's stooge" when the Soviet team lost to the Yugoslavs in 1952, "continues to thrive: he is now coach and political instructor of a football team." The man he so ridiculously accused, on the other hand, "was immediately fired back in 1952; good centre back he might have been, but he suffered from an inadequate grounding in political understanding." Both to drive home his point and to clothe himself in his usual epistolary disguise, Shostakovich adds, "Bobrov's political understanding, on the other hand, was admirably grounded." The composer's barely stifled rage is obvious—so much so that one really doesn't need Glikman's explanatory footnote about how angry Shostakovich was at the way "the Bobrovs and their ilk somehow managed to continue flourishing in the post-Stalin world, not only in sport but also in music and literature."

During this period Shostakovich was writing to Glikman every few weeks or months, sometimes even at weekly intervals, yet the first direct reference to his new bride, Margarita, comes in a letter dated June 22, 1958—nearly two full years after the wedding. There are two other mentions of her by name (one in an invitation issued to Glikman and his wife, Vera, to attend "a celebratory dinner . . . to mark the second anniversary of our nuptials," to be held at his sister Marusya's apartment), and then she disappears again from view. In mid-June of 1959, Shostakovich mentions the unbearable heat in Moscow and says of his summer plans: "It's possible we may go to Komarovo." One might presume that the "we" implicitly includes Margarita, as it did in the May 1958 letter about their planned trip to Paris, but according to Maxim Shostakovich's vague recollection, they had already separated by the beginning of summer. What we know for sure is that by the fall they were divorced.

Shostakovich did not even have the nerve to confront Margarita face to face. Instead, in what was surely not his finest hour, he sent his twenty-one-year-old son to announce the breakup and make the legal arrangements. "When I think about my life, I realize that I have been a coward. Unfortunately, I have been a coward," Shostakovich reportedly said to his friend and former student Edison Denisov in a late-night conversation that took place around this time. But he was speaking about politics (or so Denisov assumed, probably correctly), and not about any aspect of his personal life. Denisov himself attributes Shostakovich's cowardice to rational fear, and also to irrational love: "Another reason for his cowardice was his profound and obsessive love for his children. Many of the bad things he did in life were done on behalf of his children." Yet the bad thing he did in asking Maxim to deal with his divorce from Margarita was certainly not "on behalf of" anyone but himself. It was the less amusing side of the same pain-evading strategy he manifested in that note to Nina, when he instructed her to "Tell the librettist to f—— off" during his absence.

Just as we can only guess at why Shostakovich married Margarita, we can only guess at why he divorced her. There is just one pertinent if indirect clue, and that is the fact that in May of 1959 he started working on a quartet dedicated to his first wife's memory. Nina would have turned fifty that May (she had been born in 1909, which meant that she was only forty-five when she died), and this anniversary was the ostensible occasion for the quartet. Did his thoughts turn to Nina in mid-1959 because the marriage to Margarita was already in ruins by then? Or did the date alone suggest the idea of a memorial quartet, causing him to focus on what Nina had meant to him and thus making him question the value of her "replacement"? We will never know. All we are left with is the Seventh Quartet itself, which he finally finished in March of 1960.

The Quartet No. 7 in F-sharp Minor is the first quartet Shostakovich wrote in a minor key. (It was after finishing this one that he apparently told Dmitri Tsyganov he hoped to write a full cycle of twenty-four quartets, one in each of the major and minor keys.) It is also, at twelve minutes or less, the shortest of all his quartets. But it packs into its three short movements a great deal that is new to his work. Innovative without being self-promoting, moving but never theatrically so, lucid, analytic, sometimes quiet, often strong, the Seventh Quartet is an apt tribute to the woman it commemorates.

It begins in Allegretto with a little tune on the first violin—a rather tuneless tune that keeps breaking off, interrupted by a quiet but firm three-beat pulse, as of a persistent visitor knocking at the door. Whether because of the knocks themselves, the minor mode, or the constant stoppages, this movement is initially somewhat anxiety-producing. Soon we are in the hands of the cello, though, which takes over in a much more forceful and melodic manner. (In 1959, as he was starting to think about this quartet, Shostakovich was also writing the First Cello Concerto for his dear friend Mstislav Rostropovich to perform. So the cello, always an important instrument for him, had recently become even more so.) "The cello is definitely *brave*," I noted in one of my earliest responses to this quartet, and that perception has only been confirmed by repeated hearings.

The entire second movement is very quiet and at times distinctly spooky. (A single brief passage of glissando on the cello and viola, for instance, is so quiet you almost don't hear it, but when you *do* hear it, the swift, soft, upward glide makes the hairs rise on the back of your neck.) By comparison, the third movement is fast, frantic, and loud. Certain harsh, high-pitched strokes on the violins and viola sound like cries or even shrieks; there is an overall feeling of chaos, frenzy, and impending crisis. This spirals down into a somewhat stronger version of the three knocks—the arrival of the bad news—which is followed by a return to the quiet feeling of the second movement. We move from there back to the first movement's pizzicato tune, exactly reproduced here, and then we are at the end, which—as in the first movement—is carried by the cello, ultimately joined by the other three. Unlike the second movement, which breaks off so suddenly that we seem to be still in midmeasure, this last movement closes by fading away to silence.

The overall feeling of the quartet is of something stripped down as far as possible. Its brevity, its narrow chromatic range, the way two instruments playing together are made to sound like one—all this emphasizes the idea of small, less, "minor" in its everyday meaning. Even the increased dependence on pizzicato in this quartet is a sign of this same tendency, for the plucked string is itself the most reduced form of the instrument, the string without its bow. And yet the result is not minimalist or abstract; instead, this kind of reduction, like that of a long-cooked sauce, has the effect of condensing and therefore intensifying the content—in this case, the emotional content. If the Fifth Quartet is a Poussin landscape, the Seventh is a Goya ivory, one of those miraculous, delicately etched, deeply unnerving images in which the painter brought everything that concerned him into the scope of a few square inches.

Something cut short. Smallness and quietness made powerful and intense. A cycle in which the beginning comes back at the end. Ghostly otherworldliness and pensive interiority. The bravery of a single voice. It does not take much to hear the connection between these musical elements and Shostakovich's feelings about Nina. But one needn't depend on such parallels to get at the atmosphere of this piece. What Shostakovich is doing here, possibly for the very first time, is to use abstraction and pattern, rather than melody, to suggest narrative qualities like character, story, and meaning. In Quartet No. 7 he weirdly combines the highly abstract strategies of Quartet No. 5 with the personal, memorializing role of Quartets No. 2 and 4.

The Seventh Quartet is not the most moving of his string quartets, though it is filled with feeling. It is not asking for sympathy, nor is it crying tears over its own sorrow. Instead, it is trying to work something out: the mood is contemplative and even analytic rather than helplessly despairing. I get the feeling Shostakovich wrote this one for himself, to decide what he really thought and felt. There is no sense of external display here, no sense of an audience to his mourning. And it seems to me there is no sense of guilt either, unless one hears it in those harsh third-movement cries—but those strike me as something closer to passionate grief, an unwilled outburst that is almost immediately quelled. Time is in part what helps him quell it, but so does music, and not just this music, but also the distance provided by the intervening Sixth Quartet.

On April 30, 1960, Shostakovich wrote to Glikman, "The Beethoven Quartet is now studying my Seventh Quartet. The rehearsals are giving me great joy. In general, however, life is far from easy. How I long to summon the aid of the Old Woman so inspiringly evoked by the poet in his *Horizon Beyond the Horizon*, published in the Party's Central Organ *Pravda* on 29 April 1960." The old woman, Glikman tells us, is death, and Shostakovich's typically ironic way of disguising his despair (by cleverly making the despised *Pravda* serve as the "book" behind their secret book code) does not reduce the darkness of his wish. Yet while his death-wish is real and sincerely meant, so is his "great joy"—for once the thing itself, and not the mockery of it that this phrase so often conveys in his letters to Glikman.

If the Sixth Quartet is in part about the discomfort of happily surviving one's dear dead, then the Seventh Quartet is (among other things) about the comfort of truly mourning them. That such mourning might also contain an element of envy and longing—a sense of having been left out in the cold, condemned to survive—should not surprise us at all, for Shostakovich is the master of having it both ways, of looking simultaneously toward life and toward death. "Altogether life is hard," he had written to

Glikman some years earlier, in 1957. "But maybe it will be over soon; after all, I am over fifty. Nevertheless, my blooming health and my mighty organism hardly allow much hope for an early curtailment of my earthly activities." The tone here is so carefully balanced between humor and despair, self-mockery and self-preservation, that even a close friend like Glikman would have found it hard to define the sentiment exactly.

Nocturne

All the autobiographical and social aspects examined so far may
be vital to an understanding of where the music comes from;
but if we want to know where it goes to—how it penetrates the
inner lives of those who hear it—then it is to the processes of
artistic shaping that we have to turn.

—DAVID FANNING,
Shostakovich: String Quartet No. 8

A nd now something began to shift in Shostakovich's life—
some need, or some opportunity, that was connected to
his reliance on the string quartet. In the first fifteen
years after the war, he had turned to quartets only intermittently,
producing one every three or four years, as if they were merely a
private indulgence, a sideshow, a diversion from the main events
of his musical life. But now, in 1960, he suddenly finished two
quartets in one year: first the Seventh, which he completed in
March, and then the remarkable Eighth, which he wrote at
white-hot speed during the early part of July.

More attention has been paid to Shostakovich's Quartet No. 8

in C Minor than to all his other quartets combined. In the fifty years that followed its premiere, it became one of the most frequently programmed pieces of twentieth-century chamber music written by any composer. Almost from its first appearance, string players found themselves longing to play it, and audiences loved it even if they did not generally love "modern" music. The initial round of music critics raved about it (including a very young Solomon Volkov, who was present at its first performance in Leningrad on October 2, 1960, and who dates his obsession with Shostakovich back to that occasion). And then, over the subsequent decades, musicologists took apart its every detail, exhaustively examining all its methods and allusions. Surgically dissected in this way, it began to seem a corpse of its former self, a mere schema of a quartet rather than a vital piece of music. Its popularity did not help in this regard, either: in certain august circles, the much-loved Eighth Quartet came to be regarded as a kind of "music for dummies."

Perhaps it will seem perverse of me to suggest that many of these problems have arisen from the fact that the Quartet No. 8, practically alone among the quartets, has been viewed mainly as an aspect of its composer's autobiography. After all, what am I doing but casting a biographical eye over Shostakovich's string quartets, as if this were a reasonable way to look at music? Why, then, do I want to call a halt to it on the Eighth Quartet?

It's partly a matter of balance. All musical pieces—all artworks, let us say, if they are the products of an individual consciousness—stem from and reveal some aspect of their maker's life and personality.

Certain kinds of artworks have an even more intimate relation than usual to the person who created them, perhaps because of the artist's own attitude toward them, or the circumstances under which he created them, or the absence of other outlets for his self-expression, or the nature of his particular artistic language, or a whole host of other factors operating singly or, more likely, in combination. I believe Shostakovich's string quartets are this kind of artwork: I think if they are examined closely, in the context of his daily existence, they can give us a form of access to this extremely veiled artist, however tenuous, that we otherwise might not have.

But I do *not* think that the meaning of the string quartets (if music can be said to have meaning at all, in that sense) can be found in a one-to-one correlation between the life and the work. It is this kind of point-by-point translation which gives biographical criticism a bad name, causing other kinds of critics to call it, with reason, "reductive" or "vulgar." Criticism is, by its nature, reductive: at the very least, it reduces nonverbal artworks to words (or, if it is literary criticism, it reduces complex, ambiguous artworks to narrower, more linear descriptions of those artworks). As for vulgarity—well, one person's vulgarity is another person's *Lady Macbeth of the Mtsensk District*. On the critical front, the effort to avoid all tinges of vulgarity can often result in a form of etiolated, academic lifelessness that is as untrue to a living artwork as its vulgar opposite would be. Still, there has undoubtedly been something vulgar and reductive in the critical eye brought to bear on Shostakovich's Eighth Quartet.

Part of this is the composer's own fault, for describing the piece, in a now-famous letter he wrote to Isaak Glikman, as a memorial to himself. And part of it is his fault for inserting so many obvious "clues" in the work, as if to suggest to his more boneheaded admirers that solving the clues would produce some kind of definitive answer. This kind of tease was, I think, typical of Shostakovich, especially during this period—a period that began with the Fifth Quartet and the Tenth Symphony, and that seems to have reached its pinnacle in the Eighth Quartet. Though he went on to use quotation, anagram, and other such devices in some of his later works, the offered significance in those cases tended to be more available, less highly personal, and in general less cryptic than in the Quartet No. 8.

But part of the problem involves a combination of factors that cannot be laid directly at Shostakovich's door. These include the romantic circumstances of the quartet's composition—he wrote it in just three days, shortly after having been pressured against his will to join the Communist Party—as well as the intensely personal feelings it has evoked in those who subsequently heard it. The Russians at that first Leningrad performance clearly felt it was about them and their sense of despair in regard to their own particular moment in history. So did the New Yorkers, it seemed, with whom I listened to it at Alice Tully Hall in 2006, and so, presumably, did the San Franciscans, Londoners, Parisians, Berliners, Bostonians, Leipzigers, and Vancouverites who attended the various Shostakovich quartet cycles offered during that centennial year. Why, then, should they not also assume that it was "about" Shostakovich in an equally personal way? It is easy to confuse the autobiography of reception with the autobiography of creation, to imagine that the composer (or writer, or painter) simply put in the same feelings that we later took out. This is not how art works, but part of its beauty and cunning is to make us *believe* that this is how it works.

And for those who knew about it, there was that Glikman letter to back them up in this belief. Shostakovich wrote the letter on July 19, 1960, a few days after returning from a trip to Dresden, where he had gone to work on a film score for his friend Lev Arnshtam's movie *Five Days, Five Nights*. "Dresden was an ideal set-up for getting down to creative work," he told Glikman:

> I stayed in the spa town of Görlitz, which is just near a little place called Köningstein, about 40 kilometers from Dresden. A place of incredible beauty—as it should be, the whole area being known as 'the Switzerland of Saxony.' The good working conditions justified themselves: I composed my Eighth Quartet. As hard as I tried to rough out the film scores which I am supposed to be doing, I still haven't managed to get anywhere; instead I wrote this ideologically flawed quartet which is of no use to anybody. I started thinking that if some day I die, nobody is likely to write a work in memory of me, so I had better write one myself. The title page could carry the dedication: 'To the memory of the composer of this quartet.'
>
> The basic theme of the quartet is the four notes D natural, E flat, C natural, B natural—that is, my initials, D. SCH. The quartet also uses themes from some of my own compositions and the Revolutionary song 'Zamuchen tyazholoy nevolyey' ['Tormented by grievous bondage']. The themes from my own work are as follows: from the First Symphony, the Eighth Symphony, the

[Second Piano] Trio, the Cello Concerto, and *Lady Macbeth*. There are hints of Wagner (the Funeral March from *Götterdämmerung*) and Tchaikovsky (the second subject of the first movement of the Sixth Symphony). Oh yes, I forgot to mention that there is something else of mine as well, from the Tenth Symphony. Quite a nice little hodge-podge, really. It is a pseudo-tragic quartet, so much so that while I was composing it I shed the same amount of tears as I would have to pee after half-a-dozen beers. When I got home, I tried a couple of times to play it through, but always ended up in tears. This was of course a response not so much to the pseudo-tragedy as to my own wonder at its superlative unity of form. But here you may detect a touch of self-glorification, which no doubt will soon pass and leave in its place the usual self-critical hangover.

One cannot miss, I think, the dourly playful, complicatedly self-mocking, Samuel Beckett–like tone here. ("*If* some day I die"? Not a sure thing, then.) Yet, aided and abetted by Glikman's editorial notes—which append to this letter the detailed story of Shostakovich's diabolical dance with the Communist Party in late June and early July of that year—numerous generations of critics *have* missed it, or at least ignored it. Shostakovich's real despair at having finally capitulated to the powers that be (for reasons that can never be known for sure, though they probably included extra-heavy pressure by the Party, the absence of any kind of protective wife, and copious amounts of alcohol) gets equated, in this interpretation, with his mock-despair over the "pseudo-tragedy" of his "ideologically flawed quartet." That he cried real tears over the music is probably not in doubt; and he was to cement this apparent connection between his own unspeakable sorrows and the Quartet No. 8 by responding with fraught silence when the Borodins, on a later occasion, played through the quartet at his home. "When we finished playing, he left the room without saying a word, and didn't come back," Valentin Berlinsky reports. "We quietly packed up our instruments and left. The next day he rang me up in a state of great agitation. He said, 'I'm sorry, but I just couldn't face anybody. I have no corrections to make, just play it the way you did.'"

Already, the myth of the highly personal and somewhat secret motive behind this quartet was gaining force. But it was to reach its apogee in a story put out by Lev Lebedinsky, a sometime friend of Shostakovich's whose self-glorifying versions of events often appear less than reliable. "It was his farewell to life," Lebedinsky says of the Eighth Quartet. "He associated joining the Party with a moral, as well as physical, death. On the day of his return from a trip to Dresden, where he had completed the Quartet and purchased a large number of sleeping pills, he played the Quartet to me on the piano and told me with tears in his eyes that it was his last work. He hinted at his intention to commit suicide. Perhaps subconsciously he hoped that I would save him. I managed to remove the pills from his jacket pocket and gave them to his son Maxim, explaining to him the true meaning of the Quartet." But Maxim, though he agrees that Shostakovich wept when he was forced to join the Party (he remembers this because it was only the second time he saw his father cry, the first being when Nina died), has repeatedly and emphatically denied the story about the sleeping pills.

The damage was done, however, and the myth of the Eighth Quartet as suicide note survives in the popular imagination. It is easier, somehow, to think of the sensitive artist as simple victim than to acknowledge the complicated range of emotions at work in the real Shostakovich, who was above all else a survivor. No, not above all else: he was a survivor *and* an able spokesman for the dead and victimized, perhaps even at times their representative. It was part of his contradictory character, as both a musician and a man, that he could have it both ways.

The Quartet No. 8 is officially dedicated "in memory of the victims of fascism and war." To evade the public nature of this stated purpose, most commentators either finesse or downright deny the validity of the dedication. Shostakovich was including himself, they say, among the victims of fascism, and thereby including Stalin and the Party among its perpetrators. Or: Shostakovich was just falling back on any old tagline that would pass muster with the censors, as he had been doing since the Fifth Symphony, and he didn't mean the dedication to be taken seriously at all. But the quartets do not seem to have needed this kind of camouflage in the way that the symphonies did; it was just not necessary, in that smaller, under-the-radar context, to lead the Leaders astray. Why, then, should Shostakovich have defaced his most personal quartet with a bald-faced lie?

"Ridiculous!" sputtered Kurt Sanderling, laughing, when I asked him whether Shostakovich could have meant the dedication seriously. "What would the quotes and allusions to his earlier work be doing in a quartet dedicated to the victims of fascism?"

But why, I wondered, *did* he quote from himself, and from others? What did such quoting mean to him? "I can't answer this," Sanderling said, "but the quotations emphasize that all this is dealing with himself. It was more than with Bach's B–A–C–H. The D–S–C–H is more important to him, has more content for him."

Even the monogram, though, is not as straightforward as it might seem. The world of Shostakovich studies has become so used to the initials DSCH (which now mark the official publishing house that distributes his music, the primary journal devoted to his work, and dozens of other Shostakovich-related things) that people have started viewing the trademark as god-given; they have forgotten how arbitrary, and then how conscious, the choice of this signature was. First, Dmitri Dmitriyevich was almost not Shostakovich's name at all. His parents wanted to call him Jaroslav, but the priest who was brought in for the christening insisted on naming the boy after his father—perhaps to cover up his own ignorance of Saint Jaroslav's name day, or possibly because the name Jaroslav struck him as too foreign, too Polish. But what if the family had succeeded in its first effort? How would Shostakovich have cobbled a musically compelling signature out of that problematic J?

Nor was the transition from Shostakovich's given name to the initials DSCH at all automatic. He first had to transliterate his name from the Cyrillic into the Roman alphabet, and specifically into German; next he had to drop the second D, the one that stood for his patronymic; and only then would he be able to use the German system of notation to arrive at the four-note sequence D-natural, E-flat (called "Es" in German), C-natural, B-natural (called "H" in German). This precise sequence of sounds—close neighbors in a C-minor scale, with four different notes producing an actual if embryonic melody, one that begins with a slight rise but then ends on a dying fall—was eminently suited to the composer's own musical tastes as well as his larger aesthetic purposes. Though it echoed the earlier B–A–C–H, as if acknowledging his Baroque ancestry, Shostakovich's monogram was noticeably darker and more identifiably minor-key than Bach's. It was also more Jewish-sounding, a fact that fit in perfectly with his tendency to appropriate klezmer melodies.

It is here that the distinction between the "false" dedicatees and the "true" one begins to break down—or rather, let us say that in the Eighth Quartet, more than in any other quartet he ever wrote, Shostakovich managed to get the public meanings and the private messages, the service of the People and the critique of the People's leadership, the personal and the political, to coincide. As the Emerson Quartet violinist Philip Setzer has suggested, "The fact that he uses his own initials was not just a personal note, but a way of saying 'It's us, it's Russia—it's the tragedy of Russia too.'"

On the face of it, the Party leaders could hardly complain about a work dedicated to "the victims of fascism and war," to whom they themselves were always building gigantic monuments. And yet who were the primary victims, or at least targets, of German fascism? Why, none other than the Jews, against whom the Russians had recently been waging their own vigorous campaign. (Nor was the other part of that dedicatory phrase any more innocently straightforward, for from a Dresden-based perspective, the "victims of war" would certainly have included the many thousands of German civilians killed in the Allied firebombing of that city.) And the music of the Eighth Quartet itself bore out this Jewish connection, for when Shostakovich quoted from the Second Piano Trio—the work dedicated to Sollertinsky—the passage he chose was the one based on klezmer music. This is not to say that the reference was exclusively Jewish. With this particular allusion, Shostakovich was accomplishing several different aims at once. He was commemorating and mourning his best friend, the man who had characterized the Soviet persecution of Shostakovich's music as a "pogrom." He was casting his mind back over his own past, recalling the wartime years that had marked his biggest musical triumphs as well as his harshest sorrows. But he was also giving voice to a particularly large contingent of fascism's (and for that matter Communism's) victims, the murdered Jews. So if present-day Jewish audiences in New York are moved by what they accurately perceive as klezmer echoes in a quartet dedicated to "the victims of fascism," who is to say that they are being misled by the dedication? The various meanings suggested by this quartet do not exclude each other; they are simply layered far more deeply than most audience members (or most commentators) will acknowledge.

Structure, which includes both coherence and discontinuity, is one of the key methods Shostakovich uses to produce this layering effect. In his book-length study of Quartet No. 8, David

Fanning has intelligently suggested that the composition is "rich in cinematographic continuity techniques" such as flashback, fast forward, slow motion, jump cut, and the like. The analogy no doubt occurred to Fanning after he learned that Shostakovich's earliest sketches for the quartet were done on pages on which he had written, and then crossed out, "Five Days, Five Nights"—that is, the name of the film score he should have been composing when instead he was writing this quartet. But Fanning's observation also stems from the way the quotations in the Eighth Quartet work: the early flashback to the First Symphony, followed by the fast-forward overview of his later musical life (the Eighth Symphony, the Second Piano Trio, the Tenth Symphony, the Cello Concerto), leading eventually to the jump cut between the somber revolutionary song and the beautiful, delicate aria from *Lady Macbeth*. Along the way, we get flickers of personal portraits—Sollertinsky, Rostropovich, Nina—but each goes by so quickly as to be indistinct, almost indiscernible.

Though any description makes the Eighth Quartet seem to be made up entirely of quotations (as the schoolboy said of *Hamlet*), the actual experience of listening to it is not that at all. If you know the sources in question, it is rather like watching the opening-night performance of a play whose many rehearsals you have witnessed. All the little bits and pieces suggested by the director, all the untaken paths and underlying interpretations, are still there, but they go by so quickly as to merge completely into the ongoing life of the piece, which has become something new when set free on its own.

And if you do not know the quotations and allusions, the Eighth Quartet works anyway, works all the better, possibly, because you are not burdened with an excess of knowledge or expectation, but can simply respond to the music for what it is. It is in the nature of allusion—good allusion, effective allusion—that its apprehension should not be essential. As the critic William Empson remarked in writing about a poem by Andrew Marvell, "It is tactful, when making an obscure reference, to arrange that the verse shall be intelligible even when the reference is not understood." Empson goes on to say, in regard to the poem's "brotherless Heliades," that if you have forgotten, "as I had myself, who their brother was, and look it up, the poem will scarcely seem more beautiful; such of the myth as is wanted is implied." The same is true, naturally, of Shostakovich's Eighth Quartet, and it might be salutary for veterans of the piece, musicians and musicologists alike, to try to listen to it occasionally with ears that aspire to ignorance.

The Quartet No. 8 in C Minor is not one of Shostakovich's longer quartets; it lasts only about twenty minutes. But like the grandest of his works in this form, it contains five movements in its relatively small span. Perhaps because the movements flow into each other without a break, or because they echo each other so often, or maybe because the overall feel of the piece is one of stateliness and measured pace, there is no sense of rush or undue haste. Only one of the movements—the second, an Allegro molto—manifests the composer's usual degree of frantic anxiety, and here it has been radically circumscribed. And though the characteristic Shostakovich melancholy is obviously present, especially in the three slow movements, it has been shaped, contained, and somehow addressed by the extremely repetitive structure of the work.

The first four notes sound the theme that will repeat itself throughout the quartet. If we do not know much about Shostakovich, we will not recognize these as his four initials, but that doesn't really matter: we can hear that this four-note sequence is the work's emotional core. It begins on the cello, and the other instruments soon join in, one at a time, but not at regular intervals. Instead they pile up on one another, voice upon voice, until they all come together at once, and the effect at first is rather like that of a bell tolling, not ominously, but with quiet sadness.

Eventually we can discern a tune, played in the higher registers against a background of lower notes. It is an attractive tune, and we do not need to know it is from the First Symphony to be attracted to it; the melody itself *feels* personal, *feels* like a single voice. This sequence repeats itself later, as do many other elements in the movement, but especially and most emphatically those four recognizable notes. This constant return to familiar tunes and patterns is reassuring rather than the reverse. It is not obsessive, or if it is, it is an obsession we share: the repetition makes us feel that we are being located, steadied. Throughout this opening movement, simplicity and solemnity are shown to be interconnected, with both put into the service of deep feeling.

The second movement plunges us suddenly into an anxiety-ridden, almost hysterical mode, with the pace, the register, and the dynamics all on the rise. Those same four notes are back again, but now they sound less like a tolling bell and more like an SOS, crying out for help. They are followed by a klezmer melody, and though it too is frantic, it also has a quality of ironic, sardonic pleasure, like the dark, fearful joy of a Hasidic dance, or the remembered humor of a good joke told by one's dead best friend. And then, in movement three, we get the kind of creepy, dissonant waltz that Shostakovich had used as far back as Quartet No. 2. This version is neither as inviting nor as danceable as the ghostly tune he wrote for the third movement of that earlier quartet; but if it is less alluring, it is also less frightening, for there is not as much to lose now, when even death has become familiar.

The powerful fourth movement, which is in many ways the climax of the quartet, weaves together three audibly distinct elements: a slow, folk song–like tune that is, in fact, the revolutionary song "Tormented by Grievous Bondage"; a beautifully sweet melody, marked *dolce* on the cello part, which turns out to be the aria from *Lady Macbeth*; and an emphatic series of three-beat "knocks" that constantly interrupt the action in an ever more threatening way. These same knocks (they are created by having three eighth notes, followed by a rest, played percussively on all or most of the instruments at once) appeared in a more subdued form in Quartet No. 7, but nobody has thought to obsess about them there. Here, in the Eighth Quartet, they have variously been identified as gunfire, falling bombs, the KGB knocking at the door, and the secret signal given by those inside when the KGB is *about* to knock at the door. I don't care which of these, if any, they represent; what bothers me is that everybody feels obliged to jump on the latest hobbyhorse at the same time, as if the series of three beats could only mean one thing. Eventually, when history has died away sufficiently for us to listen to the music itself, these notes will manage to acquire their own inherent significance as something loud and threatening which intrudes from the outside, endangering the quiet peacefulness of the tuneful bits. In both the melodies of this movement, but particularly in the lovely transmuted aria, one can sense Shostakovich trying to drown out noisy externality with quiet interiority, as if, in the battle between loud intrusiveness and gentle reflectiveness, the internal forces might actually win.

By the time we have reached the fifth movement, we are ready for a rest, and Shostakovich gives it to us—not only in the resolution embodied in the return to the opening four-note canon, but literally, in occasional full-measure rests where all the instruments fall silent at once. This is the first time he has done this in a quartet, inserting a complete silence before the end of the piece, as a palpable presence in the melody. In this final movement, quiet reflectiveness *does* seem to have won out over noisy percussiveness, to the point where even the soft notes, feeling themselves to be too loud, temporarily disappear into the silent spaces. Maybe because of these unusual pauses, and maybe because the fugue is now allowed to complete itself (rather than being broken and erratic, as it was in movement one), the final movement of the Eighth Quartet has a remarkable feeling of closure. Fanning calls this "transcendence," and though I understand what he means, I would not use precisely that word—not, at least, in the religious or spiritual sense that we might say it of a Beethoven quartet. The feeling at the end of Quartet No. 8 is more human that that; what we are being offered is not consolation or redemption, but companionship.

When it returns in the fifth movement, the four-note motif is recognizable to us as some kind of signature, even if we do not know that it is literally one. We have heard it come back again and again throughout the piece, signaling *Here I am* and then *Here I am, still.* But now, at the end, even this seems to have changed. The here-I-am feeling has been dimmed and submerged, the Song of Myself turned into a kind of Notes from Underground, an expression on behalf of the damaged and oppressed, voiced by an idiosyncratic, solitary figure who nonetheless speaks for the rest of us. The Eighth Quartet does not, by its end, feel like a personal story; it does not feel like a story at all. Instead it feels like what it is, musically—a canon, a round, that simple musical structure which appears in both folk and classical music, and to which a variety of social and historical meanings have accrued over the centuries.

What might some of these meanings be? That music takes place in time. That time both repeats itself and goes forward. That companionship is essential and beautiful, but not finally proof against the void. That memory is a form of companionship. That simple things can be complex in the profound feelings they convey. That repetition is consoling. That even an exact repetition is never just the same thing over again, because time has changed the meaning, as has the very fact that we've been through it before. All this is there in the Eighth Quartet, and uninstructed audiences have repeatedly found it there for themselves, decade after decade.

There remains the question of Shostakovich's membership in the Communist Party, which—whatever its bearing on the Eighth Quartet—was clearly an important and troubling subject for the composer. The question is actually three questions. Why, in 1960, did the Party suddenly try again to capture him within its official embrace? Why, this time, did he give in to the pressure to join? And why, having submitted to the pressure, did Shostakovich find his capitulation so unusually painful? Over the years, he had lent himself to many other concessions, misrepresentations, and betrayals of principle in order to protect his family and his livelihood, so it is not at all clear why this one alone should have induced what his friends repeatedly described as an emotional breakdown.

By 1960, Shostakovich's stature within the world of Soviet music, and hence Soviet cultural life in general, was as high as it had ever been. He was on cordial terms with Khrushchev, and he was often asked to head up official festivals and delegations. His 1959 trip to the United States, in the midst of the Cold War, was a kind of coast-to-coast cultural ambassadorship, meant to counter foreign qualms about the revelations of Stalin's abuses and the brutal 1956 quelling of the Hungarian Uprising. His Eleventh Symphony, which premiered in 1957 under the title "The Year 1905," had taken on a manifestly patriotic theme. (His Twelfth, which he began in 1959 and was to finish in 1961, dealt even more patriotically—if even more flatly and routinely, in musical terms—with "The Year 1917.") And in April of 1960 Shostakovich was granted perhaps the highest official accolade of all: he was elected First Secretary of the newly formed Composers' Union of the Russian Federation, the organization representing composers on the republic level—a new counterpart to the existing USSR-wide Composers' Union, which had caused him so much trouble in the Zhdanov years, and which had been led since early 1948 by Shostakovich's frequent antagonist and occasional ally, Tikhon Khrennikov.

And yet there was something not quite right about his relationship to the Party's official power. "He was treated as a threat. He wasn't trusted. He was not in their system of ideas," his widow, Irina Antonovna Shostakovich, told me. When she first met him, shortly after he had finally become a Communist Party member in 1960, he told her he had been "blackmailed" into joining. But what could they have used to blackmail him? "Prevent the performing of his music," she said. "He already knew what this would be like, from *Lady Macbeth* and the Zhdanov period."

In English, the word "blackmail" suggests the threat to reveal some unsavory information, a crime or sexual indiscretion or something of that sort committed by the person who is being blackmailed. But that does not seem to apply in this case. The Communist Party did not possess any dark secrets about Shostakovich. His crimes and misdemeanors were all too public, both the "crimes" he had committed *against* the Party (like writing formalist, bourgeois music) and those he had committed on its behalf (like denouncing Stravinsky and other modern composers at the 1949 conference in New York). With such public indiscretions on his record, Shostakovich was not a likely subject for blackmail, and probably a more accurate translation of what the Party was doing to him in 1960 was "threaten." The threat needn't have been overt and probably wasn't: it could simply have been suggested to him that it would be better if he joined, or that it was his duty to join, and the implications would have been evident to everyone.

"'How is it possible that our Number One composer is not a member of the Party?'" Kurt Sanderling mimicked, giving me his own version of the probable Party-line speech. Sanderling, who had moved to East Berlin in 1960 and who saw Shostakovich on the composer's subsequent trips to the German Democratic Republic, was at pains to distinguish the political climate in the two countries. "The difference between the Soviet Union and the GDR was this," he said. "In the Soviet Union you were forced to support the system publicly, and the higher you were, the louder you were forced to shout." As First Secretary of the newly formed Russian Federation Composers' Union, Shostakovich was very high up indeed, and it seemed inconceivable (to the Party, at any rate) that the man holding this position of honor and responsibility should not be a Communist.

Why Shostakovich gave in to the pressure at this point, when he had not done so before, can never be known for sure, but it seems likely that at this lonely moment in his personal life—after his marriage to Margarita had broken up, and before he had met Irina—he felt particularly exposed. Margarita, if she had done nothing else, had protected him by being a Party member herself. Before that, Nina, with her intelligence and practicality, had dealt with all such matters on his behalf, to the extent they could be dealt with at all. Now he was alone, with no wife to shield him. Perhaps he got drunk and signed something; perhaps he simply got tired of fighting the unending battle. Certainly his friends did their best to help him in this crisis. When, in June of 1960, he showed up in Leningrad in a state of emotional collapse, Glikman urged him simply to skip the official convocation at which he would be made a Party member—to address the problem, that is, by evading it—and at first this seemed to work. But by September of 1960 Shostakovich had given up and joined the Party officially.

The primary cause, if we have to assign one, was probably his old nemesis, fear. "I don't know how not to be afraid," he said to Stravinsky when they finally met, a couple of years after these events took place; and though the context was not political (they were talking about conducting one's own music), Shostakovich's remorse about his 1949 denunciation may have lent a political edge to his remark. But he was always talking about his own

fears—of authority, primarily, whether manifested in a local po-
liceman or the Party leadership—and it would not have surprised his close friends to learn that fear had made him give in to
this pressure. "He was only a man," Sanderling temporizes. "He
was a coward when it concerned his own affairs, but he was very
courageous when it concerned others."

Sanderling may have forgiven him, but Shostakovich seems
not to have been able to forgive himself. I think Laurel Fay is
right when she says that his distraught reaction to his own capitulation "strongly suggests that the demons Shostakovich wrestled
with were his own, that he had crossed his own line in the sand."
After all, there were many prominent musicians, including
friends of his like David Oistrakh and Aram Khachaturian, who
had joined the Party for career or other reasons, with no apparent diminishment of Shostakovich's admiration for them. Moreover, it was not as if he himself were innocent of political compromise: he had done practically nothing *but* compromise since
1937. He must have told himself, though, that at least he would
never join the Communist Party, that however low he sank in
other respects he would not betray his principles to that extent.

One can get a sense of how such principles might have oper-
ated from the memoirs of the Polish poet Aleksander Wat, who
spoke with semi-rueful pride when he announced, many decades
after the fact, "I didn't join the party. . . . I committed the most
motley acts, but I didn't join the party. To some degree that was
a question of my character, inborn or developed: I knew that if I
were a member of the party, I would be surrendering my mind."

This was not an uncommon attitude among artists and intellectuals, even those who, like Wat, were initially enthusiastic about the Party's goals. Shostakovich himself probably harbored exactly that feeling of "inborn" resistance, of inescapable moral distaste. And then, to his own surprise and distress, it turned out he was capable even of this capitulation.

The realization that he was this weak must have been a terrible one for him. What had previously sounded, to his ears and others', like explicit mockery when he voiced it—the mouthing of the Party line, in speech after speech after speech—now came to seem frighteningly like his own official voice. The mask was seeping inward. His response to this, as to so many other events in his life, was a feeling of overwhelming shame. If he could deplore his occasional bouts of heavy drinking by saying, "Today I feel dreadful and disgusting," one can only imagine the degree of self-disgust he felt in regard to this far more significant violation of himself.

In practical, day-to-day terms, however, joining the Party made very little difference in Shostakovich's life. As Sanderling points out, he was already doing most of the things entailed in Party membership, "like giving speeches (which he didn't write: they were either delivered from above or written by Glikman and other friends). As a deputy of the Supreme Soviet," Sanderling continued, "he would show up and take care of an old lady who needed a toilet seat. When he was finally forced to join, his consolation was that he would have the chance to do good things for other people." Perhaps—though it is hard to picture Shostakovich getting much satisfaction out of being the local fixer.

If his spirits sank drastically in the months following the initial decision, they began to recover as other aspects of his life improved. His two professorships, lost during the Zhdanov period, had not been restored to him after Stalin's death, but in 1961 the Leningrad Conservatory invited Shostakovich to begin conducting a monthly composition class for graduate students. Despite the trying commute (it was eight hours in an overnight train, or a quicker but less convenient trip by airplane), he took pleasure in the work, and he kept it up for three years, until the "mighty organism" weakened still further, making constant travel an impossibility. The teaching allowed him to have a direct influence on a whole new generation of Russian composers, including Boris Tishchenko, with whom he stayed in touch for the rest of his life, and Alexander Mnatsakanyan, who became the head of the composition department at St. Petersburg Conservatory. It also earned him a sufficiently good salary so that he could continue supporting his growing number of dependents.

In the fall of 1961, Shostakovich was living in the family apartment at 37-45 Kutuzovsky Prospect with both his grown children, their spouses, and his two grandsons. (A third, Galina's second son, was born soon after, in 1962.) This was the same "very good" apartment to which he had moved with Nina and the children in early 1947. It was located on what was, and still is, essentially the Champs-Élysées of Moscow—"a broad avenue that has housed Russian dignitaries since the 1950s and now boasts designer boutiques," as a recent guidebook puts it. But what had seemed a magnificently large space for a family of four

was becoming a bit cramped for the extended family, and Shostakovich was finding it difficult to get the quiet and privacy he
needed to compose. So in April of 1962 he gave the old family
apartment to Galina and moved to a five-room flat that had been
allocated to him in the new Union of Composers residence, just
down the street from the Moscow Conservatory. The new apartment, as he wrote to Isaak Glikman on April 10, was "Apartment
23, 8-10 Nezhdanova Street . . . Nezhdanova Street is what used
to be called Bryusovsky Pereulok" (as, indeed, it once again
is today). He explained, somewhat irrelevantly, that "the late
Nezhdanova was a coloratura soprano," and then added, much
more relevantly: "It is terribly sad to be moving; so much is
bound up with the apartment we are leaving"—the "we" referring to Maxim and his family, who were moving with Shostakovich to the new flat.

But if sadness and regret were attached to the move, so were
new pleasures and conveniences. His neighbors in the Composers' Union building included not only Sergei Shirinsky, the cellist from the Beethoven Quartet, but also Mstislav Rostropovich
and Galina Vishnevskaya, who lived in the flat next door. And
whereas previously he had to be driven everywhere from the
rather out-of-the-way Kutuzovsky Prospect, now he was within
walking distance of many things—not only his friends' apart-
ments, but also the Conservatory's Small Hall, where concerts
took place almost every night and where many of his string quartets received their premieres.

It was on the staircase leading up to the Small Hall, if Lev Lebedinsky can be believed, that Shostakovich was first introduced to Irina Antonovna Supinskaya. "Once," reports Lebedinsky, "he said to me, 'You know that girl in glasses, I've taken a shine to her. I'd like to get to know her better, but I haven't been introduced.'"

> The girl in question worked as a literary editor under my charge at the publishing house. I promised to introduce her, but deliberately put off doing so. However, one night we were coming up the stairs at the Small Hall of the Conservatoire, and there she was talking to some other lady. As I greeted her, Shostakovich hovered at my side, whispering in my ear, "Do introduce me." How could I avoid it? Then he said, "I'll give her my telephone number straight away."
>
> "Go ahead," I said, pleased that he was consulting me.
>
> Soon afterwards they started meeting. I was very happy for him, although I wrongly assumed that this new relationship would only be short-lived. After all Irina was already married to an older man. But one day Shostakovich told me that he had proposed to her. He needed a woman to help him in his life.

Why Lebedinsky was so averse to this relationship is not clear, but soon after Irina moved in with Shostakovich, in mid-1962, the friendship between Lebedinsky and Shostakovich began to fade. Lebedinsky's explanation is that "as their life became more bourgeois, their home became open to a different class of guest, which didn't exclude officials. For this reason our meetings became rarer, and eventually I decided to terminate our friendship, rather than give in to compromise." But this image of Irina as bourgeois home-making opportunist does not tally with what we get else-where. Galina Vishnevskaya, for instance, reports on the first time Shostakovich brought Irina to visit her and Rostropovich:

It was the first time they had appeared anywhere together. She was very young, modest, and sat all evening without raising her eyes. Seeing that we liked her and approved of his choice, Dmitri Dmitriyevich grew more and more relaxed and lighthearted. All at once, like a little boy, he shyly took her hand. Never had I known Shostakovich to act out of an inner impulse like that, and touch another person—man or woman. At most he would pat his grandsons on the head.

That petite woman with the quiet voice proved to be a vigorous mistress of the household, and quickly organized the life of that huge family. It was with her that Dmitri Dmitriyevich finally came to know domestic peace.

Shostakovich himself described Irina Antonovna in two letters to Glikman. The first, on June 24, 1962, refers to his recent marriage (though in fact the tie would not become legal until November, when Irina's divorce came through). "My wife's name is Irina Antonovna," he writes; "I have known her for more than two years. Her only defect is that she is twenty-seven years old. In all other respects she is splendid: clever, cheerful, straightforward and very likeable. . . . I think we shall get on very well, living with one another." And then, on July 2, Shostakovich offers a fuller description:

Irina is very nervous about meeting my friends. She is very young and modest. She works from nine to five as a literary editor with Sovyetsky Kompozitor publishers. She can't say her r's and l's. Her father was Polish and her mother Jewish, but they are both dead. Her father was a victim of the cult of personality and violations of revolutionary legality. Her mother died. Irina was brought up by an aunt on her mother's side, the same one who is inviting us to stay with her where she lives near Ryazan—I have forgotten the name of the place. Irina was born in Leningrad. Well, that's a brief sketch of her. She was in a children's home, and for a time even in a special children's home [that is, for children of "enemies of the people"]. All in all, a girl with a past.

The young wife was also, of course, a young stepmother, and for the first two years that Irina lived with Shostakovich at the Nezhdanova Street apartment, Maxim, his wife, Lena, and their small son, Dmitri Maximovich, all lived there too. Though the flat was considered extremely luxurious by Soviet standards, it must have been very cramped as a residence for five people. The situation was reminiscent of Shostakovich's own first married apartment, the one he had shared with his mother, except that here the ceilings were far lower and the rooms less grandly proportioned than those in the Leningrad flat. (Soviet luxury, in other words, was not on the same level as pre-revolutionary comfort.) Eventually, when a place became available, Shostakovich and Irina bought a separate apartment for Maxim's family in the same complex, since Maxim, as a professional conductor, was eligible to reside in this musicians' building.

"Was he close to his children?" I asked Irina Antonovna when I met her in 2008. By this time the shy, nervous girl in glasses had become a calmly confident, surprisingly attractive woman in her mid-seventies, recognizably the same person as the one who stood at Shostakovich's side in all those old photographs, but not at all what I had expected.

"He loved them a great deal." She paused before continuing.

"But he had a position which was typical of many parents—that his children should have everything, and not go through what he did. I don't think it's the right way. When children are guarded from difficulties, they grow up infantilized. It's difficult for them to face the realities of life."

I reminded her that, to judge by at least one letter, it was her own difficult childhood which in part attracted Shostakovich to her.

"I would say that there were parallels in my past and Dmitri Dmitriyevich's past which made the understanding between us easier," she agreed. "In his case it was his father's early death, being hungry in St. Petersburg, quite a hard life. And I had the same—lost my parents when I was young, the Leningrad siege, a war childhood, which also involved hunger." And they had even more in common than that: they had both, it turned out, been evacuated to Kuibyshev during the war, though as a seven-year-old child she of course did not come into contact with the already famous composer. "We even discovered later that we had lived on the same street," she recalled with a small smile. Listening to this capable, intelligent woman speak about her late husband, I sensed for the first time what none of the photographs or anecdotes had been able to give me. I thought I understood, that is, what had drawn them to each other, and it was nothing so simple as his desire to be taken care of, or hers to find a replacement father. It was all much more personal than that.

On May 28, 1964, Shostakovich completed his Ninth Quartet, which was dedicated to Irina Antonovna Shostakovich. When I asked her some forty-four years later whether she could see anything of herself in the quartet, she shook her head. "No. But *he* said it was there. He started to write it almost the moment I appeared in his apartment, and he said my image was reflected in it. But he didn't say how. I didn't go that deeply into it. Maybe he was just happy that things were going well—not to be alone in this life, and that he felt safer."

For someone listening to the Quartet No. 9 in E-flat Major out of the blue, without any prior immersion in Shostakovich's quartets, it would be difficult to detect a sense of safety or well-being. Like all his quartets from the First onward, this one is anxiety-ridden, jumpy, unnerving, filled with dissonance and disconnection; if anything, it is even more so. But compared to the Eighth Quartet, the Ninth has a kind of antic glee, a novel feeling of dark vitality mingled with the more familiar fears and hesitations. And unlike every quartet since the Second, it ends with a bang—not only by closing with an extremely long and varied Allegro movement, but also by finishing that movement firmly, loudly, and emphatically, with the quartet's six-note theme bowed *fortissimo* on all four instruments. If this is not optimistic enthusiasm (it never is, with Shostakovich), it is at any rate vigor and resurgence.

In at least one important respect, Irina Antonovna's influence was crucial here: with her in the house, he was finally able to finish the quartet. We know, from various kinds of external evidence, that Shostakovich had been working on some version of a Ninth Quartet since 1961. In October of 1961 he told Glikman he was writing a quartet in "the *russe* style" (Glikman noted the phrase in his diary); and then, on November 18, Shostakovich wrote to him, "I finished the Ninth Quartet, but was very dissatisfied with it so in an excess of healthy self-criticism I burnt it in the stove. It is the second time in my 'creative life' that I have pulled a trick like that: the first time was in 1926, when I burnt all my manuscripts." Less than a year later, when he was publicly interviewed about his current projects, he mentioned that he was "working on the Ninth Quartet. It's a children's piece, about toys and going out to play. I am planning to finish it in about two weeks." And when the Beethovens, in the summer of 1962, announced their forthcoming Leningrad season, they included the new Ninth Quartet among the works that would be played. Yet this piece failed to materialize, either that year or the next, and when Shostakovich finally gave them the finished quartet in 1964, he told them it was a new composition, completely different from the one he had been working on two years earlier.

To judge by the unfinished Ninth Quartet that was found among his papers long after his death, Shostakovich was right to burn or suppress his abortive efforts. We don't know whether this first-movement fragment comes from the burnt *russe* quartet, the later "toy" quartet, or some other version entirely, but from the opus number assigned to the draft ("op. 113," it says, in the neat Roman handwriting Shostakovich used for all his musical notations), we can be pretty sure that its composition fell somewhere between the completion of the Twelfth Symphony (op. 112) and the completion of the Thirteenth Symphony, which eventually became op. 113. This places it in either late 1961 or early 1962. Other than its key of E-flat major, this Allegretto first movement has virtually nothing in common with the finished quartet (or, for that matter, with any other finished chamber work by Shostakovich, even his most youthful). Sticking dolt-ishly to the 4/4 rhythm inscribed on the opening measures, the music consists almost entirely of an unrelenting march, and as such it could seem either "Russian" or toy soldier–like—it could come, that is, from either of the two abandoned quartets. What it resembles, more than anything else, is a finger exercise for young piano students: it has neither the feel nor the sound of something written for strings. Repetitive to an almost unbeliev-able degree, the fragmentary opening movement displays no vi-tality and no musicality, even (or especially) of the "false note" kind.

The finished Ninth Quartet could not be more different. Played in five uninterrupted movements, the Ninth has the grandeur of the Third or Fifth Quartet, mingled with something wilder and more spontaneously playful. The music's essential strategy seems to be to find as much variety as possible within the basic structure of repetition. And here, perhaps, is where the Quartet No. 9 grows not only out of its official predecessor, the Eighth Quartet, but also out of the aborted, fragmentary version of the Ninth. The idea of repetition, as an idea, is present in all three. In the Eighth, it is used in the service of memory and profundity, like the tolling of a bell or the plangency of voices in a round. In the fragmentary Ninth, it is not used in the service of anything; it just sits there, a thing in itself, squashing the music with its implacable force. It's as if Shostakovich had to push the idea of repeating something as far as it could go before he could break through on the other side, into the realm where repetition becomes something like its opposite: variation, unpredictability, controlled chaos.

We don't know where we are in the Ninth—that is part of what is suggested by those strange, uncatchable transitions between movements. And each of the transitions is surprising in a different way, as if, having performed one trick, Shostakovich wants to trick us again by doing the opposite. This trickster mode, the sardonic laugh from above or below, can be felt all through the quartet: in the "trumpets" that surface briefly in the third movement and emerge triumphantly at the end, and that are not, of course, trumpets at all (perhaps, in that case, they are not triumphant, either); in the impossible-to-follow rhythms of the fifth movement, where the second violin often seems to be playing in an entirely different quartet from the other three instruments; and in the "funhouse" feel—more scary than fun— that infuses the Allegro passage in which the pizzicato chords thrum against the first-violin melody. Humor mingles constantly with threat, and reassurance is undermined by uncertainty. The tone of the whole quartet is not so much ambivalent as oppositional. Two contradictory states of mind are brought into being at once, and whether things will end well or badly is anyone's guess.

People (and they include many serious musicians) who object to Shostakovich's ironic, sardonic mode often act as if such attitudes are incompatible with deep feelings and tragic awareness, as if one couldn't be funny and serious at the same time. Such doubters should take a close look at Shakespeare—all of Shakespeare, but particularly *Hamlet*. Any good production of *Hamlet* will do, but the best, for these purposes, is probably the 1964 film version directed by Grigori Kozintsev, with a score by Dmitri Shostakovich.

By the time he wrote that music for Kozintsev, Shostakovich had been working on *Hamlet*, in one way or another, for most of his adult life. In 1932, at the age of twenty-six, he composed the incidental music for a radical stage production directed by Nikolai Akimov. In 1954 he produced a different score for Kozintsev's theatrical version of *Hamlet* (a score that, according to Laurel Fay, was essentially recycled from the Kozintsev/Shostakovich production of *King Lear*, staged in 1941). But his music for Kozintsev's 1964 filmed version was entirely new. As an artwork itself, the score supported, elaborated, and in some places dominated the marvelous movie it was designed to accompany. "Shostakovich's music serves as a great example to me. I could not direct my Shakespearean films without it," Kozintsev was to write, and he went on to specify its particular virtues:

> What is its main feature? A feeling for tragedy? Indeed, an important quality. . . . Philosophy, an intrinsic concept of the world? Of course. . . . But it's a different feature that is important, and one that's hard to describe in words. Goodness . . . virtue . . . compassion. . . .

In Russian we have a wonderful word: virulent. No good exists in Russian art without a virulent hatred of all that degrades man. In Shostakovich's music I hear a virulent hatred of cruelty, of the cult of power, of the persecution of truth.

Kozintsev doesn't mention it specifically, but humor is a definite element in this virulent tone. In the film of *Hamlet*, that humor takes its cue from Shakespeare's words (as translated into Russian by Boris Pasternak), and particularly from Hamlet's antic disposition. The same figure who jokes obscurely about hawks and handsaws finds himself dissolving into a combination of suppressed laughter and profound melancholy as he listens to the gravedigger talk about mortality. Watching the mobile, sensitive, nervous face of Innokenti Smoktunovsky, the actor playing Hamlet, we might find ourselves recalling Kozintsev's description of Shostakovich in terms of what he called "the hypersensitivity of his skin"—that is, "his instantaneous vulnerability, the palpitating contact of his nervous structure with the outer world, and the extraordinary receptivity of his organism." And yet this is also a man who is "never offended when asked to write exactly one minute thirteen seconds of music, and when told that he must fade the orchestra to make way for dialogue at the twenty-fourth second, and bring it up again at the fifty-second to synchronize with a cannon shot." Kozintsev's Shostakovich, like his Hamlet, is both a team player and an isolated individual, a public figure responding to public demands as well as a neurotic, vulnerable artist-soul. "He leads two lives," the director said of his composer friend: "the exterior life of everyday conversation and behavior, where he notes down football results in a large accounting book, and lays out endless games of patience," and "simultaneously, his inner life," which "runs like an incessant working motor, an ever-open wound."

If we imagine that we can hear a connection between these Hamlet-like qualities and the multifaceted Ninth Quartet, perhaps that is not only our imagination. For in the sketch Shostakovich made for the finished Quartet No. 9, buried amid the dots and squiggles that characterized the embryonic versions of his scores, is the single Cyrillic word denoting "Hamlet." Shostakovich's sketches are worth a study of their own, but nobody has done one yet, because the Shostakovich family has yet to release the sketches from the archive. After briefly showing me the draft of the Ninth, all Olga Dombrovskaya would say about the sketches was that they looked absolutely different from each other, "depending on whether he is seeking for something—if he knows the result, there are not so many sketches." (Apparently Shostakovich did not practice what he preached in his composition classes: as Dombrovskaya pointed out, he told his students to have the entire composition in mind before setting down the first note on paper, but he himself often did otherwise.) In the case of the difficult Ninth Quartet, which he started over from scratch several times, he seems to have kept the sketch pages in two different piles, for reasons known only to himself. Some of these pages have diagonal lines drawn through them—possibly, Dombrovskaya felt, as a way of marking that he had already incorporated those bits into the quartet.

And what was he telling himself with that single word "Hamlet," scribbled on its own in a blank space at the end of a series of notes? Why, simply to insert a part of his recently completed film score into the quartet at that point, Dombrovskaya presumes. Maybe. Probably. But I wonder if he was also dropping a hint to himself about the whole mood of the Ninth Quartet, offering himself a literary, cinematic, and musical model that could serve as a possible path through the thicket of contradictions.

In any case, *Hamlet* was not the only key. At least one more element lies buried at the heart of the Quartet in E-flat Major, and it too stems from his experiences in the early 1960s. In the fall of 1962, in his capacity as head of the Russian Composers' Union, Shostakovich organized and ran the group's Fourth Plenum, which focused on the topic of jazz and popular music. Five months later, Nikita Khrushchev was still complaining about the unpleasant sounds he had been subjected to at the jazz concert held at the Kremlin, which he had attended at Shostakovich's invitation. It was "the kind of music that gives you a feeling of nausea and a pain in the stomach," Khrushchev said during his March 1963 meeting with representatives of the artistic intelligentsia.

In responding to this complaint at the meeting, Shostakovich made his usual soothing, conciliatory, anodyne remarks. But he evidently stored up a different reaction, for jazz makes a distinct if phantomlike appearance in the Ninth Quartet. It is there, perhaps, in the sense of spontaneity and unexpectedness, in the disrupted rhythms, the small and large cacophonies, the repeated uses of variations on a theme; but it is also there, quite definitely, in a single moment of pizzicato that occurs toward the end of the third movement. It is hard to say precisely why this plucked chord sounds so jazzy—whether it is the particular combination of pitches on the viola and violin, or the way it rhythmically interrupts the bowed sequence that precedes it, or the fact that it is followed by a punctuated series of pizzicato beats, or all of the above plus more—but it is so noticeably a jazz moment that it stops the ear every time. And this is true whether you are hearing the Alexander Quartet's recording or the Emerson Quartet's, the Beethovens' or the Borodins'. What is astonishing is that the Party watchdogs missed it. But that, for Shostakovich, was the beauty of the string quartet medium. He could toy with cacophony, immerse himself in irony, indulge in all his darkest, least acceptable moods, and not be called unpatriotic, because nobody who cared about such labels was listening to these compositions.

They were listening instead, in the period immediately preceding this quartet, to his latest symphony and his revived opera. And if op. 114 (the number he assigned to the updated *Lady Macbeth* under its new name, *Katerina Izmailova*) was eventually an unqualified success, op. 113 was another matter entirely. Shostakovich's Thirteenth Symphony, based on five poems by the rebellious and self-proclaimedly "precocious" poet Yevgeny Yevtushenko, premiered on December 18, 1962, to a resounding silence in the press. (There was one small notice about it on the morning after the first performance; that was all.) Up until the very day of the Moscow premiere, the composer and his performers didn't even know whether the symphony would be allowed to go on: it didn't receive Khrushchev's approval until the afternoon of the 18th itself. A second Moscow performance took place two days later, and then a few more scattered performances occurred in February and March of 1963. After that, the Thirteenth Symphony was quietly dropped from the repertory—not because of any official ban, but because everyone understood that it was too hot to touch, politically.

What made it politically dangerous was the language of the poems, which is what had drawn Shostakovich to the project in the first place. The first and longest movement is an Adagio setting for "Babi Yar," Yevtushenko's now-famous poem against Russian anti-Semitism. "They smell of vodka and onions. . . . They guffaw 'Kill the Yids! Save Russia!'" are some of its lines about the perpetrators of pogroms, and though this was the movement that caused all the trouble—including officially imposed rewrites of the text—other sections seem equally problematic. "Humor," the Allegretto second movement, has the title character, humor itself, captured as a "political prisoner." "Fears" (a Largo movement) talks about the bad old days of "an anonymous denunciation . . . a knock at the door." And the final movement, a strangely despairing Allegretto setting for the poem "A Career," muses about an unknown, unsung scientist in Galileo's time who "was no more stupid than Galileo," who also "knew that the earth revolved, but he had a family." Cheery stuff for a man with Shostakovich's history of real fears and forced compromises.

We know from his letters, and from the fact that he under-took this obviously dangerous work, that the poems affected the composer very personally. But sincerity and even bravery do not guarantee aesthetic success. The Thirteenth Symphony, to my ear, is filled with the kind of bombastic urgency that makes you want to resist its patently commendable sentiments. The compo-sition features a rather tuneless bass solo line against a background of heavy male chorus and portentous orchestral accompaniment, replete with clashing cymbals, whirring tambourines, and ring-ing church bells. It is more like a hymn than a symphony, and at times even more like a melodramatic movie soundtrack. Still, its aes-thetics are not what caused the problem with its reception. Shosta-kovich had always been allowed, even encouraged, to produce bom-bastic symphonies, as long as the ostensible political content was the approved one. Here he was asking for trouble, and he got it.

Two prominent singers—one who toyed for months with the idea of performing the piece but finally refused to do it, another who rehearsed up until the day of the premiere but then failed to show up—backed out on Shostakovich, and he was forced to rely on the alternate bass to put across the solo. More impor-tantly, his old friend Yevgeny Mravinsky, who had premiered most of his symphonies from the Fifth onward, refused to con-duct the Thirteenth. Explanations for this vary. A number of people believed that Mravinsky's wife, a noted opportunist, got him to turn down the assignment because it was too much of a political hot potato, and that she gave him his excuse by point-ing out to him that he never conducted choral music, only "pure music." Kurt Sanderling, who worked closely with Mravinsky for many years, felt that this was not an excuse, but the truth: Mravinsky was uncomfortable with the idea of conducting a chorus as well as an orchestra, and the huge effort it would have required from him, especially with a new work like this, would have taken more time than he had available, given that his orchestra was about to go on a major foreign tour. Sanderling insists to this day that Mravinsky's motive was not political. But Shostakovich clearly felt that it was, and he broke with Mravinsky over it—a break that was perpetuated, even after the composer himself patched it over, by some of his musician friends. Here is Mstislav Rostropovich, for instance, placing the incident in the context of Shostakovich's overall attitude about loyalty: "I knew that if he were to write something for cello, he would automatically turn to me, even if I had forgotten how to play. As far as Mravinsky was concerned, Dmitri Dmitriyevich would have trusted him with all his works till the end of his days if Mravinsky had not proved himself to be an unprincipled turncoat."

In the face of Mravinsky's refusal, Shostakovich gave the Thirteenth Symphony to Kirill Kondrashin, who, with his Moscow Philharmonic Orchestra, had presented the much-belated premiere of the Fourth Symphony in December of 1961. Now he eagerly accepted the assignment to conduct the Thirteenth, and it was in fact due to his enthusiasm (he even, quite courageously, praised the symphony in print) that the piece received not only its Moscow premiere but also its few additional performances in early 1963.

According to Glikman, there was a huge discrepancy between

the public's response at the premiere—"At the end of the finale the audience rose as one man and erupted in tempestuous applause, which seemed to go on forever"—and the officially imposed silence that followed. Nor did Shostakovich allow the Party disapproval to dampen his own pleasure in this symphony ("if it is indeed a symphony?" he asked parenthetically in one of his letters). For the rest of his life, he and Irina celebrated July 20, the date he had completed the Thirteenth, as an important anniversary. The fact that its composition had lightened a month-long hospital stay in the summer of 1962, which coincided with his "honeymoon" in the marriage to Irina, may have had something to do with his strenuous affection for the Thirteenth, but so did its shoddy treatment at the hands of the Party. In this respect, it had joined company in his mind with his other victimized works. "He used to say he liked all of his works, because if he didn't like them, he wouldn't have written them," Irina Antonovna told me. "But of course he thought more and felt more about those works whose fate was tragic."

Chief among these was *Lady Macbeth of the Mtsensk District*, which had remained one of the compositions dearest to his heart. Since the mid-1950s, Shostakovich had repeatedly tried to get it staged again in some form or other. He revised it for a suggested Leningrad performance in 1956, only to have it rejected in March of that year by a ministerial committee set up specifically to "audition" it. The opera was then proposed but not, in the end, performed by both the Kirov Opera in 1957 and La Scala in 1958. Finally the Düsseldorf Deutsche Oper put on the original

Lady Macbeth in November of 1959, announcing that this would be the last such performance before the introduction of a new version, which the composer had called *Katerina Izmailova* after the opera's heroine.

After several delays and complications—Tikhon Khrennikov actually had to speak on the opera's behalf to get it through the Composers' Union—this update received an "unofficial" premiere at the Stanislavsky-Nemirovich-Danchenko Theater on December 26, 1962. The official Moscow premiere then took place at the same venue in January of 1963, at which point the opera was widely acknowledged, inside Russia and out, as a formerly mistreated masterpiece. From the moment *Katerina Izmailova* became the accepted text, Shostakovich refused to give his permission for any variant production, including the original *Lady Macbeth*. Whether he did this out of active preference for the new score or fear of political reprisals surrounding the old is not entirely clear, but he does seem to have liked the new one well enough to personally supervise performances all over Europe. Eventually he even invited Galina Vishnevskaya to play the title role in the film version, which came out in 1967.

The opera's manifest success should have made the composer feel vindicated, and on some level it probably did. But on another level there was a nagging feeling that he and his opera should never have had to go through all this in the first place. When Yevtushenko, who attended the premiere, wrote a poem about it called "Second Birth," Shostakovich was pleased and honored by the attention but disturbed by the title: "My music did not die," he told Glikman, "and therefore did not need to be born a second time." More tellingly, although he now planned to return to the opera form and announced that he was immediately embarking on a version of Mikhail Sholokhov's *And Quiet Flows the Don*, nothing ever came of this or any other opera project. His music for *Lady Macbeth* may have survived, but something seems to have died in Shostakovich when Stalin and his henchmen destroyed that early triumph. And just as the success of the Fifth Symphony had driven home to him what he had sacrificed in giving up the Fourth, the rousing success of *Katerina Izmailova* may well have cut both ways, reminding Shostakovich of all that had been torn away from him when *Lady Macbeth* was suppressed.

His response, in any case, was exactly what it had been in 1938: to retreat from the large-scale efforts that had caused him so much unwarranted pain, and to devote himself instead to the string quartet. In 1938 he hardly knew what he was doing. By 1964 he had become a master of the form, so much so that he could produce two astonishingly inventive quartets in the space of half a summer. On July 20, 1964, less than two months after the completion of the Ninth Quartet, Shostakovich finished the Quartet No. 10 in A-flat Major.

The Tenth Quartet is at once Shostakovich's harshest string quartet and his friendliest. That peculiarly sardonic harshness expresses itself most strongly, though by no means exclusively, in the Allegretto furioso second movement, whose loud, fierce opening comes as quite a jolt after the delicate close of the first movement. From this sudden start, the music just keeps getting louder and fiercer. A series of braying chords (which can sound like either a donkey's hee-haw or a train's double whistle, depending on which instrument plays them) represents the most extreme version of what the composer does throughout this section, assaulting our ears with purposely unmelodic noises. And yet even this difficult movement is intensely rhythmic, as is the quartet as a whole: the piece almost invites choreography, its rhythms are so foot-tappingly regular. Nor is the perceptible rhythm the quartet's only friendly sign. There is also the way the first and last movements have a similar texture, enclosing us in that welcoming sense of return. And then there is the little tune that arises early in the fourth movement and companionably stays with us, reappearing after numerous side steps and digressions, sometimes in broken or altered form, but always recognizable, always coming back, until at the end it slows to a quiet halt. If Shostakovich ever deigned to reassure, the Tenth would be his most reassuring quartet; since he does not, its darkness is at any rate pierced by flashes of something else, something that makes us feel less alone.

Like the Ninth Quartet, the Tenth is dedicated to someone alive, and to someone close to Shostakovich. Unlike the Ninth, it is dedicated to a very old friend. Moisei Weinberg had stood by the composer through all the tragedies, all the losses, all the compromises, and all the reconciliations of his adult life. It was to Weinberg's house that he went on that January day in 1948 when he was first condemned by the Zhdanov committee, and it was there that he confessed his envy of the dead man, Weinberg's father-in-law Solomon Mikhoels. It was to Moisei and his wife, Natalya, that Shostakovich turned for help in breaking the news of Nina's death to Maxim. And the favors and kindnesses went both ways: when Moisei Weinberg was arrested on trumped-up capital charges in 1953, he and his wife temporarily signed over guardianship of their daughter to Nina and Dmitri Shostakovich, and when Weinberg was released later in 1953, partly through Shostakovich's intervention with Beria (though mainly because of Stalin's death), the guardianship papers were ceremoniously burnt. Weinberg felt that Shostakovich had saved his life; and Shostakovich, in turn, understood the extent to which Weinberg had suffered politically for being affiliated with the "Shostakovich school" of composers. "Weinberg was one of his closest, dearest friends—close to his soul," Olga Dombrovskaya told me. "Shostakovich and Weinberg shared all their compositions with each other. They dealt with each other as equals, even though Shostakovich was so prominent, and older."

"There was a bet between Weinberg and Shostakovich," Kurt Sanderling said, "about which would be the first to finish more quartets." When Shostakovich completed the quartet dedicated to Irina Antonovna, in May of 1964, each man had written exactly nine quartets: they were now neck and neck in their race. So the Tenth Quartet is both a generous gift and a competitive one (and even the competitiveness is part of the generosity, for it acknowledges that they are indeed "equals"). In pouring everything he has into this one additional quartet, which he wrote from start to finish in less than two months, Shostakovich is gambling his whole pile of chips on a single roulette number, a single roll of the dice—and, somewhat to his own amazement, he wins. But while the composer may revel in his temporary victory and his temporary spate of luck, he is also conscious of how many other times he has been and will be less triumphant, less lucky. The humor and good humor in the Tenth Quartet are weighted and mediated by their opposite, which in this case is neither blank despair nor anxious hesitation, but a firm, strong awareness of how cruel and terrible life can be. If the Tenth Quartet feels whole and unified in its tone, this is partly because its cheer is still dour, its gratitude cautious. It is, in short, not an uncharacteristically optimistic Shostakovich speaking to us here, but the same steely-eyed, grave-hearted man we've known all along. That too is part of its friendliness, its companionableness—the fact that this quartet renders the composer's essentially divided nature so honestly and so accurately.

Interestingly, this quartet, despite its Jewish dedicatee, uses no klezmer melodies of any kind. If Kurt Sanderling is right, and if Shostakovich associated Jewish music with tragic experiences, then this would seem to be further evidence that the Tenth is one of his less tragic quartets. And indeed, by the time we get to the final movement, the music itself almost seems to be celebrating: we are comforted by the resurgence of the contrapuntal theme from the opening movement, and we are also delighted in a different way by the friendly little fourth-movement motif that won't go away, that insists on keeping us company. Survival through the inevitable cycles (of life, of history) is not the only point here. Things can come around again, *will* come around again, and that is neither good nor bad in itself. It is the companions with whom we experience these memories and returns—the companions of our youth, who are almost like our other selves but are thankfully *not* ourselves—that make these circularities tolerable or intolerable, joyful or empty. If loyalty is at the center of Shostakovich's personality, then so is the rejuvenated pleasure that only a certain kind of loyalty can bring.

That is what we hear in the last few notes of the Tenth Quartet, as the little tune, played in a high register on the first violin against the softly fading high notes of the other three instruments, stutters to its close. The stutter is not a misstep, but a winding down, as of a clock; the ending is not abrupt or tragic or frighteningly final, but quiet and somehow expected. It is like watching the day come to its close, knowing that tomorrow will be another day like it, or possibly not like it at all, but at any rate another day.

And yet, despite its aspect of quotidian reassurance, despite its circularities and reminiscences, despite its deep companionableness, the Quartet in A-flat Major also feels like the last of its kind. Something has ended here, not just for today but for good; a phase of life that was both terrifying and significant has finally come to a close. Or so it seems when I listen to it now. But perhaps this is just retrospective imagination, the result of looking back on the Tenth Quartet from the vantage point of what was to follow.

⋛ 5 ⋚

Funeral March

You know, the "Beethovens" no longer play so well. But when
I see that they are still together, it gives me a feeling of
security—I know that everything in the world is still all
right, because they continue to exist.

—SHOSTAKOVICH,
as reported by Mstislav Rostropovich

B y the fall of 1964, the outward forms of Shostakovich's
daily life had taken on pretty much their final shape. He
and Irina were comfortably—indeed, by Soviet standards, luxuriously—settled in the Nezhdanova Street flat. The
apartment had been remodeled after Maxim and his family
moved out, and it now included four rooms plus bath and
kitchen, the latter presided over by Maria Kozhunova, Fenya's
niece, who also did all the daily housecleaning. At the front of
the flat, just inside the door that led in from the lift, was a formal, rather bare reception room in which Shostakovich received
official visitors, answered (with the help of a secretary) a huge
number of requests through the mail, and otherwise carried out

his duties as a deputy of the Supreme Soviet—duties that, by all accounts, he took quite seriously. Just past the reception room lay a separate dining room, and beyond that a large bedroom, on the wall of which hung a Pyotr Vilyams painting called *The Bathers* that Shostakovich had brought from the Kutuzovsky apartment; it portrayed, in profile, a couple of earthy, sexy, heavy-bodied women whose figures manage to suggest what might have happened if Cézanne or pre-Cubist Picasso had crossed paths with Socialist Realism.

All the rooms in the apartment were pleasant and nicely furnished, in some cases with custom-built Karelian birch woodwork that went far beyond anything the normal Russian citizen could afford. But the only room that truly radiated a sense of expansiveness and elegance was the composer's study, which was so large it took up one whole side of the flat. Though it contained a grand piano—in fact, *two* pianos in the later years, after Rostropovich gave him a Steinway for his sixtieth birthday—Shostakovich did almost all of his composing at his desk. This was a massive, elegant piece of furniture that faced out the room's windowed side; when he was working, it was generally filled with various-sized piles of paper. Among the other items arranged on its broad, rectangular surface were an ornate box for his playing cards, a beautiful old clock, and an abacus. He probably used the abacus when working out the complicated mathematical details of his compositions. The cards were there for his frequent games of solitaire. As for the clock, all his life he was obsessed with precise timekeeping: he insisted that all the household clocks be set at exactly the same moment, and he was punctual to a fault—an uncommon fault, among Russians.

On one wall of the study hung the Vilyams painting *Nana*; other walls were filled with framed posters announcing Shostakovich's various premieres and performances. Behind his back and next to the doorway—in other words, out of his sight as he wrote—was a large, ladderlike piece of wooden equipment that the Russians call a "Swedish wall," which Shostakovich used for his prescribed muscle-strengthening exercises. And in a corner of the room, placed high enough on a shelf so that it overlooked the desk from some distance, was a larger-than-life white plaster bust of Beethoven, sculpted by Gavriil Glikman, Isaak's brother, and presented to Shostakovich as a gift. The bust had occupied a similar post in the Kutuzovsky apartment, and Shostakovich had taken care to reinstall it when he moved, so that Beethoven's characteristically frowning gaze could continue to fall directly on his writing table.

An equally fierce supervisory presence haunted his country-house study. In 1960 Shostakovich had purchased a dacha at Zhukovka, about thirty kilometers outside Moscow, and when Irina Antonovna married him in 1962, she began remodeling the small house so that he could write in peace on the second floor, even when his grandchildren were visiting. (Eventually, as his health weakened, she had an elevator installed and—to meet the legal requirements for such equipment—had herself trained as an elevator operator.) In the Zhukovka study was another large desk, on the surface of which lay several pictures preserved under glass. It was an odd, personal assortment of faces. Bach and Hemingway were neighbors here, and next to them sat Shostakovich's relative by marriage, the eminent critic and children's writer Kornei Chukovsky, whose grandson Yevgeny had married Galya. On the other side of the table were photos of the composer's son, Maxim, the conductor Rudolf Barshai, and the soprano Galina Vishnevskaya. But dominating the center of the desk, in the largest picture by far, was a gigantic full-length portrait of Modest Mussorgsky, glaring straight out at the viewer with his hypnotic, glittery, dark-browed eyes. Mstislav Rostropovich, who, together with Vishnevskaya, had also acquired a dacha in Zhukovka and who often visited Shostakovich there, once glanced down at the desk and said to him, "But why do you have this picture of Mussorgsky here? Why not on a wall somewhere?" To which the composer reportedly replied, "Slava, you can't imagine how many of my works I put in the wastebasket when I look at his eyes."

Aside from these two permanent homes, there were other locations to which Shostakovich and Irina frequently traveled. For a number of summers they went to Dilizhan, in Armenia, a place so lovely that it caused the composer to write to Glikman, in a voice that lacked any traces of his typical irony, "I have come to the conclusion that there is nothing more beautiful than the Earth" (to which he added, with his characteristic musical allusiveness, "I think constantly of Mahler's *Song of the Earth*"). Shostakovich also made frequent trips to the composers' retreat at Repino, near Leningrad, where he was able to meet Glikman,

Kozintsev, and other Leningrad friends. In addition, there were intermittent travels abroad to attend foreign premieres or receive honors and awards.

And, increasingly, there were the stays in hospitals and sanatoriums to deal with Shostakovich's ever worsening health. Aside from the weakened right hand, for which he returned to the hospital numerous times in the 1960s, these ailments included a broken left leg (resulting in an extended hospital stay in late 1960), great difficulty in climbing stairs or boarding buses, the nervous twitching that had plagued him for decades, and a more general neurological fear of movement ("I should like not to drop dead with fright every time I step on the escalator in the Metro," he confided to one friend). No one had yet diagnosed the source of these problems, nor had any of the many doctors Shostakovich consulted succeeded in curing them. By 1964 they had already become a routine if deeply resented aspect of his life, and though he at times expressed the hope that he would once again be healthy, another side of him—his more realistic self, perhaps—seemed aware that things could only get worse.

Yet even as Shostakovich's circumstances were taking on a semblance of permanence, certain things in his world were also changing dramatically. In October of 1964 Nikita Khrushchev was suddenly removed from his post as Party leader and replaced by Leonid Brezhnev. Shostakovich's only reported response to the event was in his usual sardonic vein—"Well, Sergei Mikhailovich, now we will most certainly enjoy an even better life?" he apparently said to a friend he met on the street the day the news broke—and there was no direct connection, at least at first, between his own life and this sudden shift at the top. Still, it did signal a kind of sea change in the way the USSR, or for that matter Russia, was governed. Every previous Soviet leader, not to mention all the preceding tsars, had been removed from office by death alone; the idea that a former ruler could go on living as a private citizen was an almost Western novelty.

More local but, to Shostakovich, of much more immediate importance was the personnel change that occurred around the same time in the Beethoven Quartet. For over forty years—since the quartet's founding at the Moscow Conservatory in 1923—the same four men had been playing together, and for twenty of these years they had been premiering Shostakovich's string quartets. Now, in the fall of 1964, the violist, Vadim Borisovsky, was forced by ill health to retire. And this frightening development (frightening because of its general intimations of mortality as well as its practical impact on the ensemble) took place exactly when the Beethovens were about to start rehearsing the Ninth and Tenth Quartets for a scheduled November premiere. Shostakovich had just handed over the scores to Dmitri Tsyganov, and rehearsals were about to begin at Sergei Shirinsky's flat, when the violist was suddenly forced to withdraw.

Fyodor Druzhinin, who was brought in to replace Borisovsky, gives his account of the transition:

> When my teacher, Vadim Borisovsky, became so ill he could no longer play, I was asked by Dmitri Tsyganov to help them out by reading through with them Shostakovich's two new quartets, the

Ninth and the Tenth. Tsyganov told me that Shostakovich was impatient to hear what he had written. He gave me the copied parts at the Conservatoire at around lunchtime, and I was to come that evening at seven o'clock to the flat of Sergei Shirinsky for a play-through.

I arrived at quarter to seven, worried that I might be too early. However, when I entered the room, to my horror I saw not only all the other musicians in their places, but Shostakovich in an armchair right next to my empty place. This modest "sight-reading session" turned out to be a three-hour endurance test. Not only was I replacing my teacher in the Beethoven Quartet, but I was having to sight-read sensing the presence of the composer beside me— and I mean sensing, as I didn't dare look at Dmitri Dmitriyevich.

When we had played the last chord in the Ninth Quartet, Dmitri Dmitriyevich said in a satisfied voice, "Masters are playing." Thus my place in the Quartet was assured for the forthcoming premieres of these quartets.

As the autumn wore on, most of the rehearsals took place in the reception room of the Shirinsky flat, but some of them were held in Shostakovich's nearby study—a space large enough to hold a string quartet and a small audience, along with everything else. Druzhinin goes on to describe Shostakovich's unusually calm demeanor in these intimate sessions, as opposed to his nervous appearance outside them. "The relaxed atmosphere of these rehearsals had a very beneficial effect on Shostakovich," the violist reported. "When he was amongst strangers, especially if there were present people ill-disposed towards him, his critics, other composers, or simply someone he didn't know, his nervous tension never slackened. His body kept twitching, his mouth drooped dolefully, his lips trembled and his eyes exuded such oppressive tragic energy that he was frightening to look at." But alone with the Beethovens, "he was a different person. . . . He was calm but concentrated, ready to smile and joke."

The Ninth and Tenth Quartets received their joint premieres on November 20, 1964, in the Small Hall of the Moscow Conservatory, an intimate, pleasant, rather plain auditorium located up three flights of stairs in the main teaching building, just down the street from the complex that held Shostakovich's and Shirinsky's flats. Though it was a far more public occasion than the rehearsals had been, the performance thus had a familial or at least neighborly aspect. The hall itself held fewer than five hundred people—a small portion of them on pewlike benches in the steeply raked balcony, but most sitting in the simple, straight-backed seats that filled the flat, wooden floor of the main room, facing the waist-high stage. On the evening of November 20, the composer, his wife, and his two children, along with various friends and in-laws, sat on the right-hand side of the first row. From the picture that was taken of the occasion, it appears that both Irina and Shostakovich were biting their lower lips nervously during the performance. But their anxiety, for once, was needless: the response to these two quartets, on this occasion and others, was overwhelmingly positive.

Still, dread remained an appropriate prevailing emotion, for there was always another blow waiting to descend. Ill health and retirement had not, it turned out, been the worst card fate could deal out to the Beethoven Quartet; that had been held in reserve, only to appear less than a year later. In August of 1965, while he was chopping wood at his dacha, Vasily Shirinsky suddenly and quite unexpectedly died of a stroke. "He bent down, then straightened up and passed away," his niece Galina Shirinskaya recalled. "He was a very healthy man, never drank or smoked— one wife, one child, very happy and successful life. Unlike the others, who made tons of mistakes, he was always 'correct.' His death was a shock; it was like thunder from a clear sky. Everybody was more or less sick except him. To die at the age of sixty-five was too early for him."

The second violinist, though absolutely essential to the makeup of any string quartet, might be expected to play a supporting rather than a leading role. But according to Shirinskaya, her uncle was the core of the Beethoven Quartet, both its primary mover and its ultimate arbiter. "His authority was absolutely indisputable in the Quartet," she said. "His words were law— though I wouldn't say that he used his authority very often. But if there were any arguments, his word was final." And this was not only because he was slightly senior to two of the three other players, nor even because he was a "first-rate personality" and a "very good composer" himself ("Dmitri Dmitriyevich respected his talent as a composer," Shirinskaya noted). It was also due to the fact that Vasily Shirinsky's own work had been the basis for the founding of the Quartet.

In 1923 these four young musicians gathered together in public for the first time to perform Vasily Petrovich Shirinsky's diploma work, a string quartet composed as his conservatory graduation exercise. Vasily Shirinsky and his violist, Vadim Borisovsky, were twenty-three years old; their first violinist, Dmitri Tsyganov, and their cellist, Sergei Shirinsky, were only twenty. They were all close friends, and two of them, the Shirinskys, were brothers. (Actually, they were half-brothers, for while they shared the same mother, they had different fathers. Vasily's father had died shortly after he was born, and his mother, an accomplished Viennese pianist, soon married Shirinsky, who gave his last name to her infant son; Sergei was born a few years later. Their respective instruments—violin for Vasily and cello for Sergei—had been chosen for them at birth by their mother, who had dreams of performing trios with her musician sons. And she ultimately got her wish: "They performed for quite a long time together and toured during the Civil War," Galina Shirinskaya said of her grandmother's, her uncle's, and her father's youthful days.)

Vasily Petrovich's graduation quartet was performed before an examining board of eminent musicians and composers, including that same Nikolai Myaskovsky—teacher of Shebalin and Khachaturian—whose work was ultimately condemned, along with Shostakovich's, by the 1948 Zhdanov Decree. "And the examining board admired their performance so much," Shirinskaya said, "that they recommended they work together and name the quartet after the Moscow Conservatory." This is how the original Moscow Conservatory Quartet came into being, and it played under that name until the early 1930s, when a change in the Conservatory's name (it briefly honored one of the old Bolsheviks, Feliks Kon, before he too fell out of favor) caused the players to ask for a new name, the Beethoven Quartet. "Beethoven was in favor with the Soviet leaders," Shirinskaya drily observed, though that can't have been their sole reason for choosing his name. Others, including members of the Quartet itself, have suggested that Beethoven and Shostakovich, as the nineteenth- and twentieth-century masters of the string quartet form, ultimately became the twin patron saints of the Quartet—the two composers whose work was repeatedly performed, together and apart, over the course of the Beethoven Quartet's career. This subliminal and at times explicit pairing of Beethoven's quartets with Shostakovich's was one of the many gifts they brought him as a group.

"Starting with the Second Quartet, they were doing his pre-mieres," Irina Antonovna Shostakovich reminded me, explaining the composer's strong affection for these players. "They were part of his whole life, and he considered their performance to be adequate to his ideal." (In this she was actively contradicting the sense one gets from Rostropovich—and also, at times, the Borodins—that it was loyalty rather than respect for their playing which kept Shostakovich with the Beethovens to the end.) "And he loved them as personalities," she added, "and they loved him." As to what distinguished the Beethoven Quartet's performances from anyone else's, Irina Antonovna commented: "In my opinion—which is not that of an educated musician, but just a listener—what made them special was that when they played they were listening to each other, as opposed to being individuals."

Yet it was as individuals, with one quartet dedicated to each of the original Beethoven players, that Shostakovich now proceeded to honor them. I do not think he necessarily intended to compose all four of these quartets when he began; he was not in the habit of planning beyond the very next quartet, and it was the death of Vasily Shirinsky which now plunged him into the Eleventh. But I think that, once started, the series of four individually dedicated pieces, one for each man and each instrument, unfolded with increasing inevitability.

The Quartet No. 11 in F Minor is the quietest, most broken, most passively depressive quartet Shostakovich ever wrote. And that is saying a great deal. There is a pervasive and deepening sense of sorrow throughout this final period, even in the symphonies, but especially in the quartets. Yet when that mood appears elsewhere, it is at least punctuated occasionally by rage, or wit, or melody, or allusiveness, or something else that, if it does not lighten the mood, at any rate convinces us that a strong-willed individual is still alive in the music. No such inhabitant peeks out at us from the Eleventh Quartet. It is like the empty ruin of a once joyous house, a crumbling, disintegrating memorial to lost happiness. No attempt, at least that I can discern, has been made to commemorate the personality of the strong, hearty, infectiously talented man to whom it is dedicated; the quartet is entirely devoted to his death, as if that sudden blow had erased not only everything that came before, but also everything that was to come after.

In its seven short sections, some barely more than a minute long, the quartet tries over and over to get going again, only to fail each time. Nothing quite works as a stimulus—not the weird, slithery glissandos that are suddenly introduced into the Scherzo section, nor the juddering sixteenth notes that run all through the Etude. Extreme measures are invoked only to be despaired of: the corpse remains a corpse. At times the music feels willfully inert, as the Emerson Quartet discovered when they tried to liven it up a bit. "He makes it sound so boring," said Eugene Drucker, alluding to the string of repetitive notes Shostakovich inserted in the Scherzo. "We tried it like this"—he demonstrated, humming a more staccato, more interesting version of the passage—"but we decided that wasn't right. So we make it sound as plain as possible, almost annoying. To me it always sounds like a Suzuki exercise."

The Eleventh is Shostakovich's least tuneful quartet, as if melody itself had gone out of the world when Vasily Shirinsky left it. (And not just the chamber music world, it seems: this fractured, distressed, forsaken feeling also pervades the haunting Second Violin Concerto, written during this same period.) In accord with the sense of overwhelming meaninglessness, many of the quartet's seven named sections convey the opposite of what they promise. The Scherzo is neither happy nor light. The Humoresque could not be less amusing. The Recitative is so far from imitating the sound of a human voice (especially if you recall what Shostakovich can do with violin recitative—what he *did* do, in Quartet No. 2) that it seems especially perverse of him to have chosen that title. Squalls and caterwauls and braying sounds, faintly reminiscent of the hee-haw cacophony in the Tenth Quartet, are what substitute for speech in this Recitative movement. But that, of course, makes its own kind of sense, in that death (and perhaps, for Shostakovich, this death in particular) is indeed unspeakable.

Only in the Elegy do we get something that resembles its title. At the very end of this movement—which, at just over four minutes, is the longest of the seven, and clearly the heart of the work—Shostakovich gives us a few measures that briefly appease our hunger for soothing melody. And he does so in a way that exactly replicates his sense of loss. A little ten-note tune is initially carried by the first violin, which by this time is playing all on its own. The same sequence of notes is then repeated (though with a slight addition at the end) by the second violin, also playing alone. But whereas the first violin is playing loud enough to be heard clearly, only declining toward the end of its sequence into a quieter dynamic, the second violin begins softly and diminishes to nothingness. By having the second violinist play the little melody *con sordino*—that is, with a mute on the strings— the composer essentially turns him into a ghost.

This is the only place where the second violin's role is so obviously singled out. Elsewhere it is used mainly for its rhythmic capacity, or occasionally as a companion to the first violin, which most often carries the independent musical line. This is not, in other words, a quartet designed to showcase the position of second violin. It is not Shirinsky's specific performance role that is being commemorated here, but his entire presence in the group, a presence that—as both the music of this quartet and the words of Galina Shirinskaya suggest—was the foundation for everything else. The piece appears to be asking whether, under the circumstances, any kind of music is still possible. When, in the Scherzo, the two violins disappear for long sequences, the question seems to be: what would a world without violins be like? And then the cello too drops out, leaving the viola chugging on alone, but doggedly, unmelodically, as if even the viola's ability to play expressively derived somehow from the now-departed violin.

In the Finale, Shostakovich lets the first violin carry the last note, just as he had let it begin the Introduction. But whereas the opening measures gave promise of a tune—though it turned out to be a broken promise, as all the promises in this quartet are— the final measures offer instead a single very high, very quiet note. A violin's highest register, played close to the bridge on the fourth and highest string, is almost out of our normal hearing range; in other words, it is only half there at its best. And the way Shostakovich uses it here, the ghostly high note dies out so gradually and indistinctly that we cannot actually pinpoint the moment when it ceases to be audible. It is the most *morendo* of his chronically *morendo* endings. But because it closes a quartet in which nothing ever really happened, the silence has an almost positive force. It is like the ending of Beckett's novella *The Lost Ones*, where the undefined, unindividuated creatures of the title, encased in a cylinder pervaded by a "faint stridulence" and forced to carry on their repetitive actions for an eternity, are at long last allowed to rest—that is, they are allowed to die. "So much roughly speaking for the last state of the cylinder and of this little people of searchers one first of whom if a man in some unthinkable past for the first time bowed his head if this notion is to be maintained" is Beckett's final sentence. The blessed finality of it comes across as deeply, idiosyncratically, impersonally moving, but it can only do so if you have been through all the frustrating depressiveness of the preceding sixty pages.

The same, I think, is true of the silence at the end of the Eleventh Quartet. Like Beckett, Shostakovich has scraped away everything that lay at his disposal, all the tricks and tools of his artistic trade, in order to render up honestly and feelingly the nothingness that is death. For musicians who play these quartets all the time, this bareness comes to seem a special virtue. "The Eleventh is actually one of my favorites of all the quartets," commented Philip Setzer, who takes the second violin role when the Emersons play this piece, "I think because it's built with so few tools and ingredients." Elizabeth Wilson feels the same way: "It implies a lot without saying very much," she said of this quartet.

If the strategy is Beckett-like in its modernism, it is also Shakespearean in the grandeur of its self-renunciation. What we are offered is not quite the "poor, bare, forked animal" of *King*

Lear, for Lear is mad and the ragged creature he addresses in that scene is playing mad, while Shostakovich is burdened with an overabundance of sanity. And it is not *The Tempest*'s "Now my charms are all o'erthrown," for Prospero, in making that final speech, is actually asking for our applause, whereas the Shostakovich of the Eleventh Quartet couldn't care less what we think. But there is something of the dethroned monarch here nonetheless, something of the powerful wizard who has purposely renounced his magic.

It's possible that Shostakovich himself was aware of the Shakespearean overtones. At any rate, when he scheduled this quartet for its May 1966 premiere in Leningrad, he put on the same program a very old piece of his—a musical setting of Shakespeare's Sonnet 66—that had rarely if ever received a public performance.

Sonnet 66 begins, "Tir'd with all these, for restful death I cry." The poem was the basis for one of the *Six Romances on Texts of W. Raleigh, R. Burns, and W. Shakespeare* that Shostakovich composed in 1942, when he was living in Kuibyshev. According to Irina Antonovna, this particular piece was suppressed because "the authorities saw some allusions to the USSR in the sonnet." Their attention may have been attracted by the lines deploring:

> . . . art made tongue-tied by authority,
> And folly, doctor-like, controlling skill,
> And simple truth miscalled simplicity,

And captive good attending captain ill.
Tir'd with all these, from these would I be gone . . .

Or perhaps they were offended by the references to "gilded honor shamefully misplaced" and "right perfection wrongfully displaced." In fact, there's barely a line in the sonnet that *doesn't* seem to refer to Stalin's Soviet Union. But by 1966, even if the prevailing atmosphere was no longer that of the Thaw, there was nonetheless sufficient latitude for Shostakovich to feel he could schedule this sonnet in the first half of his program, along with newer songs written to satiric verses by Sasha Chorny and texts from the humorous magazine *Krokodil*. The plan was for Galina Vishnevskaya, who had premiered the Chorny verses five years earlier, to reprise them on this occasion, while a young bass named Yevgeny Nesterenko would sing the even more recent *Krokodil* songs. And then, after an intermission, the reconstituted Beethoven Quartet would play both the Quartet No. 1 and the new Quartet No. 11.

By the time he finished writing the Eleventh Quartet, on January 30, 1966, Shostakovich knew that he could once again depend on the Beethovens to premiere it. After Vasily Shirinsky's sudden death, his place as second violinist had been taken by Nikolai Zabavnikov, a student of Dmitri Tsyganov's who also happened to be the son-in-law of a famous pianist, Maria Israilevna Grinberg. Zabavnikov was "a very interesting person, very educated and knowledgeable, naturally a wonderful violinist, very intelligent and modest," reported Galina Shirinskaya (who, as a promising young pianist herself, began helping the Beethovens to rehearse the Shostakovich piano quintet at around this same time). "He talked little but knew much," she went on, "and was fanatically faithful to Shostakovich and to the Quartet." With the aim of training and preparing its two new members, Zabavnikov and Druzhinin, the Beethoven Quartet now proceeded to rehearse its whole repertory, and particularly the full cycle of Shostakovich's quartets to date. It was probably at one of these sessions—after the death of Vasily Shirinsky, but before the composition of the Quartet No. 11—that Druzhinin saw Shostakovich weeping in response to the Third Quartet.

By 1966 Shostakovich had essentially given up performing because of the problems with his right hand. But for some reason, perhaps inspired by the Beethovens' contagious sense of "renewal," he decided that he himself would play the piano accompaniment to Nesterenko's and Vishnevskaya's singing. The performance was scheduled for May 28 and 29 at the Glinka Hall in Leningrad—an identical program both nights, with the songs in the first half and the new quartet (preceded by his oldest one) in the second. "I am terribly nervous about my part in the concert, but I very much want to try," he wrote to Glikman on April 27. "I am afraid, though, that I shall not be able to manage. . . . When I think that the concert is not that far off, my right hand starts to go on strike altogether."

In the event, however, he did manage to perform his piano parts on May 28, despite the fact that he was still "terribly nervous" up to the very evening before. But his accomplishment—which included not only the playing itself, but also the overcoming of his now-habitual nervous fears—came at a tremendous cost. Glikman, who was present at the Leningrad premiere, gives his account of the evening:

> 28 May was one of those stiflingly hot, sticky and humid Leningrad days that Shostakovich had always found very trying. In the Glinka Hall, the Small Hall of the Leningrad Philharmonic, there seemed to be no air at all to breathe. It was uncomfortable enough in the light jacket I was wearing, but for Shostakovich, in tails and a starched shirt, it must have been unbearable. On top of this he was under tremendous stress, and when a very young Nesterenko, nervous as he might well be at being accompanied by the great composer himself, twice fluffed his entry, Shostakovich's face showed real panic. With a huge effort of will, he mastered himself and the performance continued.

Glikman tell us that "the new Eleventh Quartet was encored" and that the concert itself was a success overall. "But the appalling heat and the extreme nervous tension had taken their toll," he continues, "and Shostakovich was taken ill during the night." He was rushed to the hospital, and when the report finally came back from the doctors the next day, the diagnosis was a heart attack.

Shostakovich survived, this time. But it was a terrifying warning, and he became a different kind of invalid from that moment onward. For one thing, his doctors forbade him ever to smoke or drink again, and though he tried to obey (with mixed success), he confessed to enjoying life much less without alcohol. The two-month hospital stay that followed the heart attack was succeeded by a month-long stay in a sanatorium, and this too set a kind of pattern of illness. He was barely well enough to attend his own sixtieth-birthday celebration on September 25, 1966, but he did manage at the last minute to put in an appearance at the Large Hall of the Moscow Conservatory, where Maxim was conducting the First Symphony and Rostropovich was premiering the new Second Cello Concerto.

For the rest of 1966 and much of 1967, Shostakovich was in and out of hospitals and clinics. His physical state dominated his existence during this period, and though he was sometimes capable of writing music while hospitalized (the Thirteenth Symphony, for instance, had been composed almost entirely during his 1962 hospital stay), it was a full eight months before he was able to finish a new work—in this case, a song cycle based on the poetry of Alexander Blok. And even that accomplishment did not cheer him up much. In the same February 3 letter which notified Glikman of the newly completed *Seven Verses of A. Blok*, Shostakovich also mused darkly about mortality, his own and others':

> I am thinking much about life, death and careers. . . . For instance, Musorgsky died before his time. . . . Tchaikovsky, however, should have died earlier than he did. He lived slightly too long, and for that reason his death was a terrible one, or rather his last days were. The same applies to Gogol, to Rossini and perhaps to Beethoven. . . . I expect you will read these lines and ask yourself: why is he writing such things? Well, it's because I have undoubtedly lived longer than I should have done. I have been disappointed in much, and I expect many terrible things to happen.

At other times, though, Shostakovich could be drily humorous about his own physical impairment. Writing to Glikman about the two doctors—a surgeon and a neurologist—who examined him during one of his hospital stays in the fall of 1966, he displayed in full his old sense of Gogolian irony. "They both pronounced themselves extremely satisfied with my hands and my legs," he announced. "At the end of the day, the fact that I cannot play the piano and can only walk upstairs with the greatest of difficulty is of no importance at all. After all, nobody is obliged to play the piano, and one can live perfectly well without going upstairs. The best thing to do is sit at home and not mess about with stairs, or for that matter slippery pavements."

And then, in September of 1967, after a rather troubling summer during which, despite his long country walks, "my legs seem to be getting worse," he fell and broke his right leg—that is, the leg which had *not* been broken in 1960. From his hospital bed in Kuntsevo he wrote to Glikman: "Here is a general report. Target achieved so far: 75 per cent (right leg broken, left leg broken, right hand defective. All I need to do now is wreck the left hand and then 100 per cent of my extremities will be out of order.)" The dour mockery probably had a special appeal to ears attuned to the "targets" of the Five-Year Plans, but the gallant humor is evident to everyone, and the tone is worthy of Mark Twain. Twain did, in fact, once write a brief comic sketch about dispensing romantic advice to a girl whose fiancé had lost various parts of his body—a delicate matter that involved "the lifelong happiness of a woman and that of nearly two-thirds of a man." But Shostakovich's joke is even more trenchant than Twain's, in that he makes himself the butt of it.

His broken leg kept him in the hospital for most of the fall of 1967; the cast wasn't taken off until December, and then he had to learn to walk again. But by early 1968 Shostakovich was back in Moscow attending concerts and seeing friends. In the first few months of 1968 he often visited Leningrad as well, staying in the composers' retreat at Repino for most of the month of March, and there he was finally able to finish his Twelfth Quartet. While he was still in the midst of it, he reportedly said to Glikman, "It's funny, but I always feel that whatever opus I am working on, I shall never finish it. I may die suddenly, and then the piece will be left unfinished." But on this occasion, at least, such fears turned out to be groundless. Nor were his hands in such bad shape as to render him incapable of privately performing his own compositions on the piano. On March 16, 1968, "Dmitri Dmitriyevich played through the profoundly dramatic Twelfth Quartet to Venyamin Basner and me at Repino," noted Glikman. "He was in high spirits at the time."

As well he might have been. If audiences in general are fondest of the Eighth Quartet, musicians, musicologists, and professional Shostakovich admirers, to the extent they can be forced to choose a favorite at all among the quartets, tend to lean toward the Twelfth. The biographer Laurel Fay, explaining to me that the string quartets had been her "entry point" into Shostakovich as well as the subject of her Ph.D. dissertation, said that she was fond of all the quartets and preferred different ones at different times, but then volunteered, "I *love* the Twelfth." Elizabeth Wilson appears to feel the same way: "In no other work did Shostakovich so uncompromisingly condense his thinking, bending and manipulating the thematic material and reconciling the resulting conflicts within the taut framework of his structure, achieving a work of unrelenting dramatic force and intensity," she noted in *Shostakovich: A Life Remembered*. Alan George, the violist of the Fitzwilliam Quartet, observed in an essay about interpreting the quartets that the Twelfth is "the ultimate examination of the performers' interpretive powers, in that it confronts them with a resourcefulness, a range of expression and imaginative colouring, unmatched elsewhere in the series." And Shostakovich himself told the violinist Dmitri Tsyganov, to whom he dedicated the Twelfth Quartet on the occasion of his sixty-fifth birthday, that he thought it had turned out "splendidly," and that it was really more like a symphony than a chamber work.

Structurally, Shostakovich is doing something completely new in the Twelfth, just as he had in the Eleventh, with its seven brief movements. But if the Quartet No. 11 represents a period in which musical structure (along with everything else) is breaking down under the pressure of an annihilating despair, the Quartet No. 12 in D-flat Major embodies a fierce attempt to create some kind of new order out of that chaotic disintegration. A relatively brief first movement gives way to a second and final movement that is monumental in its length and scope, seeming to cover in its vast twenty-minute span every pace from *adagio* to *allegretto*, every mood from harshness to tenderness, and every sound from sweet melody to blaring dissonance. It incorporates a large number of virtuosic tricks, from trills and arpeggios to rapid, obsessive pizzicato and skirling, unnerving, on-the-bridge bowing, but the virtuosity does not register as such. On the contrary, everything in this movement, indeed in this quartet as a whole, exists for the sole purpose of expression—by which I mean not just the *espressivo* of a musical passage nor the emotional register to which that technique leads (though both those things are present here), but a more literal kind of expression, whereby wordless, unspoken feelings are described and made palpable by the music. *Sense can be made of this sorrow*: that is the meaning that comes through in the Twelfth Quartet.

And the odd thing is that Shostakovich accomplishes this by borrowing from a musical system that had, in many ways, exactly the opposite expressive aims. Generations of critics have recognized in the opening passage of the first movement (a cello solo whose strange melody is repeated or alluded to throughout the rest of the quartet) a classic twelve-tone row. What this means, in practice, is that each of the cello's first twelve notes is one note out of the twelve-tone scale represented by all the black and white keys in a piano's octave; when taken together in sequence, these cello notes add up to the kind of "series" that a twelve-tone composer would use to create the underlying building block for an entire work. But Shostakovich does not develop his initial row serially; on the contrary, it seems to exist in and for itself, almost as an adventurous dare or a faintly allusive joke, but one with very serious purposes.

Whereas Arnold Schoenberg invented his arithmetical serialist technique in order to break the hold of Romanticism on music, Shostakovich is using a variant of the technique to do something that is very different: that is, to create a strange form of melody that is at once strikingly novel and intuitively accessible. He is developing his own musical language, but he is doing so with the idea of speaking to us more directly, more honestly, and more nakedly than ever before. And because his language is at once so capacious and so idiosyncratic, he can absorb multitudes (the lessons of traditional harmony, the expressive power of Romanticism, the dissonance of modernism, even the rules of serialism) and still sound exactly and only like himself. If there is something introverted about Shostakovich's music, it is not the introversion of a clique that seeks to communicate only with those who are similarly enlightened, but the much more personal introversion of an artist who plumbs his own depths in order to bring up material that can be meaningful to all of us, initiated and uninitiated alike.

Given that the official Soviet position was a firm and resolute condemnation of "decadent" Western serialist and atonal techniques, it was somewhat bold of Shostakovich to introduce a twelve-tone row into his own composition (though he was hardly breaking new ground, since many of his younger colleagues and a few older ones had already done it). It was also, in his typical fashion, somewhat duplicitous, for earlier in the 1960s he had published a number of articles attacking the twelve-tone method. In "Bourgeois Culture Is Bankrupt," for instance, he asserted:

Very typical of modernistic trends today in Western music are
so-called "dodecaphonic" and "concrete" music. By the way, one
can hardly call either trend "music," both dodecaphony and
"concrete" music being founded on dogmas, and dogmas can
have nothing in common with art. Little wonder that the music
produced by the exponents of these dogmas is nothing but a
mannered technical experiment devoid of any real beauty.

And in "Dodecaphony Shatters Creativity," he went even further: "*This dogma of dodecaphony does nothing but kill the composer's imagination and the living soul of music* [his emphasis]. In
such a system of 'creating' music based on the 'total' organization of sound, the composer's role is quite pathetic."

Like all of Shostakovich's published statements, these ones
pose many problems. For one thing, he probably didn't even
write the essays himself, though he allowed his name to be attached to them. For another, as he had demonstrated over and
over again, he could be depended on to voice the politically necessary comment even if it went against his personal convictions.
But we cannot even be certain whether and to what extent these
assertions *did* violate his convictions. He might readily have
agreed, for example, that "dogmas can have nothing in common
with art," though the meaning he gave that phrase would have
differed from the official Soviet interpretation. And perhaps he
even believed that twelve-tone serialism, as strictly practiced by
Schoenberg and his most obedient acolytes, could hamper the
composer's creative role. What Shostakovich was doing in the
Quartet No. 12 was not to capitulate to serialism's rigid rules, but
to adopt certain aspects of the twelve-tone approach as an en-

hancement of his available palette. If it could be justified by its relationship to the rest of his musical intentions, he felt, then any compositional tool was fair game; and when Tsyganov voiced concerns about the explicitly serial elements in this quartet, Shostakovich apparently answered him by saying, "But one finds examples of it in Mozart's music."

In any case, to focus on the twelve-tone elements is to ignore what is most powerful and moving about the Twelfth Quartet: the way it dramatizes, acknowledges, and also resists its own sadness. The piece begins with a cello solo that, with the addition of the viola and the first violin, soon becomes a trio, while the second violin sits motionless for what seems a very long time. Shostakovich may have dedicated the Eleventh Quartet to the memory of Vasily Shirinsky, but it was only in the Twelfth that he finally managed to embody that missing and much-missed figure, in the person of the silent second violinist. And when the second violin finally does enter the music, it is at an extremely subdued (not to say ghostly) level, as one of three pizzicato players thrumming quietly in the background of a first-violin solo.

Except for that initial second-violin silence, nothing in the Twelfth Quartet lasts long. But there is none of the juddering, incapacitated stop-startedness that marked the Eleventh; instead there is a strong sense of flow, and resurgence, and even completion. After the lassitude of the Eleventh Quartet, these four instruments are now back in business together, allowing each other to take over solo roles at times, but mainly existing in relation to one another. And that in turn brings a sense of solidity, almost of equability, to this otherwise difficult musical world. Late in the first movement, for instance, long after the second violin has joined the others, there is a passage where the two violins both sit it out for a while, as the viola and the cello carry on alone. But this time it feels like rest, not death: we know the violins will eventually return. And when they do, they give us one of the most melodious, affecting passages in the quartet, a series of pure, high-register tones that seem to correspond to the visual impression of a pale, clear light piercing briefly through the darkening gloom.

Melodiousness, especially in its most lyrical, attractive form, was a complicated issue for Shostakovich. He had rebelled against it twice, for two different reasons: once when the admired European modernists of his youth had dismissed it, and again when the cultural dictators of his middle years had demanded it. In one typically satiric letter to Glikman, for example, he commented on "A. A. Zhdanov's inspiring directives to the effect that music should be melodious and graceful." For Shostakovich, as for all the serious composers who had been suppressed and persecuted under the Zhdanov Decree, these directives made it impossible to take melodiousness seriously. And yet the irony—one of the many in his life—was that Shostakovich himself had a significant talent for tonal melody, and had to work hard to suppress it.

One of his most effective strategies in this regard was the frequent insertion of the false note. I am not saying Shostakovich did this just to defy Zhdanov and the other cultural watchdogs.

His "wrong" notes were, on the contrary, a crucial musical discovery. They offered him a way of solving the central compositional problem that faced him: how to express true feeling in an environment where tonal melody had been robbed of truth, but also where atonal music had largely been robbed of feeling. This false-note approach would not have been evident in the work of a Western, serial composer, because one has to hear a ground-level tonality in order to detect its violation. So we in the audience, we who are able to notice and respond intuitively to the dissonant notes, are Shostakovich's necessary collaborators in this regard. In other words, his is a music that takes as its departure point our innate sense of musical expressiveness. And nowhere does this become more apparent than in the Twelfth Quartet.

In the second movement especially, everything gains additional meaning by being placed in proximity with its opposite. The feeling of dissonance and dark, harmonically ambiguous tunelessness that Shostakovich uses elsewhere is present, but although it is not entirely pleasurable, it somehow feels less anxiety-ridden than in the earlier quartets. If he is driven here, it seems to be by his own internal demons and angels rather than by something oppressing him from the outside. But even to distinguish inside from outside, willed from driven, seems false to the mood of the Twelfth Quartet, where, despite the vast scope and constant changeableness, everything essentially moves in one direction, as if with one unified aim.

That sense of impulsion, or propulsion, leads us eventually to what may well be the most emphatic and is certainly the most conclusive of Shostakovich's quartet endings. Out of a chaos of trills and harsh voices—repetitions and returns of earlier patterns that have now been pushed to an extreme—comes a sequence of strong, even, rapidly bowed notes, with all the instruments playing in unison, their different strands satisfyingly resolved in a major-chord harmony. This happens twice just before the ending, in a brief, suggestive manner, and then it happens a third time in a final, showstopping way. For once in Shostakovich, you can actually feel the end approaching: it announces itself, and then it announces itself again, and then it is there.

The emotion this creates is a kind of glorious, almost visceral excitement, very much like the feeling we get from the wave-like endings in certain Beethoven quartets. And indeed, it turns out that Shostakovich's Quartet in D-flat Major is the only one of his quartets to share an opus number with a Beethoven work for string quartet. The Twelfth is Shostakovich's op. 133, the same number that Beethoven assigned to his "Grosse Fuge"—and though the correspondence cannot have been fully intentional (that is, the opus number cannot be chosen at will), its significance would not have been lost on Shostakovich. It's even possible that the idea for the Twelfth's disproportionately long final movement was suggested to him by the numerical connection with Beethoven's op. 133, which began its life as the final movement of another quartet, op. 130. That Shostakovich was indeed thinking in terms of opus numbers at the time he wrote the

Quartet No. 12 is indicated by the wording of his mordant comment to Glikman, where he refers to his fear that "whatever opus I am working on" will not be finished before he dies.

The Twelfth Quartet's ending may display Shostakovich at his most dramatic, but there is an equally theatrical passage buried deep within the second movement. The earlier of its two Moderato sections begins with a pizzicato solo on the first violin—naturally enough, given that the violin is the featured instrument in this quartet. But it turns out to be a very strange solo indeed. Starting slowly, with brief pauses between the notes, and then gradually escalating in volume and speed until it verges on the hysterical, the pizzicato solo is little more than an alternation between two notes, which eventually change to two other notes, and thence to a couple of others, and so on, almost ad nauseam. There is something idiotic-sounding in this relentless, forced, increasingly obsessive repetition, and technically it is quite difficult to perform—not so much because of tricky fingering or rapid timing, but because it requires such intense participation on the part of the performer. "I get a blister on my finger because you have to play it so loud," reported Eugene Drucker, who takes the first-violin role whenever the Emersons perform the Twelfth.

And the emotional demands are even greater than the physical ones. "You have to really get into character, like an actor—on the spot," explained José Maria Blumenschein, the young violinist who has played the pizzicato passage in the Vertigo Quartet's performances. "If you just play it, it's dull." Alan George detected something similar, though from the perspective of a relative bystander. He referred to "the charged atmosphere" produced by "a passage in the second movement of the Twelfth Quartet, in which the main argument is sustained, mostly solo, by the first violin's pizzicato—I myself, being a silent viola player at this point, am particularly conscious of the extraordinary electricity given off by this music, and have learnt to appreciate the importance of remaining absolutely involved in the drama." Even the man for whom this quartet was written, and to whom it was dedicated, singled out that pizzicato passage in talking about his personal connection with the work. "Shostakovich praised my playing in the funereal episode of the second movement, in the lengthy violin pizzicato section, where one seems to hear the tread of death itself," Dmitri Tsyganov said—a comment he led up to with the remark, "It was as if he reached the very core of my musical nature."

If Vasily Shirinsky had been the foundation stone and hidden leader of the Beethoven Quartet, Dmitri Tsyganov was its public face, its official front man. It was he who most often dealt with the public, giving interviews and announcing the Quartet's upcoming seasons, and it was also he who dealt directly with Shostakovich. When each string quartet was finished and copied out, the composer handed the scores to Tsyganov, who in turn distributed them to the others. And during the bleak period of the Zhdanov-imposed silence, when Shostakovich wanted to hear his quartets played aloud, he wrote to Tsyganov about it: "Dear Mitya," began a note from September of 1950, "My birthday is coming up, and I want you and your friends to make me a gift. Please play the Fourth Quartet."

There was also a specifically musical aspect to Shostakovich's dependence on Tsyganov. Because of the nature of what he was doing in the string quartets—because they were, in a sense, his speaking voice—this particular composer was more than usually reliant on the capacities of his first violin, the instrument most often used in recitative. Christopher Rowland, a violinist with the Fitzwilliam Quartet, has said of the Second Quartet that its "extended recitatives leave Shostakovich more vulnerable to the expressive eloquence of the performer than at any other time." That performer was, in the original instance, Dmitri Tsyganov, for whom the Recitative and Romance movement was explicitly written, as the composer confirmed much later ("Yes, indeed it was, Mitya. I wrote it for you"). Rowland goes on to theorize that the reason for Shostakovich's "constant recourse to recitative" may well have been "the sublimation in instrumental terms of his strong dramatic vein." In other words, because the disastrous fate of *Lady Macbeth* had derailed his opera career—a career at which he would clearly have been a natural—he was diverting that talent into a different channel, substituting the violin's voice, as it were, for the soprano's. This is plausible, if probably not the whole story. It does, at any rate, suggest the close connection between Shostakovich's patently observable dramatic tendencies and his writing for the first violin, a connection that Tsyganov reinforced in his comments about the pizzicato passage in the Twelfth Quartet.

And yet even this does not fully convey the extent of Tsyganov's importance to Shostakovich. Yes, he was the conduit by which the composer mainly dealt with the group, and yes, he was the key player on whom those crucial recitatives depended. But he was also the man who, by virtue of his own will and desires and pragmatic nature, had kept the Beethoven Quartet going in the face of illness and death. It was he who gave the scores for the Ninth and Tenth Quartets to Fyodor Druzhinin that fall day in 1964, and asked him to come by for a read-through that very evening. It was he who recruited his own student, Nikolai Zabavnikov, to play the second violin for the group after Vasily Shirinsky died. Without Tsyganov's active involvement and indeed insistence, the others probably would not have had the heart to go on. "I remember him being a fanatic," Galina Shirinskaya said of Tsyganov. (She also remembered him as "a stunning violinist" and "a wonderful professor" who encouraged and developed musical distinction in his students.) It was precisely this fanaticism, which gave him the strength and devotion needed to keep the Beethovens alive, that Shostakovich was in part commemorating with the powerful, stirring, deeply coherent Twelfth Quartet.

During the six-month gap between Shostakovich's completion of the Twelfth and its premiere by the Beethoven Quartet in September of 1968, the world inhabited by the composer, and indeed by all of his compatriots, grew noticeably grimmer—or perhaps it would be more accurate to say that the grim nature of the regime they lived under made itself more visible, more undeniable. In August of 1968, Russia invaded Czechoslovakia, quelling the hopes for new political and artistic freedoms that had been embodied in the Prague Spring. If this represented a low point in the USSR's relationship with the West, it also signaled a transition in the internal political environment of the Soviet Union. For older figures like Shostakovich, the retreat from Khrushchev's "thaw" to Brezhnev's "stagnation" was a frightening indicator, a hint that conditions could well be moving back toward the repressiveness of Stalin's era; and Shostakovich's impulse, in such circumstances, was to keep his head down. But among a younger generation of Soviet artists and intellectuals, something new—the possibility of expressing political and aesthetic disagreement with the government in a manner that was risky but not, as in Stalin's time, necessarily fatal—began to take the place of the old quietist strategy.

In 1968 this dissident movement was still in its infancy, but the invasion of Czechoslovakia strengthened and hardened it, driving a wedge between the cautious Shostakovich and the more vocal proponents of the new attitude. As Aleksandr Solzhenitsyn remarked, after he thought of getting major Soviet cultural figures to sign a letter of protest about Czechoslovakia, and then thought better of it: "The shackled genius Shostakovich would thrash about like a wounded thing, clasp himself with tightly folded arms so that his fingers could not hold a pen." The choice

of Shostakovich's name, though pointedly insulting, was probably not personal (if such a distinction can have any meaning
under such circumstances): that is, Solzhenitsyn knew Shostakovich slightly through their mutual friend Rostropovich, and
though they were certainly not close, Shostakovich had on occasion tried to use his position to help Solzhenitsyn. But these
prior connections would have struck the outspoken writer as irrelevant. It was Shostakovich's visibly compromised stance, as
well as his high standing among the country's artistic elite, that
made him such a useful target for the dissidents' disdain.

On the public level, at least. Privately, Solzhenitsyn's attitude
toward Shostakovich was apparently much more complicated.
"He was very fond of him," said his son Ignat Solzhenitsyn,
speaking to me in 2009, a few months after his father's death.
"He loved his music. He gratefully acknowledged his genius. He
warmly sympathized with the plight that Shostakovich found
himself in. But to understand is not to condone. I'm sure he
wished Shostakovich had more fight in him."

But if the older Solzhenitsyn was impatient at times, the
younger one—who is a professional musician now based in
Philadelphia—often finds himself empathizing with Shostakovich. "He was a deeply shy man, introverted, with a profound
inner life, a *very* profound inner life," Ignat Solzhenitsyn said
with conviction, though he was born too late to have known the
composer personally. "He was not that kind of dissident, not
that kind of person. But neither were 99 percent of the people.

It is very easy to sit in the West and say, 'Oh, he should have done this, he should have done that.' So I for one have great sympathy with him.

"Something else I should say," he went on. "To the extent we're comparing my father and Shostakovich—what my father did was extraordinary, but by the time he was functioning publicly in this way (after surviving the camp, after *Ivan Denisovich*), he was functioning at a whole different level, in a whole different environment. How old was Shostakovich when *Lady Macbeth* was pulled? He was thirty, he was twenty-nine. And it's not just about age: going up against Stalin in that environment was a whole different ball of wax. That Shostakovich in 1968—an old, broken man, not old in years, but in health—that he should have the same vitality as my father, who was fifty going on thirty, was not really in the cards."

It's not clear to me that Shostakovich at *any* age would have wanted to take on the role of zealous crusader in the Solzhenitsyn mode. Nonetheless, it is definitely true that by 1968 the composer, though only sixty-two, already seemed an old man—in his own view, perhaps, more than anyone else's. In his letters and his reported conversation we can see his thoughts turning more and more to death: not only his own encroaching demise, which began to seem ever more present to him, but also the deaths of those he had sadly and somewhat guiltily survived. During August of 1968 Shostakovich and Glikman paid a visit to the grave of Mikhail Zoshchenko, who had died in poverty exactly ten years earlier. And then, in the midst of a prolonged hospital stay in February of 1969, the composer became preoccupied with memories of his friend Sollertinsky. "It is incredible to think that twenty-five years have passed since he died," he wrote to Glikman, who had recently attended an event commemorating Sollertinsky at the Composers' House—where, according to Shostakovich, "you did something very important in reminding everyone that Ivan Ivanovich Sollertinsky was one of the most dedicated and tragic personalities of the century as well as one of the wittiest."

In this same letter, dated February 17, Shostakovich mentioned to Glikman that he had just completed the piano score of a new work. "It cannot really be called an oratorio," he wrote from his hospital bed, "since an oratorio is supposed to have a chorus, and mine doesn't. It does have soloists though—a soprano and a bass." This unclassifiable work, in which he pursued his mortality-obsessed train of thought in settings of poems by Lorca, Apollinaire, Küchelbecker, and Rilke, was soon to become known as Shostakovich's Fourteenth Symphony.

Like the Thirteenth Symphony, this one depends heavily on text, but it does so in a way that is extremely moving and remarkably coherent rather than slightly platitudinous. Designed for a chamber orchestra, the music is quieter and more painful than that of the Thirteenth. The Fourteenth is not an easy symphony to listen to, for its sequence of melancholy recitatives— alternating between a mournful bass and an otherworldly soprano, which carry us from Lorca's "De profundis" to Apollinaire's "The Suicide" and beyond—constantly forces us to attend, and

attend again, without ever relaxing into any kind of vague contemplative mode.

The final poem in the symphony, Rilke's "Conclusion," reads
in its entirety:

> All-powerful is death.
> It keeps watch
> even in the hour of happiness.
> In the world of higher life it suffers within us,
> lives and longs—
> and cries within us.

If this is not as overtly political as the Yevtushenko words that
accompanied the Thirteenth, it is nonetheless shockingly rebellious, for melancholy and despair were not acceptable Socialist
Realist sentiments. To acknowledge death as Shostakovich is
doing here is to place the individual's fears and sorrows at the
forefront of human experience. There can be no socially designed
solution to this "eternal problem," as Shostakovich called it in
his March 19 letter to Glikman (where he added, with characteristic wryness, "I cannot say that I am wholly resigned to this
event").

This symphony with songs had two obvious ancestors: Mussorgsky's *Songs and Dances of Death*, which Shostakovich had
been listening to just before he went into the hospital, and
Mahler's *Song of the Earth*, which he had loved for his entire
adult life. But there was also a third influence in the mix—that
is, Britten's *War Requiem*, a work Shostakovich first heard in
1963. "I have been sent a recording of Benjamin Britten's *War*

Requiem," he wrote to Glikman in August of that year. "I am playing it and am thrilled with the greatness of this work, which I place on a level with Mahler's *Das Lied von der Erde* and other great works of the human spirit. Hearing the *War Requiem* somehow cheers me up, makes me even more full of the joys of life." That "somehow" gives away the fact that Shostakovich is entirely serious here, even while he is also mocking his own dour incapacity for unmitigated joyfulness.

In dedicating the Fourteenth Symphony to Benjamin Britten, Shostakovich was not only acknowledging the *War Requiem* as its forerunner; he was also cementing a friendship that had begun in September of 1960, when the two composers sat together at Rostropovich's London performance of the First Cello Concerto. Britten subsequently visited Moscow on official tours in 1963 and 1964, after which he and Peter Pears made a number of private visits to Russia at the invitation of Rostropovich and Vishnevskaya. Their visit at Christmas and New Year's of 1966–67 involved long, intimate, laughter-filled meals attended by all three couples, with serious musical conversation interspersed with silly British party games, at which Shostakovich apparently excelled. "Dmitri and Irena Shostakovich were there, punctual as always, and we exchanged presents," Pears noted in his diary. "Shostakovich in good form, talkative, nervous, Irena gentle, quiet, a marvellous foil for him." That was Christmas in Moscow; at New Year's, in Zhukovka, Shostakovich hosted a screening of an "ancient copy" of Charlie Chaplin's *The Gold Rush* at his dacha, complete with appetizers and "a quick nip of vodka" (this despite the still-recent heart attack), before the party moved off to the Rostropovich house for the main course.

"Despite obvious differences in temperament—Britten was warm and affectionate with those whom he trusted, Shostakovich nervous to the end—the two quickly found sympathy with each other, and their connection may have gone as deep as any relationship in the life of either man," observes Alex Ross in *The Rest Is Noise*. This despite the fact that they had no language other than music in common: Shostakovich spoke virtually no English, and Britten knew little or no Russian, so all of their pleasant times together had to be mediated by multilingual friends such as Rostropovich. As for the musical link between them, Ross cleverly surmises that "Britten's psychological landscape, with its undulating contours of fear and guilt, its fault lines and crevasses, its wan redeeming light, made Shostakovich feel at home." I have no doubt that this was true, though the fear and guilt would have stemmed from very different sources in the life of each man. In any case, the Fourteenth Symphony was Shostakovich's grateful response.

By this time, even though he was still a deputy of the Supreme Soviet, Shostakovich had become such a problematic public-artist figure that his new work sometimes had to struggle for a premiere. That seems to have been the case with the Fourteenth Symphony, which eventually received its official premiere in Leningrad in September of 1969, under the baton of Rudolf Barshai, with the vocal parts sung by Galina Vishnevskaya and Yevgeny Vladimirov. Before that, however, there was a much smaller, unofficial premiere, attended by invitation only, in the Small Hall of the Moscow Conservatory. Scheduled as a "rehearsal" beginning at noon on June 21, this performance by Barshai and his musicians (including a replacement soprano for Vishnevskaya, who had not yet learned her part) was both a vetting opportunity for the music-world authorities and a chance for the composer to hear his work played in full.

As his health worsened, Shostakovich had become particularly anxious to hear his compositions performed as soon as possible, since he always feared he might die between the work's completion and its premiere. With the Fourteenth Symphony this level of superstitious fear may have been greater than usual, not only because the symphony itself was explicitly about death, but also because Shostakovich viewed this piece as the pinnacle of his career to date, the "turning point" toward which all his recent work had been leading. In this instance, though, it was not Shostakovich who died, but a Party functionary, Pavel Apostolov: the apparatchik very prominently left the Moscow Conservatory concert midway through the performance, in what was initially interpreted as an angry gesture but was later disclosed to be the beginnings of a fatal heart attack. In private music circles much was made of this irony, which was viewed as a kind of unwitting but effective table-turning on the part of the erstwhile persecuted Shostakovich, but according to Glikman the composer himself never once gloated or laughed about it.

Shostakovich's own health, though it had seemed to hold steady for a while, began to plague him again in late 1969 and throughout 1970. Earlier in 1969 he had learned about and then briefly met with a Dr. G. A. Ilizarov, a surgeon who ran a clinic in Kurgan where at least one seriously injured athlete had apparently been restored to complete health. Before he could even schedule a stay at the clinic, however, Shostakovich was diagnosed in November of 1969 as suffering from a rare form of poliomyelitis. Since this meant that his problem was a "nerve" disease rather than a "bone" disease, it was not clear that Dr. Ilizarov could do anything for him. Nonetheless, he persisted in his plans to stay at the Kurgan clinic, and for much of 1970 he was in and out of Ilizarov's hospital. The contrast between the tone of his letters to Glikman, which report constant progress under the doctor's care, and Glikman's own observations, which suggest no improvement at all, is heartbreaking. It is as if Shostakovich were willing himself to believe in an impossible cure. And perhaps at times the self-deception succeeded, for there is a photo taken in 1970 that shows him performing on the piano for the hospital staff—an activity that surely would have been beyond him at the low moment in November 1969 when he received his polio diagnosis. But such improvements, if they ever existed, were intermittent and ultimately fleeting.

On another front, though, there was definite progress. In August of 1970, between two of his stays at the Kurgan clinic, Shostakovich announced that he had finally completed his Thirteenth Quartet, a project he had begun a year earlier. This quartet, which highlighted the role of the viola, was dedicated to the

Beethovens' original violist, Vadim Borisovsky, on the occasion of his seventieth birthday.

If the Twelfth Quartet is strikingly innovative in its form, the Thirteenth Quartet is downright strange. Composed of a single movement lasting about eighteen and a half minutes, the Quartet No. 13 in B-flat Minor is possibly Shostakovich's most unnerving work for string quartet. "The Thirteenth Quartet is indeed a harrowing experience for all involved," wrote the Fitzwilliam's Alan George, who played the viola part in one of the very first performances of this quartet outside the USSR. After performing it repeatedly for decades, he felt that "many listeners have been truly frightened by it, and even the most resilient emotional temperament could hardly fail to be at least uncomfortably disturbed by it."

Allied with both the death-ridden Fourteenth Symphony, which preceded it by a year, and the film score for Kozintsev's *King Lear*, which Shostakovich finished just before the quartet, the Thirteenth is at once bleak and inventive, despairing and disruptive. Its horrors are those of the human condition, particularly as they manifested themselves in the twentieth century, but they are also the funhouse horrors of dancing skeletons and rattling bones. Creepiness has been elevated to the highest form of art here. At the same time, novelty has been pressed into active duty in the service of emotional seriousness. The tricks in this quartet are never just tricks: whatever pleasure they give on the level of invention is balanced, indeed weighed down, by the chilling sadness they help to convey.

Melancholy is a pervasive feeling in the Thirteenth Quartet, as it is in all the quartets of this late period. Yet the person who was closest to Shostakovich at the end of his life, Irina Antonovna, emphatically denied that he himself was melancholic. "No," she said when I asked her, "he was quite a settled person. And he was quite a strong person, with a strong character." Perhaps this was just the widow's understandable effort to protect her husband from any suspicion of neurotic weakness—an accusation that might have been a particularly unpleasant one during the Soviet years, though I had not thought of it as an accusation. Or perhaps in her presence he truly was a settled person. It doesn't really matter. The man and the music are not identical, and in this case the man himself presented many contradictory faces to the world, even to the world of his intimates. All we can be sure of is that he understood melancholy and knew how to convey it in his music.

In a period like the one Shostakovich lived through, the right to feel and express sadness takes on a political dimension. I am not saying that Shostakovich wrote mournful music as a gesture of protest. He wrote it for numerous indecipherable reasons of his own, both biographical and aesthetic (if the two can ever be separated in an artist); among other reasons, he wrote it because it gave him the opportunity to tell the truth. That this music continues to mean something to us suggests that the sadness he was expressing was neither specifically autobiographical nor limitedly historical. And yet there was something quite pointed about the emotion, too, in its own time and place: under a regime that prescribed "optimistic" and "positive" as the only acceptable modes, it took a certain courage to write as pessimistically as Shostakovich did in the Thirteenth Quartet. If the man who wrote it often came off as a coward in the public, political sphere, so much the more reason to notice his bravery in the more intimate realm of his chamber music.

For Shostakovich, mood and instrument precisely coincided in the Quartet No. 13: he was thinking about death almost constantly at this time, and the viola's sonorous voice was inherently suited to such thoughts. Moreover, he had reached the point in his dedications where, having already honored the Beethovens' two violinists, he was practically obliged to write quartets for the other two players, which meant that the retired violist was an obvious choice as dedicatee. And yet to write a quartet for Vadim Borisovsky was also, in a way, to write one for Fyodor Druzhinin, the young replacement violist who would actually play the work. So the piece contains a kind of life-in-death or death-in-life quality, an acknowledgment that the world goes on without us even though we are no longer there. And that too is frightening, maybe even more frightening than the opposite, fantastical idea that we wipe it all out when we go.

Borisovsky was himself poised on this terrifying brink between being and non-being, participation and removal. He had retired in 1964 because of severe ill health, so it was somewhat remarkable that he was still alive in 1970, and indeed he was to die two years later at the age of seventy-two. But even in retirement he was still a towering figure, perhaps even Lear-like in the context of twentieth-century viola music. (Lear too, it could be said, retired before his proper time.) As head of the viola department at the Moscow Conservatory, principal violist with the Bolshoi Theater's orchestra, noteworthy soloist, and of course founding member of the Beethoven Quartet, he had a profound influence on the development of the viola repertory. Several generations of Soviet composers wrote works specifically for him, and his fame extended even outside the USSR's borders: "The world Union of viola players! Borisovsky is their chairman," Paul Hindemith (himself a violist as well as a composer) announced from Berlin in 1927. In 1969, on the verge of writing the Thirteenth Quartet, Shostakovich summed up his feeling for this longtime colleague by saying, "If asked what exactly attracts me most in Borisovsky's personality, I would answer: Everything."

The composer's way of honoring his old friend was characteristically ambiguous and contradictory, for the violist is at once the star and the victim of this quartet. His solos are marked by twelve-tone rows that never develop fully, either serially, as they would in a Schoenberg-influenced piece, or tonally, as they might in earlier Shostakovich; instead, they dead-end into disturbingly dissonant chords. His opening few measures are performed absolutely alone, with the rest of the instruments sitting in silence, as if his were the only voice in an otherwise empty world. "It's as if you're on a darkened stage and the spotlight is on one or two instruments at a time," the Emersons' Eugene Drucker has commented about Shostakovich's strategy here. "I don't know if he sat down and said, 'I'm lonely and life is bleak,' but that's the feeling that this conveys." And at the close of the quartet, where the violist has a longer, more melodic, at times deeply haunting solo, he ends by being subsumed into the violins' high-pitched crescendo, with which his own eerily high note finally merges.

But the most memorable aspect of the Quartet No. 13 lies at its core, in a passage which does not particularly showcase the viola. Bracketed by two slower sections that somewhat mirror each other, the central *Doppio movimento* segment of the quartet displays all of Shostakovich's most unnerving, least familiar musical techniques. For instance, in a weirdly jazzy episode—"that very sinister passage that sounds like a jam session from hell," as Drucker puts it—the instruments all seem to get up and shake their bones at us. Here the cello plays a rhythmic pizzicato that sounds just like a walking bass line in jazz; the first violin emits a series of high-pitched three-beat stutters that recall the ominous "three knocks" of the Seventh and Eighth Quartets; the second violin trades off pizzicato runs with the instruments on either side of it; and the viola maintains a thrumming, eerie tremolo in the background.

The strangest element in the piece, though, is the highly unusual sound of wood clicking lightly on wood. This *col legno* percussion is produced by tapping the wooden part of the bow on the belly of the instrument; the notation for it in the score is a small x descending from a vertical line. Played by only one in-strument at a time, initially with a substantial gap between beats, the sound is unearthly and unsettling. It also *looks* very odd, if you are watching the piece played live.

I have only been able to locate a few earlier examples of this tapping-on-the-belly type of *col legno* (as opposed to the more standard wood-on-strings version, which was used by a number of well-known composers, including Mozart, Mahler, Ravel, Berlioz, and Prokofiev, not to mention Shostakovich himself). That clicking sound first appears as far back as the seventeenth century, in Heinrich von Biber's weird *Battalia* for strings and continuo, and then it reappears in several works from the 1960s, including pieces by George Crumb and Krzysztof Penderecki; according to Laurel Fay, the Penderecki could well be the im-mediate source for Shostakovich, since he was familiar with the compositions of the Polish musical avant-garde. There's also a similar strategy in the overture to *Il Signor Bruschino*, where Ros-sini had the strings tap their wooden bows on their then-wooden music stands—though Shostakovich's taps are significantly darker and scarier than Rossini's obviously lighthearted ones. Wherever he got it from, Shostakovich proceeded to make the hollow wooden sound into something that is uniquely and eminently suited to the eerie atmosphere of the Thirteenth Quartet.

Not every string player who undertakes the Thirteenth has been willing to follow the composer's instructions about how to produce this sound. The Fitzwilliam Quartet members, for in-stance, who were nervous about possible damage to their valuable instruments, habitually played these percussive beats by hanging a cheap violin from the stand and hitting *it*. But this method not only affects the sound quality in an unfortunate way (in the Fitzwilliam recording, the resulting "thwack" is far too loud); it also ruins the visual effect of seeing the musicians attack their own instruments. For the point, of course, is psychological as well as visual and auditory. We need to feel that there is something truly at stake in the gesture—a serious possibility of loss, the presence of real fear—if it is not to descend into the merely comical. That the strategy had its comic aspects is made clear in the description Shostakovich apparently gave when he first presented the Thirteenth Quartet to his potentially censorious colleagues at the Composers' Union: "I wrote a short lyrical quartet with a joke middle," he told them. But Galina Shirinskaya, who heard him utter these words at that unveiling, also recalls that he told the Beethoven Quartet during their rehearsals that the *col legno* device referred to "the lash of a whip in a concentration camp." Both stories could be true, of course, but neither can simply be taken at face value, since a certain amount of irony is inherent not only in the composer but in the device itself.

So what *are* those weird-sounding taps doing in the Thirteenth Quartet? It is a question that all performers of the piece inevitably confront. "It may have something to do with the jazzy atmosphere," commented Eugene Drucker, who performs the second-violin role when the Emerson Quartet plays the Thirteenth. "It expands the sonic palette. And there's also something creepy about it. I think it's an extension of the three-beat pattern, those three repeated notes of the same pitch." Drucker went on to confess that, unlike his Emerson colleagues, he didn't precisely follow the directions about hitting the instrument's belly. "I hit my chin rest," he said, "but the other guys all hit the body of their instruments. It only costs about fifty dollars to replace a chin rest."

"I remember we joked with Shostakovich about the implication that the original first violinist must have had a more expensive instrument than his colleagues (the first violin is not called upon to do any tapping)," wrote Alan George. The Fitzwilliams, too, had asked themselves why these taps were there, and according to George, "the only certain reply is that, from experience in rehearsal, the music sounds far less effective without them. . . . The effect of the return of these taps during the awful stillness of the viola solo at the end is often shattering, even when one knows they are coming." This last observation is quite true: as unnerving as the strange clicks may be when we first hear them, they are particularly horrifying when they come back at the end, where they quietly, intermittently, but persistently sound a threat that we thought had been safely banished. That threat could be death (Elizabeth Wilson notes that many Russians associate the tapping sound with "the last act of farewell, the sinister sound of the final nailing down of the coffin lid"), but it could also be some other kind of horror inflicted by humanity on itself; with music, we do not have to choose.

The first time I listened closely to a recording of the Thirteenth Quartet, an odd thing happened to me. I was alone in a sixth-floor apartment in New York, with the double-paned windows tightly closed, straining to hear the near-silences that punctuated the piece, and straining too to discern the new kinds of sounds that made up the non-silences. When the music stopped (it was at the end of one of the Emerson discs), I took the CD out of its player and inserted the next one in the series, meanwhile putting my finger on the stop button so as to give myself time to prepare for a new quartet. Yet even as I pressed down my finger, I imagined that I could hear the beginning of the probable next piece, a low, buzzing, near-silent note that fell perfectly within Shostakovich's late-quartet range. I looked again at the CD: it was not playing. I listened again, and then I went to the window of the apartment, where it became clear to me that what I was hearing was a power saw, or an electric generator, or some other street-level construction noise that was dimly making its way up five flights of stairs and through two panes of glass.

Zhdanov thought that Shostakovich's music sounded like "a piercing road-drill," and so, apparently, did I. Just as the Soviet censors had feared it would, his adventurous composing managed to turn the sound values upside down, so that noise became music and music noise. But the result was not, as the fearful might have predicted, the complete annihilation of structure, or form, or even pleasure. Pleasure is still there in the Thirteenth Quartet, even amid the strangeness and the anxiety, and it stems partly from the work's formal coherence. One could almost dance to that "jam session from hell," it is so cunningly structured; as Eugene Drucker pointed out, "It's fugal, so it's jazzy and fugal at the same time." In fact, the truly frightening thing about the Quartet in B-flat Minor is how unexpectedly enticing its weirdest passages are.

To be drawn against one's will into music like this is to perceive how powerful a grip Shostakovich had on his material, and therefore on his audience. No wonder he had to disguise his Quartet No. 13 as "a short lyrical quartet with a joke middle" when he presented it to the musical commissars; they would have been appalled if they had understood what he was really doing. But the audiences understood. At the December 1970 premiere in Leningrad, the audience members rose to their feet when the brief quartet ended and remained standing until it was played again. And in the spring of 1971, when Benjamin Britten—along with Peter Pears, Elizabeth Wilson, and Susan Phipps—heard the Thirteenth in a private performance held at Shostakovich's apartment, he too asked to hear it repeated. Then, according to Fyodor Druzhinin (who had just played the viola part to much acclaim), "Britten, moved and shaken after hearing the Thirteenth Quartet, kissed Shostakovich's hand."

The two composers were to meet one more time after this, in the summer of 1972, when Shostakovich and Irina, on an official trip to Dublin and London, took a side visit to the Aldeburgh home of Britten and Pears. Britten was working on the opera *Death in Venice* at the time, and he showed the score of the unfinished work to Shostakovich—a rare and generous gesture of intimacy, which Shostakovich fully appreciated. Even the silences between them would have been freighted with meaning at this point, for both men were in ill health, and each fathomed the extent to which death was not an abstract or academic subject for the other.

When he visited Britten in 1972, Shostakovich was in the midst of his own compositional dry spell, one of the longest he had ever experienced. It was set off, apparently, by his second heart attack in September of 1971—yet another serious health scare which again led to two months of hospital stay and an additional month in a sanatorium, accompanied by the usual injunctions to give up all artificial stimulants. "I have been warned to cut out alcohol, nicotine, strong tea and strong coffee completely from my diet," he wrote to Glikman on November 28, 1971. "This is most distressing to me."

Luckily, he had completed his Fifteenth Symphony in July, a good two months before the heart attack, when he was feeling relatively strong and well. This vibrant work, which turned out to be his final symphony, was in some ways a return to form: it had the vigor of the First, the ambiguity of the Fourth, and the extreme dynamic shifts and movingly quiet interludes of the Eighth, mingled with something all its own. From the opening pings on a triangle to the hair-raising chords at its close, the Fifteenth Symphony is more enigmatic and possibly more com-

plex than any he had done before. But according to Kurt Sanderling—who conducted the Fifteenth at its Berlin premiere in
1972 and then performed it more than a hundred times, all over
the world, during the rest of his career—Shostakovich "sent it
into the world under a wrong flag. He introduced it as a tiny,
small symphony, as a toy shop, so they couldn't understand what
they were hearing." This was no doubt a purposeful mask, like
the lyrical-joke label he applied to the Thirteenth Quartet, and it
allowed Shostakovich to get away with a great deal of musical
idiosyncrasy. But it has also, over the succeeding years, resulted
in a thorny interpretive thicket, with conductors staking their
reputations on (for instance) the decision about whether the
ending should be played cheerfully and assertively or quietly and
mournfully.

One of the most prominent features of the Fifteenth Symphony, at least from a listener's point of view, is its tendency to
quote from other material—from Beethoven and Wagner, in a
somewhat veiled way, and also quite blatantly from the most
famous passage of the *William Tell* overture, which sounds its
highly familiar theme several times over the course of the first
movement. What, I wondered, did the Rossini quotation in particular mean to the composer? Irina Antonovna Shostakovich,
discounting any particular meaning, pointed out that "he had a
wonderful memory, and he knew a lot of different composers'
work. It was 'in his luggage.'" But Kurt Sanderling felt the reference might have a deeper significance. "Freedom," he suggested.
"He was well-read, and in the Schiller poem William Tell is a

national hero of freedom. So as a symbol of freedom, possibly."
This seems a reasonable conjecture and needn't contradict the
other associations Shostakovich had with Rossini—for instance,
as a composer who had lived beyond his proper span, producing
nothing for the last thirty years of his life; or, alternatively, as the
man responsible for some of Shostakovich's favorite operas; or,
possibly, as a wit who had done his own fair share of blatant
quotation, in *Il viaggio a Reims* and elsewhere. Shostakovich
himself apparently told Glikman, about this and the other allusions in the Fifteenth, "I don't myself quite know why the quotations are there, but I could *not*, could *not*, *not* include them."

The first conductor to whom Shostakovich entrusted this
work was his own son, Maxim, who had performed his father's
symphonies before but had not yet handled a premiere. Now he
was ready, the composer judged. "He has become a real conductor, and in five years' time he will achieve even more," the pleased
but demanding father predicted in a letter dated December 30,
1971. Despite his relatively recent release from hospital, Shostakovich had been attending all the rehearsals, commuting into
the city and back from the nearby Zhukovka dacha; on the basis
of what he had heard, he felt that "if Maksim is on form, as I
hope he will be, the symphony should sound as it was intended
to." The premiere took place in the Great Hall of the Moscow
Conservatory on January 8, 1972, and Shostakovich declared
himself immensely satisfied.

But he longed for a Leningrad premiere as well, and he nervously asked Glikman to intervene with Mravinsky to make sure

it would happen. "I should like you, please, *tactfully* to find out if and when it is due to be performed. It is rather awkward for me to do it myself," he wrote on April 2, 1972. "I am worried that Yevgeny Mravinsky's creative personality may not be in complete sympathy with the work, and that he may therefore treat it as cavalierly as he did the Thirteenth Symphony and the Second Cello Concerto." To this same letter, in a postscript that began with remarks about his bad health, Shostakovich appended the thought: "I miss you very much, and, strange to say, I miss Leningrad as well. Whenever I see the Neva or St. Isaac's Cathedral etc. on television or at the cinema, tears come to my eyes." He may have spent half a lifetime and most of his adulthood in Moscow, but he was still a Petersburger at heart—imbued, however tenuously, with the slower, less brash, more refined, more European, and somewhat less nakedly political sensibility that, even to this day, distinguishes St. Petersburg from the more long-standing capital to the south.

And Leningrad, it turned out, missed him, for Mravinsky scheduled the Fifteenth Symphony with alacrity, and its premiere at the elegant Great Hall of the Leningrad Philharmonic took place on May 5. Shostakovich was in attendance, prominently seated in one of the boxes, and it seemed to Glikman "as though many people had come not only to hear the symphony but to see its much-beloved composer." As in Moscow, the audience reaction to the piece was extremely warm, and Shostakovich was forced to endure the pain—both physical and mental, at this point—of bowing onstage in response to a lengthy ovation.

The Leningrad performance apparently healed the breach between Shostakovich and Mravinsky, for by March of 1973 the conductor was paying a social call on the composer at Repino. This turned out to be an extremely important visit, for at Shostakovich's suggestion the two men indulged in a drop of vodka together, in defiance of strict doctors' orders. And that drink, in turn, somehow freed up whatever had been blocking Shostakovich, or so he seemed to believe. At any rate, he began work the very next day on his Fourteenth Quartet, and a month later, on April 23, he completed it. It marked the end of the long compositional dry spell that had begun in July of 1971, and he was delighted.

During the ocean voyage that he and Irina made across the Atlantic a few months later—ostensibly so he could collect an honorary doctorate from Northwestern University, but actually to consult American doctors about his health—he was still floating on the pleasure induced by thoughts of his new quartet. And even though the American news was not good (the doctors assessed his condition as "incurable," diagnosing a combination of neurological disorder and heart trouble), he returned to Russia eager to attend the Beethovens' rehearsals of the Fourteenth.

As Druzhinin remembers it, the composer himself played a part in the very first rehearsal. The Beethovens had arrived at Shostakovich's Moscow flat "without our second violinist, Nikolai Zabavnikov, who was ill." At this point

Dmitri Dmitriyevich opened up the score at the piano and said that he would play the second violin part himself. So in this unusual formation we read through the whole quartet. When the rehearsal was over, Dmitri Dmitriyevich was visibly excited. He got up and addressed us with these words: "My dear friends, this has been for me one of the happiest moments of my life: first of all, because I think the quartet has turned out well, Sergei" (the quartet was dedicated to the cellist, Sergei Shirinsky) "and secondly I have had the good fortune to play in the Beethoven Quartet, even if I only played with one finger."

In distinct contrast to the three quartets that preceded it, the Quartet No. 14 in F-sharp Major displays some of that rare quality of happiness. It is a mingled, rueful, Shostakovichian kind of happiness, so it doesn't sound unmitigatedly joyful or mindlessly content, but it *does* sound warm and alive. That long period of intractable silence appears to have produced as its end product something novel—perhaps it is simple gratitude at the renewed possibility of self-expression—that informs this quartet and no other.

We are back to the melodic vein here: away from the harsh dissonances and the flirtation with twelve-tone rows, past the need to shriek or clatter or pine away in the face of death. The cello is allowed its full voice, its full range of emotional expression. One could almost imagine we are back in the Recitative and Romance section of the Second Quartet, except that if you play the two quartets side by side, you will see what a long way we've come since then. It's not just that the cello solos are darker than the violin's, or that the quieter parts are infinitely more subdued than in the earlier quartet; it's also that Shostakovich's whole relationship to melody has been altered by the extremely discordant phase through which he's just passed. Lyricism is never a given in the Fourteenth Quartet. It has to be rediscovered, almost reinvented note by note, and the resulting tunefulness is cautious, guarded, liable to sudden disappearance, and only briefly—in what he called, speaking to the Beethovens, "my Italian bit"—sublimely beautiful.

"We think of that as being a reference to Mahler," said the Emerson Quartet's Eugene Drucker, speaking about Shostakovich's "Italian" passage. "It's about halfway through the second movement of the Fourteenth, and then it comes back near the end of the third movement. At the end it's in F-sharp major." According to Drucker, the home key (a key that Mahler, too, used in order to express life-loving, death-facing longing and desire in his unfinished Tenth Symphony) has a great deal to do with what makes the Fourteenth Quartet feel the way it does. "I've always felt that the F-sharp major of the first and last movements expresses a relative brightness within the landscape of his late works," Drucker remarked. But the word "relative" is important here, for no one listening to the Quartet No. 14 could fail to hear that it also sounds very melancholy and uncertain.

Paul Epstein, in his program notes to the Emersons' performance of the Fourteenth, refers to this quartet's "very contemporary sense of doubt," and then goes on to quote a pertinent remark by the Russian poet Joseph Brodsky: "In the business of writing, what one accumulates is not expertise but uncertainties." In Shostakovich's case, this late quartet might be seen as an example of the innocence that lies beyond experience, the moment when one can return to earlier preoccupations—both the concerns of youth and the more recent worries of aging—and see them with wiser, clearer, less naively self-confident eyes.

That the composer is indeed revisiting old ground is signaled by his use of quotation in this quartet. He reuses the same lovely aria from *Lady Macbeth* ("Seryozha, my fine one") that he had borrowed for the Eighth Quartet, only here, instead of alluding to his own past triumphs and defeats, the quotation serves as a charming, friendly reference to Sergei Shirinsky's nickname. I think I can also hear, in a few brief violin passages, a vague allusion to the opening notes of the Eleventh Quartet's Scherzo section—those irreducibly plain, "annoying" notes that were part of the memorial quartet dedicated to Sergei's dead elder brother, Vasily. The composer of the Fourteenth Quartet clearly remembers his dead: we know from his letters, with their lists of the recently departed, that he is all too aware of how many close friends he has lost in the three years since he wrote the Thirteenth (including Vadim Borisovsky, the man to whom that previous quartet was dedicated). But there is life here as well, and the wish for more of it—in particular, a passionate, unresigned longing for more years than are likely to be available at this point to either Shostakovich or his friend Shirinsky.

Sergei Shirinsky was already seventy when Shostakovich dedicated the Fourteenth Quartet to him in 1973, but though he had suffered from a serious heart condition for years, he showed no signs of giving up on his zestful participation in music and life. By this time he was on his third marriage, to a younger cellist; his daughter Galina, the product of that marriage, was his fifth child. "He had to provide for the family," she remarked in a recent conversation, and as a result "he worked at full stretch all his life." Still, he always managed to convey the sense that his work was a great pleasure to him. "He was a delightful man, always smiling and somehow big and bustling and kind," said Elizabeth Wilson, who met Sergei Shirinsky during the six years she studied cello with Rostropovich at the Moscow Conservatory. Though Shirinsky was never her teacher, she knew him through his attendance at cello club events, his presence on exam committees, and his frequent visits to listen to Rostropovich's classes. "He was a much-married man," Wilson went on, "and that was something of a joke, I believe, but I could see that women would be attracted by his warm and outgoing personality. In the quartet this always appeared in contrast with his brother's more reserved manner. Sergei Petrovich was the most accessible of the Beethoven Quartet members." She also noted that he was "a very fine cellist" who "was of course much loved by his pupils."

Mark Maryanovsky, who studied under Shirinsky at the Conservatory in 1974, remembers him as an "'old school' teacher who took personal care of his students and even gave them dinners at his apartment before lessons, if we were not from Moscow and staying at the dormitory." The Shirinsky flat, located only a few hundred meters from the Conservatory, seems to have served as a kind of familial adjunct to the institutional halls and rehearsal rooms. It was here, in Sergei Shirinsky's home, that most of the rehearsals of Shostakovich's quartets took place, whether they were to be premiered in Leningrad or Moscow; and it was here, in the flat's large reception room, that family members like Irina Antonovna Shostakovich and Galina Shirinskaya were invited to hear the late-stage rehearsals.

"Berlinsky wrote somewhere that the Fourteenth Quartet is like a portrait of my father," said Shirinskaya, citing the Borodins' cellist. "I don't know, maybe I was too close to my father, so I don't understand and I don't see it." But she agreed that, in its focus on the cello, the Fourteenth would necessarily have had something to say about her father's character and temperament. "The instrument defines the person to a great extent," she pointed out. "My mother, who was my father's pupil, always said, 'I would recognize a cellist at one kilometer's distance.' The instrument leaves a great mark on the person." In any event, while some of the inviting warmth we hear in the Fourteenth Quartet may be the generic mellowness of the cello, perhaps a portion of it also belongs to that particularly warmhearted man who opened his home to students and quartet members alike.

If thinking about *King Lear* and death had led Shostakovich to choose the retired violist as the previous quartet's dedicatee, perhaps the knowledge that he now had to write something for his still-vigorous cellist friend—the last Beethoven to be so honored—may have helped to turn his thoughts in a temporarily more hopeful direction. Yet "hopeful" is not exactly the right word to describe the tone of this quartet (unless we are using it in the sense Kafka did when he said, "Oh, plenty of hope, an infinite amount of hope—but not for us"). Part of the way Shostakovich honored his dear friend was to mingle in the Fourteenth Quartet a strong sense of the pleasures of this life with a full awareness of how painful it will be to leave it. And Sergei Shirinsky responded in kind. According to his daughter, when "Shostakovich dedicated the Fourteenth Quartet to him, my father said a remarkable thing. They understood everything pretty well; they realized their place in the history of music. And my father was maybe one of the few who had a very realistic viewpoint. So he said, 'Well, I can die now.'"

And now this sad story grows even sadder. Shostakovich, by the fall of 1973, has become an old man—not so much in years (he turns sixty-seven that September), but in health, outlook, and appearance. In a kind of reversal of his perpetually boyish looks as a young man, he now seems ten or even twenty years older than his true age. He walks and stands with great difficulty; he cannot play the piano at all; he can barely write with his weakened right hand, though that is how he still composes the few chamber works and poetry-inspired songs that are his remaining task. The neurological illness that has caused these problems will never, he now knows, be cured. Neither will the heart condition that has already led to two severe heart attacks. And in addition to these illnesses, he has discovered within the last year that he has lung cancer—a development he makes light of in a January 1973 letter to Glikman ("they found a cyst on my left lung, and I am now getting radiation treatment to destroy it . . . so that in about three or four weeks I shall be the proud possessor of two immaculate cyst-free lungs"), but nonetheless, not a good sign.

He still has his sense of humor. And he still has an enormous feeling of affection for the excellent performers and musicians— most of them younger than he is—who have brought his work to the stage, allowing him to hear what he has composed. But because of his strange, ambiguous position in the Soviet hierarchy, as well as the changes that are gradually taking place in the way power is imposed and resisted in Russia, he finds himself more and more cut off from the younger generation of musicians, writers, and artists. They are actively in favor of free expression and creative independence, whereas he can only advise passivity and caution, the strategies that have enabled him to survive all these difficult years. "Don't waste your efforts," Galina Vishnevskaya remembers Shostakovich saying about each new act of resistance. "Work, play. You're living here, in this country, and you must see everything as it really is. Don't create illusions. There's no other life. There can't be any. Just be thankful that you're still allowed to breathe!"

But Vishnevskaya and Rostropovich, and many other younger friends as well, did not share Shostakovich's quietist attitude: they believed in taking a far more vocal stand against the Brezhnev regime. These dissident artists, joined by eminent scientists like Andrei Sakharov and Zhores Medvedev, repeatedly protested what they saw as the Soviet Union's violation of human rights. As each new case arose, Shostakovich remained silent or, worse, was seen as siding with the authorities. Finally, this difference of political opinion reached a peak in early September of 1973, when a letter publicly denouncing Sakharov was published in *Pravda* over the signatures of about a dozen major cultural figures, including that of D. Shostakovich.

Whether he agreed with or actually read or even physically signed the letter is irrelevant. For years he had routinely lent his name for all sorts of purposes to which he didn't actively subscribe, perhaps assuming that people would view such Party-line statements (as he did) as meaningless drivel. But in this case he had allowed things to go too far. The writer and activist Lydia Chukovskaya circulated a samizdat letter in which she wrote, "Shostakovich's signature on the protest of musicians against Sakharov demonstrates irrefutably that the Pushkinian question has been resolved forever: genius and villainy are compatible." And Chukovskaya was far from the only person to react this way. Younger artists and musicians began to cut him openly when they met, as Edison Denisov reveals in his description of a 1973 performance at the Composers' Union:

> Dmitri Dmitriyevich came and sat at the end of a row in the middle of the hall. Everybody had to pass by him to get to their seats. When Yuri Lyubimov went by, Dmitri Dmitriyevich got up to greet him. It was difficult for him to get up; he could hardly walk and then only with the aid of a stick. Struggling to his feet he approached Lyubimov with hand outstretched. But Lyubimov

looked him in the eye and, turning away, demonstratively sat down on his own. Shostakovich went white.

I asked Lyubimov, "Why did you do such a thing?"

He answered: "After Shostakovich signed that letter against Sakharov I can't shake his hand."

There were many others who felt the same way.

Painful as such public moments of humiliation were, they were probably overshadowed and certainly exacerbated by Shostakovich's own harsh judgments against himself. That he was capable of clearly perceiving his weaknesses and moral flaws comes through in a letter he wrote to Boris Tishchenko in February of 1974. There Shostakovich confesses to this friend and former student that he unfortunately sees a great deal of himself in Dr. Andrei Yefimich Ragin, the cowardly, pathetic figure at the heart of Chekhov's novella *Ward No. 6.* As if to sharpen the self-condemnation, the composer notes that the comparison is particularly apt "in regard to his reception of patients, his signing of blatantly falsified accounts, or when he 'thinks' . . . and much else besides." The specificity of the comparison gives weight to the charge, and one turns immediately to the Chekhov story itself to try to get a firmer sense—so rarely offered in this largely hidden private life—of how Shostakovich really viewed his own position and his own actions.

"Andrei Yefimich loves reason and honesty intensely," Chekhov tells us, in that strange combination of exterior and interior voice that informs the whole narrative, "but has insufficient character and belief in his rights to build a reasonable and honest life around him." As the head of a dirty, stinking, callously inefficient hospital for the poor, the formerly idealistic Dr. Ragin knows that his institution is "immoral and exceedingly harmful to the health of his patients," but he feels that any action would be useless, so he just resigns himself to things as they are. "To tell the superintendent to stop stealing or to turn him out, or even to abolish this unnecessary, parasitic job, is completely beyond his strength. When Andrei Yefimich is cheated or flattered or brought a deliberately falsified account to sign"—and here one draws a sharp breath on Shostakovich's behalf—"he reddens like a lobster and feels guilty, but signs the account just the same."

And then there is the matter of his "thinking," in which Shostakovich so devastatingly saw himself. Here's a fair sample of that, in a passage where Chekhov (himself a once idealistic doctor) shows us Dr. Ragin at home at the end of a workday:

> His heavy head sinks toward the book; he cradles his face in his hands and thinks: "I serve a pernicious business and receive a salary from people I swindle; I'm dishonest. But, of course, I'm nothing by myself, I'm only a part of an inevitable social evil: all provincial officials are harmful and receive salaries for nothing. . . . Meaning it's not I who am guilty in my dishonesty, but the times. . . . If I had been born two hundred years later, I would be another person."

How tempting it would have been for Shostakovich to think that about himself, just as we are tempted to think it on his behalf. Part of what is so harrowing about this story is the sympathy, or at any rate the evenhanded understanding, with which

Chekhov views his unheroic hero. This is no bug coldly dissected under a microscope, no ordinary villain viewed coolly and ironically by a safely distant narrator. We are inside Andrei Yefimich throughout; if we find ourselves criticizing him, it is through the vehicle of his own self-condemnation. No wonder Shostakovich felt himself so deeply implicated, so accurately described.

The fate Chekhov ultimately deals out to Dr. Ragin (though that overstates the degree of authorial vindictiveness, for there is nothing O. Henryish or moralistic about this seemingly inevitable tale) is that of finding himself, eventually, in his own Ward No. 6, a wretched hut that is the poorest and cruelest part of the hospital, the place where the mentally ill are kept. Somehow, in his vague and almost dreamlike way, Andrei Yefimich has wandered into the ward as a doctor and been kept there—not precisely against his will, for he has no will by this time—as a patient. "Where had Nikita taken his clothes? Now, perhaps, he would never again put on trousers, a waistcoat, and boots for the rest of his life. All this was somehow strange and even incomprehensible at first," Chekhov tells us near the end of the story. Apparently Ragin, like Shostakovich, is the victim of his own refusal to cultivate "illusions":

> Andrei Yefimich was still convinced now that there was no difference whatsoever between Belova's house and Ward No. 6, that everything in this world is nonsense and hustle and bustle; but still, his hands were trembling, his legs were growing cold, and he was uneasy at the thought that Ivan Dmitrich would soon wake up and see him in a bathrobe.

"I am almost completely helpless in the ordinary business of life; I can no longer do things like dress myself or wash myself on my own. Some kind of spring has broken in my brain," Shostakovich wrote to Glikman from his hospital bed in January of 1973, shortly after receiving the lung cancer diagnosis. Things were to get better before they got worse again: he was to write the Fourteenth Quartet a few months later, and he was even to perform a part in it on the piano—with one finger, it's true, but a part nonetheless—a few months after that. But by September of 1973 he was once again telling Glikman, "Things are very bad with my right hand: I couldn't even play 'Three Blind Mice.'" And then, in May of 1974: "At the moment I am in hospital: my hands (especially the right hand) and legs are very weak." At times he must have felt, amid all those increasingly dire hospital stays, that he had come to rest in his own Ward No. 6, from which he would not be allowed to depart.

He knew, at any rate, that the end was drawing near, for in the spring of 1974, when Mstislav Rostropovich showed him a letter he had written to Brezhnev, asking permission to emigrate with his family, Shostakovich began weeping and said, "In whose hands are you leaving me to die?" With Shostakovich too ill to move, Irina went alone to the airport in May of 1974 to see Rostropovich off. The two old friends were never to meet again.

On May 2, 1974, just before he went into the hospital, Shostakovich telephoned Isaak Glikman to say he was working on a new quartet. He finished it on May 17, despite the extreme weakness in his right hand—a disability that must have made it very difficult for him to write out the score of this rather long quartet, particularly in the last movement, where all the instruments together play an extended flurry of thirty-second notes. "Just writing that passage had to be very painful to him," says the Emerson violinist Philip Setzer, who thinks about Shostakovich's movingly admirable effort of will whenever he plays the piece.

If we can sense pain in the Fifteenth Quartet, though, it is not primarily of the physical or even narrowly psychological variety. Mortal anguish and anxious dread, though they surface occasionally, have mainly been suppressed here in favor of something more solemn and more abiding. The tone, though it builds on aspects of the Eleventh and Thirteenth Quartets, is something new to Shostakovich—more wrenching even than the Eighth, more dissonant than the recent Fourteenth, but with sporadic tuneful elements that reach back as far as the First and Third Quartets. One might be tempted to call the tone "valedictory" if that word didn't seem too smug and tidy to cover this quartet's overwhelming sorrow at leave-taking.

The Quartet No. 15 in E-flat Minor carries no dedication. Shostakovich had by now finished the four works dedicated to his Beethoven Quartet friends, and the obvious conclusion is that this piece was meant for the wishful fifth Beethoven, the one who had written himself into their group with his Piano Quintet thirty-four years earlier and had happily played his small role in the previous year's rehearsal of the Fourteenth. "I have the feeling he may have known the end was near, and this was an elegy to himself," commented the Emersons' Eugene Drucker; and many others (myself included) have felt the same way. But one can acknowledge that death is near and at the same time resist the knowledge, so even though the Fifteenth feels very much like a final quartet, one cannot be certain he meant to end his cycle there. "I don't know," answered Irina Antonovna, when asked if this was her husband's elegy for himself, "but he meant to write twenty-four, one in each key"—as if he had not, even then, given up on this project. And Laurel Fay, in her program notes to the quartets, alludes to a planned Sixteenth Quartet that would have been dedicated to the "new" Beethoven Quartet. Still, one cannot get away from the finality of the Fifteenth's tone. And why, if it were *not* about his own imminent death, would he have failed to put a dedication on it? "Who can know?" responded Kurt Sanderling. "Perhaps because it was so unfathomably terrifying that he couldn't dedicate it to anyone." The German word Sanderling actually used was *abgründig*, which carries the suggestion of standing on the edge of a precipice, looking down into the abyss.

Unlike any quartet he had written, or indeed any that he might have heard, the Fifteenth consists entirely of slow movements: six Adagios—titled Elegy, Serenade, Intermezzo, Nocturne, Funeral March, and Epilogue—to be played one after the other, with no rest in between, for a duration of over thirty-six minutes. Perhaps Bartók's final quartet, with the slow *mesto* that introduces each of the first three movements and entirely takes over the fourth, lay somewhere in the back of Shostakovich's mind. More immediately present to him would have been his own Eleventh Quartet, and also Britten's *Serenade* for tenor, horn, and strings, with which the Fifteenth shares a number of section titles: Nocturne, Elegy, Epilogue, not to mention Serenade itself. It's also possible that when he called one of the movements in this quartet Serenade, Shostakovich was thinking of the Braga "Serenade" in Chekhov's strange, death-ridden tale "The Black Monk," a story that preoccupied him in his last few years, and about which he was said to be writing an opera. "In a garden at night a morbidly imaginative girl hears mysterious sounds so weird and wondrous that she is compelled to acknowledge them as divine harmony which soars back aloft to the heavens, being incomprehensible to us mortals": that is how Chekhov summarizes the content of Gaetano Braga's well-known nineteenth-century piece, and these words (minus, perhaps, the divine part) could apply almost as well to moments in Shostakovich's quartet.

But the Serenade—both its weirdness and its wondrousness—comes later. First we get the Elegy, which, at over twelve minutes, is the longest and slowest-seeming of the six Adagio movements. "Play it so that flies drop dead in mid-air, and the audience starts leaving the hall from sheer boredom," Shostakovich reportedly told the Beethovens during rehearsals. I have witnessed audience members following these instructions to the letter, but for me the opening section of the Fifteenth Quartet has never felt boring, though it is relentlessly—I would say profoundly—repetitive. The slow tempo that pervades the movement has a

stately, processional feel, but it is a procession that is not necessarily going anywhere, and the longer it goes on, the more you
come to feel that this condition of suspension is your natural
state: you have always been, and will always be, listening to this
unfolding that has no endpoint, this movement that imitates
stasis but never quite stops. The emotional quality is very sad,
but not at all anxious. Whatever was to be feared or evaded is
over now, and no action is left to be taken. One would almost
call the feeling religious, except there is no suggestion of God or
salvation or redemption here—there is nothing religion can address, just a sense of saying good-bye, and one cannot even be
sure whether that adieu is made from this side of the grave or the
other.

The contemplative mood is suddenly broken by the series of
buzzing crescendos that open the Serenade—exaggerated de-
scendants of the similarly insectlike sounds that began appearing
in the quartets as early as the Tenth. This initial dissonance is not
at all serenade-like; in fact, it is not until nearly a third of the way
into the movement that the true "serenade" begins, with the first
violin singing its melodic, slightly eerie solo against the dry, broken strums of the other three instruments. We end the second
movement back in the realm of the buzzing crescendos, and
those long, harsh, increasingly loud strokes fill the Serenade with
a sense of aggression, anger, and resistance. That mood continues
into the short Intermezzo, where it is briefly amplified before the
third movement ends with a sweet, quiet tune that leads directly
into the Nocturne—by far the most lyrical movement in the

quartet. Here the viola plays a high, lovely, almost singing melody, and in the background the second violin and cello glide up and down in a series of uncanny-sounding eighth notes, producing something like the "etched" mode that Shostakovich used in his Fifth and Seventh Quartets. The strange unearthliness, which is already quite intense, increases about halfway through the Nocturne, and the whole atmosphere is of an otherworldly, seductive, glowing light cast upon the music: perhaps a very late, very eerie Leningrad summer twilight.

This feeling only begins to dissipate with the pizzicato notes that lead us from the end of the Nocturne directly into the Funeral March. There we hear a series of slow, rhythmic chords, assertively interrupted by eloquent solos on the part of the viola, the cello, and a very high violin, as if each member of the funeral procession in turn were raising his or her individual voice to contribute a memory about the dead person—a story about his past, a description of his character, an expression of grief at his demise. And then, after a measure of rest that is actually within the Funeral March and not after it, we reach the Epilogue, which casts a glance back at all that has come before it.

This final movement is heavily dependent on whirring, trilling sounds that together suggest a winged swarm: a strange and unsettling image, if not necessarily a threatening one. The violinist Philip Setzer hears in these swarming passages the musical equivalent of the image—"a tall black column like a whirlwind or a sand-storm"—with which Chekhov always introduced the appearance of the supernatural black monk. In Chekhov's story, the only person who sees the black monk is the ailing, mentally inflamed protagonist, who, in the end, after seeing him one last time, dies spitting blood. (Tuberculosis, one might recall, was Chekhov's own disease, and it had been Shostakovich's too in his youth.) In Shostakovich's quartet, the final movement clearly ends in some kind of death as well, with the viola sounding a diminishing trill as the other three instruments fade away to silence.

I am not sure how thoroughly the analogy between "The Black Monk" and the Fifteenth Quartet holds up; what I am sure of, though, is that both works are very pointedly and upsettingly about the way death casts its shadow back over life. The sense we get from the Quartet No. 15, as from the Chekhov story, is that everyone is finally alone. Even when we are paired, as two of the instruments sometimes are, we do not walk the same path at the same time but are forced to wander separately. We cannot save each other. We cannot even keep each other company beyond the grave. But we can mourn each other. And something of us survives death—not the body, not the soul, not anything that can make the individual feel it is still alive, but some trace of ourselves in the minds of others and in the world we leave behind. This vague consolation lends life a sweetness but also a sadness, because you cannot remember and treasure the dead without reminding yourself of their absence.

What Shostakovich feelingly realizes, in this quartet, is that there can be no settling into comfortable resignation, no weak or even fearless embrace of death, because something in us always still wants to live. Hence the tugging back and forth in the Serenade section—because the Serenade reminds us what it is to be alive, to *not* want to leave this life, whereas the Elegy was almost ready to let it all go, to sink into timelessness. Having been softened by the Elegy, made lethargic and forgetful by the it's-all-over-now quality of that first movement, we find we can be hurt again, in the Serenade, by the fact that death is the end of life.

The Fifteenth is the most cyclical of Shostakovich's quartets, not only because the Epilogue looks back over the other movements, but because the initial Elegy seems to pick up where the Epilogue left off. More than with any of the earlier quartets, I think, you can hear this one played over and over again without feeling that you are reaching a conclusion each time: its shape is that of a circle, leading back to itself. Music, of course, can and must be played again—that is its nature, which makes it somehow the opposite of life, which can't be redone, can't start over. And yet the music of a quartet, with its familial voices, its "conversation," also has an affinity with human life. This quartet in particular is filled with that sense of conversation, or at least of different voices chiming in, each with its own manner and in its own register, but with something in common to talk about. The subject of the conversation might be death's inevitability, as in the Elegy; or it might be the dying person's desire to awaken and live (as expressed in the Serenade), to resist death willfully (as in the Intermezzo). But the quartet voices are also talking, especially in the Nocturne, about death's seductiveness, about the strange beauty of an imagined otherworldliness; and they are talking, in the Funeral March, about the dead one himself—our respective feelings about him, and what his life meant to us.

The Epilogue may be a part of all this, or it may be presented from a position totally outside this human conversation. With all its whirring sounds, it definitely possesses a feeling of suspension, of remaining constantly in flight rather than settling on the ground. So the quartet as a whole contains a strange reversal: at the beginning everything is all over, but by the end it is in a state of flux. This too makes it circular, for we feel the need, at the end, to go back to that more fixed state of endlessness, instead of the more tremulous, unbalanced state in which the quartet leaves us. And this means that the music is once again set in opposition to a human life, which goes from tremulous to permanently fixed and over.

The quartet is pointing to itself as being *unlike* life. It is saying, This is what survives: not the body, not the spirit, not the individual, but these sounds, which can come alive over and over, for centuries. This self-referentiality, if one can call it that, is neither postmodern nor abstract, neither jovial nor careless, for the music knows about tragedy; it understands death, even though it cannot die. That is its final, most compelling contradiction, the paradox that makes it heartrending. The music of the Fifteenth Quartet mirrors us and, like our reflection, seems to belong to us personally, to be subject to our presence; and yet it turns out not to be so dependent on us after all. Like a mirror, it remains when we are gone—all of us, including its maker and its players and each generation of its listeners.

"He was very fearful of death," said Kurt Sanderling, speaking to me many decades later about the Shostakovich he had known. But his fearfulness (if "fearfulness" is even the right word for the complicated emotion we hear in the Fifteenth Quartet) was not just a selfish, personal fear, a dread of his own dissolution. The sorrow we hear in this quartet is as much a memorializing one as an anticipatory one; in that sense, the unnamed dedicatees might include all his lost ones, all his beloved dead, as well as himself. Death is terrible and frightening in part because it separates us from those we cared for in life, and music is somehow uniquely equipped to remind us of that, perhaps because, in its very abstraction, it allows each of us to fill the role of mourner.

In a beautiful and unusually personal passage from his essay "Marginalia on Mahler," Theodor Adorno comments that he never fully appreciated the *Kindertotenlieder* until "the first time in my life when someone I loved died." This led him to realize that

the dead may well be our children. The aura of what has not become that encircles those who died young like a halo of apparent happiness does not fade for adults either. But it is not able to enclose their distracted and abandoned life otherwise than by making it smaller. This happens to the dead through memory. . . . As they are defenseless, at the mercy of our memory, so our memory is the only help that is left to them. They pass away into it, and if every deceased person is like someone who was murdered by the living, he is also like someone whose life they must save, without knowing whether the effort will succeed. The rescue of what is possible, but has not yet been—this is the aim of remembrance.

Sollertinsky at just over forty, Nina at forty-five, Pyotr Vilyams in his mid-forties, Vasily Shirinsky at sixty-five: all were stilled at their specific moment, preserved in Shostakovich's music as his remembered dead whom he was doomed to outlive. By the time he composed the Fifteenth Quartet, he had grown older than all of them, and the works he had dedicated to them became the only life remaining to these "children" of his, the only aspect of their existence that was not merely frozen in memory.

But to cheat death in this way is not really to conquer it; on the contrary, its power is newly acknowledged every time the memorial quartet is played. And because even the dedicatees who survived Shostakovich would themselves die someday, all his quartets were destined to be transformed, eventually, into memorial quartets. Somehow, without bringing it consciously to mind, we who are listening to the music understand this, and we understand that the pattern applies to us as well. What we hear in Shostakovich's quartets is the spectral prophecy inherent in all music: it speaks only to mortal ears, so its very assurance that we are alive is also a reminder that one day we won't be.

Death did not wait long to intrude again on Shostakovich's intimate circle. On October 18, 1974, about an hour after the Beethovens had completed that day's rehearsal of the Fifteenth Quartet for its projected fall premiere, Sergei Shirinsky died suddenly of a heart attack. He had gone for a walk and then decided to take a bus to one of Moscow's parks, "but on the way to the bus stop he fell down in the street and died. He rehearsed the quartet by Shostakovich literally until the last hour of his life," recalled his daughter, Galina Shirinskaya.

Her father's death was not unexpected, according to Shirinskaya—he had been seriously ill for twelve years and had endured three previous heart attacks. But if it was not a surprise, the suddenness of the death was still a shock to friends, family, and students, many of whom must have been lulled into feeling that he would somehow beat the odds. That evening, Shostakovich called Glikman to tell him of Shirinsky's death, quoting in the course of the conversation Pushkin's line "And yet another's hour is near at hand." A month later, he was still praising Shirinsky for having died in the midst of his life: "That morning he was rehearsing, in the evening he was no more," he told Glikman when they met for dinner in Leningrad on November 14.

Glikman, at this mid-November meeting, was struck by how comparatively healthy his old friend seemed. "When Shostakovich was sitting at the table, he looked well, and when he laughed it was as though his youth had returned," he noted. "His words, together with his mimicry and gestures, brought back the Dmitri Dmitriyevich Shostakovich I remembered from long ago." But Shostakovich himself was doubtless aware that it could easily have been he rather than Shirinsky who died before the Fifteenth could be performed. He was so aware of it, in fact, that he refused to delay the premiere until the Beethoven Quartet could reconstitute itself. Instead, for the first and last time since they had begun premiering his quartets, he took away their privileged first performance and gave it instead to the Taneyev Quartet, which played the world premiere of the Quartet No. 15 in Leningrad on November 15, 1974. That was why Shostakovich was having dinner with Glikman on November 14: despite his ever-worsening health, he had come to Leningrad to hear his own premiere, thereby establishing—in his own mind, if in no one else's—that he too would be working up until the moment of his death.

The Beethoven Quartet was back in functioning order by January 11, 1975, when they gave the Moscow premiere of the Quartet in E-flat Minor with a replacement cellist, Yevgeny Altman, and with Shostakovich again in attendance, at the Small Hall of the Moscow Conservatory. Except for the fact that Dmitri Tsyganov was the only surviving original member of the quartet, it might almost have seemed like old times. But it was to prove the last occasion in the group's long association with the composer, for there were to be no more string quartets after the Fifteenth.

Yet that was not *quite* the end. Shostakovich's unique connection with the Beethoven Quartet was to influence even his final piece of music—a Sonata for Viola and Piano which he composed explicitly for Fyodor Druzhinin, the Beethovens' violist.

In the early days of July 1975, Shostakovich began calling Druzhinin on the phone and asking him about various fine points of viola playing. He eventually told the young violist that he was working on a viola sonata which he expected him to premiere, and on July 5 he called to say that it was finished. "Fedya,

I have buckled down to it, and managed to complete the Finale," he said, according to Druzhinin. "I am having the score sent to the Union of Composers to be copied, as no one could possibly read from my manuscript. As soon as the copying has been done, I'll let you have the music. I have to go into hospital now, but I'll have a telephone there by my bed, so we can talk."

The violist never did manage to get through to Shostakovich by phone; by the time he actually called, Shostakovich's condition had worsened and he had been moved to a ward without a telephone. But Druzhinin was eventually able to reach Irina Antonovna, who reassured him somewhat, and on August 6 he was told to come pick up the music at their flat on Nezhdanova Street. This he did, and it was only when he opened the finished score that he learned the sonata had been dedicated to him.

Moved and overwhelmed, Druzhinin rushed home and called the pianist Mikhail Muntyan, whose role in the performance Shostakovich had already approved. "He came flying over to my place and we thereupon started playing the sonata and continued playing it till late at night," Druzhinin later recalled. "Immediately afterwards I sat down to write a long letter to Dmitri Dmitriyevich to express my profound gratitude to him and my immense admiration for the sonata, which sounded marvellous, and to reassure him that there wasn't a note in it that could not be played. I promised to be ready as soon as possible to perform it to him, and at latest, if he approved of our interpretation, to schedule it for a concert on his birthday, 25 September."

The letter was written on the night of August 6—or, technically, the morning of August 7—and it reached Shostakovich at the hospital the next day. "It's good that you wrote to him," Irina Antonovna told Druzhinin. "Dmitri Dmitriyevich read your letter and was very pleased. It was the best medicine for him." But the medicine was only to work for a brief time. A couple of days later, on August 9, late in the afternoon, Shostakovich died of suffocation. His lung cancer had come back, and it had killed him.

The Soviet authorities, for reasons best known to themselves, withheld the news of Shostakovich's death for forty-eight hours. They then deferred the funeral a few more days so that Maxim, who had been touring in Australia, could return for it. Finally, on the morning of August 14, the composer's body was brought to the Large Hall of the Moscow Conservatory, where it lay in state until the massive public funeral began at 1:30 p.m. "My mother was there and she described the funeral as rather official—naturally, he was a big figure. Everything was very decorous, speeches as always, nothing special as far as I know," reported Galina Shirinskaya.

But another young woman, Oksana Dvornichenko, who had worked on several newsreels and documentaries about Shosta-kovich (and who was later to produce a long, detailed biography of him), gave a somewhat different account. Recently hospital-ized with a severe case of mushroom poisoning, Dvornichenko got up from her sickbed prematurely in order to attend the lying in state at the Conservatory. "She made her way through all the crowds up to the coffin," her daughter, Helga Landauer, told me.

"Nobody stopped her, perhaps because she looked so pale and sick. She said what was striking about his face was that it had this sardonic smile. Because, you know, he had this face that was like a combination of two masks—one corner of the mouth going up, the other going down, tragedy and comedy. And maybe death emphasized that."

Because August 14 fell in the midst of the summer break, many of the Conservatory musicians and other colleagues who might have attended the public ceremony were out of town. "When Shostakovich died," remembered Lev Ginzburg, a musicologist and fellow resident of the Composers' Union complex, "I was on my regular summer vacation in Latvia and could not come to the funeral." Ginzburg was writing to me in 2009, over thirty years after Shostakovich's death, but he was clearly still moved by his memories of this "rather reserved person" and his "tragic and complicated" music. "As far as I know," he went on, "it was a standard official state ceremony in the presence of some party bosses, who, most probably, were only happy—the dead composer was not dangerous any more. But musicians mourned not only in Moscow, but all over the country, because the number of his friends and admirers was big, and he had almost no enemies."

One of those distant admirers was Mark Maryanovsky, the young cellist who had studied at the Moscow Conservatory with Sergei Shirinsky, and who had met Shostakovich at the Shirinsky apartment on the night of his teacher's funeral. Ten months later, in August of 1975, he too was away in Latvia—in Riga, where he attended a Moscow Philharmonic concert conducted by Kirill Kondrashin, Shostakovich's old colleague and supporter from the days of the Thirteenth Symphony. "After break he came on stage and announced that someone called him from Moscow to tell that Dmitri Shostakovich is dead," Maryanovsky told me. "Symphony No. 10 was in program. He told us that performance will go on as scheduled but asked not to applaud at the end. I will never forget this moment, not to mention very emotional performance, when full house of people and musicians on stage moved out of the hall in total silence."

A somewhat different kind of silence greeted the ending of the Sonata for Viola and Piano when, late in the following month, it received its informal premiere on what would have been Shostakovich's sixty-ninth birthday. On that sad, solemn September 25th, a small group of intimates gathered at the Nezhdanova Street flat to hear Fyodor Druzhinin and Mikhail Muntyan perform the composer's last piece, opus 147. Packed into this thirty-three-minute composition were many of the elements his listeners had come to associate with the string quartets: the jaunty "dance" of the Allegretto following upon the spooky, etched notes of the opening Moderato; the mingling of stark dissonance with evocative melody; the alternation between slow-paced thoughtfulness and frenzied, klezmer-inspired hysteria; and above all, the vast surrounding emptiness through which a single voice, whether of viola or of piano, was required to make its hesitating, lonely way.

But unlike, say, the opening movement of the Fifteenth Quartet, which relentlessly and repetitively dwells on the subject of death, the Viola Sonata seems to include something more shimmering and magical—the moonlight, perhaps, from the Beethoven piano sonata to which it so openly pays tribute. The music is melancholy, but not painfully so. (Unless it is the pain that those first listeners must have felt, hearing this beloved voice again so soon after it had been silenced by death.) Late in the final Adagio movement there is a moment of outcry, a period of darkness, as if to confess that the equable tone cannot be maintained; but even this disturbance quiets down, by the end, into something more tuneful and soothing. One gets the feeling that both instruments now carry Shostakovich's intimate voice—the piano that had been his instrument and the viola that had not—and this in turn suggests a kind of calm renunciation, a sad but grateful acquiescence to the fact that his own lost playing hands have practically been replaced by the hands of his Beethoven Quartet friends. As the viola holds its last, gradually diminishing note against the piano's delicate, lovely, repeated pattern, we can perhaps sense a letting-go, in a closing *morendo* that is for once less frightening than peaceful. And yet the sorrow too persists, resounding in the final silence.

⧩ 6 ⧨

Epilogue

The fact is, no one owns the meaning of this music, which has
always supported (nay invited; nay compelled) multiple
opportunistic and contradictory readings. . . . But that
hopelessness of final arbitration is precisely what has given
the music its enormous social value, its terrific emotional force,
and its staying power. . . . We can never simply receive its
messages; we are always implicated in their making, and
therefore we can never be indifferent to them. It is never just
Shostakovich. It is always Shostakovich and us.

—RICHARD TARUSKIN,
Defining Russia Musically

What brought me to the quartets to begin with, I
think, was that I could feel a voice speaking to me
through them. Quite a few people seem to feel this
way, and I think it may be this very quality that has deluded so
many Shostakovich critics (myself, at times, included) into be-
lieving that they can give a unique and correct interpretation of
his works. But of course music doesn't work that way, particularly complicated, ambiguous music like Shostakovich's string

quartets. Still, there does seem to be an impulse toward communication of some kind in these works, and the fact that the message is wordless and open-ended does not stop us from feeling that it is meant specifically for us.

Even the symphonies, apparently, can produce this feeling in the right listener. "It is not interpretation," said the conductor Maxim Shostakovich, when I asked him how he went about interpreting his father's works in performance. "I *feel* him, I feel his presence always in his music. He never left me. Everything the same in his music as in life: how he talks, his anger, his humor. It was easy for me to understand what he was saying, between the notes. His quartets and his symphonies—yes, it is the same circle of feelings, just on a different scale."

But Maxim is a rare, probably singular case. People who knew the composer less well than his son did are more likely to sense his personal voice in the chamber works. "I think the quartets are his most personal and moving expressions," Kurt Sanderling has commented. "The quartets are all messages to his friends; the symphonies are messages to mankind." He counted himself, obviously, among the friends, and with good reason. But where does that leave the rest of us, who came to Shostakovich from faraway places and later times? We never met the composer, and yet we too feel that the messages in the quartets are intended for us, in a distinctly more personal way than anything that is expressed in the symphonies.

That "us," in the case of Shostakovich's quartets, includes a surprisingly wide swath of listeners: North Americans and West-

ern Europeans along with Russians and Poles, literary types as
well as musicians, people who generally dislike modern music
and those who are currently composing the most up-to-date
music themselves, the young along with the old—in short, all
kinds of audience members. Frederick Lifsitz, who is a teacher as
well as a violinist with the Alexander Quartet, notes with excitement that the quartets "are becoming more a part of teenagers'
Friday night reading sessions. These works are speaking to this
youngest generation in their own terms." And Lily Francis, the
violist of the Vertigo Quartet, confirms this from her own experience. "Shostakovich was popular in high school," she recalled
of her early exposure to the quartet music. "All the students
wanted to play it then. It appealed to people going through a
dark phase—adolescence and so forth."

Part of the appeal, for adolescents and non-adolescents alike,
lies in the combination of harsh, wrenching, complicated emotions with a relatively accessible, or at least superficially simple,
musical technique. It is not that the quartets are "easy" in the
sense of easy listening—in mood and method, they have a far
greater affinity with late Beethoven than with early Haydn—but
their texture is not as complicated as that of, say, Bartók's string
quartets. "In certain ways Shostakovich can be easier than other
twentieth-century composers to sight-read," remarked Nicholas
Canellakis, the Vertigos' cellist. "But it takes longer to know
what he's really saying—to figure out what the notes really
mean." As if to suggest that the simplicity and the depth were
two sides of the same coin, he went on to observe that the quar-

tets are "not very rich contrapuntally, or however you would say it—in terms of counterpoint. Often there are very few voices playing. And sometimes even when everyone is playing, three of the members are just holding one drone. I think that gives it a certain intimate quality."

That very plainness, though it helps account for the intimacy, may be part of what has hampered Shostakovich's acceptance into the academic canon. Or so the practicing musicians would argue. The conductor and pianist Ignat Solzhenitsyn, who teaches at the Curtis Institute, pointed out to me that "musicologists love to engage just with the technique of the work. So in the case of Bartók they can do that with great fruitfulness. With Shostakovich, there is a kind of outward simplicity of texture, simplicity of material, that beguiles certain critics, even very good critics, into a dismissive posture." Philip Setzer of the Emerson Quartet has noticed the same dismissive attitude, but feels that the critics and musicologists are now beginning to come around to the more general audience viewpoint. "For so many years his music was not taken seriously by the intellectual musical community," Setzer told me. "They saw him as a talented composer who wrote bombastic music, who sold out. Now that's changed, for two reasons. One, audiences really love even his difficult pieces. The irony is that he was forced to write for the masses and he *did*. And the other is that the more you look at them and study them, you see how much there was a tremendous intellect behind them."

Shostakovich may have succeeded in writing string quartets

for the masses—or at any rate the chamber music masses, which is a somewhat smaller group—but these pieces never make us feel we are being addressed in the aggregate. On the contrary, the four familial instruments seem to whisper directly into our ears, communing with us about our own personal sadnesses and anxieties. And this in turn calls forth a responsive feeling from music audiences, wherever and whoever they may be. "When we put a Shostakovich quartet on a mixed program," the Emersons' Eugene Drucker has noticed, "no matter whether we put it before the intermission or at the end, when people come backstage, what they want to talk about is the Shostakovich. This happens even if we're also playing something equally great, like Schubert's 'Death and the Maiden.' That is, it's not just a matter of quality. I think it has something to do with the immediacy of the music."

But where does that immediacy come from? What is it, exactly, that people are responding to in Shostakovich's quartets? Philip Setzer, when I asked him this, replied, "Like most things with Shostakovich, I think there are two answers. One is the obvious thing that the language he's speaking is one that people can understand. The other answer is more complicated, and it's that beneath everything—all the horrible compromises, all the regrets, all the guilt—I think he was a great human being under that. And I think that's what comes out in the music. It's honest, it's heartfelt. He was in such a horrible state, but he was still able to make something that was great."

Except for those who write off the whole of Shostakovich's music as an ironic mask, there is widespread agreement that a number of his works, and in particular the string quartets, carry a powerful sense of truth. But a debate rages about what, exactly, is meant by that. Is this "truth" the same thing as the heartfelt honesty that Setzer hears? Are we simply saying that the music accurately represents the man himself, or perhaps the man and his circumstances? And in that case, is this just another version of what some might call "authenticity"? Or is there some other kind of truth here, some deeper correlation between the world as we listeners perceive it and the world as the music portrays it? Many of us who love the Shostakovich quartets would be inclined, I think, to make this larger claim for it, though we would be hard-pressed to demonstrate how it works.

For some, the truth of Shostakovich's quartets is simply that which inheres in all music. "You cannot lie in music," said Valentin Berlinsky, explaining why he and his fellow Borodins could not have performed a "socialist," "optimistic" version of the Fourth Quartet for its official audition. And Galina Shirinskaya, a performing pianist as well as a conservatory teacher, recently echoed Berlinsky's view. "Music cannot lie, it cannot lie. If it lies, it is not music," she stressed.

One understands why people who lived alongside Shostakovich in Soviet Russia might want and need to feel this. "Music was the last retreat, intellectually," said Helga Landauer, who helped make the film *A Journey of Dmitry Shostakovich*. "The thoughts about death, the eternal questions, which in literature had been replaced by particular Party questions about work or whatever—music was the last muse that was not totally scrutinized." It was the only place, that is, where the most unsettling truths could still be safely if evasively expressed. That such truths were necessarily wordless is part of what allowed music, unlike literature, to be honest: language itself had been so defiled by the regime that even the word "truth"—*pravda*—had come to represent a pack of lies.

But to insist absolutely that music can never lie seems to annihilate the very distinction that would be helpful in such circumstances. After all, as the Shostakovich scholar Gerard McBurney has logically observed, "If music cannot lie, then music also cannot tell the truth." And if all music tells the truth equally, then how are we to distinguish between the honesty of, say, Shostakovich's Eighth Quartet and the relative dishonesty of his "Song of the Counterplan" or "A Toast to Our Motherland," not to mention the more complicated case of his variously heartfelt and hypocritical symphonies?

"I think in Shostakovich this question about truthfulness relates to the layers of irony," the violinist Eugene Drucker commented to me. "He's aware that people are looking over his shoulder, and he has to develop strategies to express himself. So if he's using irony to express something on the surface and something else underneath, maybe he's 'lying' to tell a deeper truth." As if to squelch the whole philosophical quandary, Drucker then brought in the opinion of a contemporary composer: "Ned Rorem says music cannot refer to anything outside itself." But he seemed to realize that this pronouncement by an American working in the Debussy-Ravel tradition might have little applicability to Shostakovich's situation, and so he returned to the central question. "Music conveys truths," Drucker conceded, "but not in the sense of a truth or a lie. That's much too narrow a definition of truth. I don't think of it on a graph where the x axis is truth or falsehood and the y axis is something else."

Fair enough. And within the arts, music is not the only one that works through indirection. Painting and sculpture often convey conflicting ideas or perspectives, and even verbal artifacts like novels, plays, and poems don't tell the truth by stating it flatly or undebatably. Masks and implications are always brought to bear whenever art addresses itself to fact and opinion. So even though art, and especially music, may be non-propositional in a logician's sense—that is, unable to make statements that are subject to proof or disproof—it can still, in a colloquial sense, be deemed capable of telling truths. Or, for that matter, lies.

"As much as I love Shostakovich—and the greatest of the symphonies are pinnacles of their kind—I think there's a greater percentage of truth in the quartets than in anything else he wrote," said Philip Setzer. "I think art definitely can lie, or at least not tell the truth. I think Shostakovich wrote a lot of lies in his music, sometimes sacrificing the whole work: maybe in a moment of weakness, maybe because he had a sense of the bigger picture and wanted to preserve his ability to keep writing music. Some of the symphonies I think were written to please the authorities." Lev Ginzburg, the Moscow musicologist who knew Shostakovich mainly through their joint activity in the Composers' Union, made a similar distinction between the string quartets, which he characterized as the composer's "intimate diary, reflecting his inner thoughts and feelings," and at least some of the symphonies (particularly the Eleventh and Twelfth, the ones written as "concessions to the rulers"), which displayed "all his mastery, but without a trace of his soul." And the youthful members of the Jupiter Quartet, in a note that accompanied a recent New York performance of the Fourth Quartet, argued essentially the same point. "He abided by the Communist Party's mandates by composing extravagant symphonies and oratorios that celebrated the Party's accomplishments," the Jupiters wrote in their program, "but then escaped to the string quartets to communicate how he truly felt."

But how, I wondered, does the music's truthfulness or lack of it manifest itself? In answering, Philip Setzer offered me a contrast between the conflicting, conflicted strategy of the Fifth Symphony and the very different kind of honesty he perceived in the string quartets. "I don't hear that as a joyous ending," he said of the Fifth Symphony's finale. "By the end of that piece, I'm just torn to shreds. And I felt that as a kid, without reading anything or knowing anything about Shostakovich. And the audience that heard it at the premiere was in tears at the end. Why does what seems to be an incredibly joyous ending leave us in tears? Because it's so extreme—it goes past the point of a joyous ending to something else."

If exaggeration and ironic bombast are the way Shostakovich

hints at his true meaning in the symphonies, something much more direct is taking place in the chamber works. "With the quartets," Setzer continued, "I guess I would call it a kind of inner truth. This music is often the most personal—it's true of the late Beethoven quartets as well. These are very intimate conversations among four people. What's interesting about what Shostakovich does with the quartets is he creates a kind of art form—a kind of style, but deeper than that—a kind of philosophy of how to say what he really wants to say by taking the mask off at certain points, and then putting it on quickly enough so he's not found out." Still, as Setzer himself acknowledged, there are always masks behind the masks: one never sees Shostakovich plain. This does not make him any the less honest, for as Oscar Wilde put it, "Man is least himself when he talks in his own person. Give him a mask, and he will tell you the truth."

"There's the whole question of who is telling us the story, as there so often is in Russian literature," Setzer observed about Shostakovich's string quartets. He went on to point out the "Chekhovian" and "Dostoyevskian" elements in the composer's approach, the way "Shostakovich often plays the role of the fool—the Shakespearean fool, the Dostoyevskian fool, the one who tells the truth." One has only to think of Prince Myshkin in *The Idiot*—or, for a different version, Shostakovich's own example of Dr. Ragin in *Ward No. 6*—to come up with a figure who fits the description. The fool in such works is not an innocent figure, or rather, his innocence is the very thing that allows him to become enmeshed in and partly responsible for the widespread symptoms of disaster and despair. And he is not the only one who is enmeshed in this way; we all are. This is why it is so important that we cannot be sure who is telling us the story in a Dostoyevsky novel or a Chekhov tale. That narrator may be an unnamed figure in the story, but he is also our mirror, our stand-in, and as a result he constantly wavers between being an integral part of the tale and observing it from the outside. He is, in this respect, rather like the composer who speaks to us through four other musicians, and whose only participation in the performance is secret, or silent, or otherwise behind the scenes.

"Writing quartet music was the closest he could come to being a poet who just picked up a pencil and wrote for himself, after playing for himself on the piano," noted Helga Landauer. "The smallest model of the universe, the first acoustic. Nothing is required for these four people to come play: they are the closest friends, they can just come. With a symphony, you have to ask how and whom. Those were the four who were always on his side."

With a quartet, of course, you also have to ask "how and whom"—how the work will be structured, for whom and to whom it will speak—but these are artistic questions only, and thus very different from the ones that need to be raised in the much more public presentation of a symphony. And Landauer's contrast is a useful one. For if the best of Shostakovich's symphonies are comparable to, say, a full-scale theatrical production of *King Lear* (complete with storms, battles, and death scenes), the quartets are much more like Shakespeare's sonnets. In fact, they are *very* like those sonnets, especially in the way they combine extreme artfulness with an extraordinary feeling of intimacy. "None of his predecessors speaks as Shakespeare does, like a voice in the next room—even like a voice in the reader's mind," writes Barbara Everett in a passage that is remarkably applicable to Shostakovich's string quartets, as is her observation that the sonnets are "at once so inward as to be enigmas for editors, yet so entirely realised as to be available to any reader who wants to experience them."

Perhaps it would finally be more accurate to say that Shostakovich's quartets resemble both Shakespeare's sonnets *and* Shakespeare's plays—or, to switch to his other favorite author, both Chekhov's stories and Chekhov's dramas. Just about everyone who has played or listened carefully to the string quartets has noticed their intensely theatrical quality. It has something to do, I think, with the way Shostakovich uses the suspenseful and the unexpected as a way of holding our attention and pushing us off-balance at the same time. As the Alexander Quartet's cellist, Sandy Wilson, has said, the "wild ride" we are taken on in the Shostakovich quartets seems both "inevitable" and "unpredictable" (a paradox that is typical, incidentally, of all great mystery plotting). There is a drama which comes through even in his quietest chamber music, and which stems from the way he seems able to transmute narrative elements like event, story, and character into musical structures. And these structures, in turn, play themselves out in a particularly stageworthy way, reminding us that their time is also our time for the duration of the piece's performance.

"His music tells a story in the way that human beings need to hear a story told," the Emersons' Eugene Drucker has observed. "There are events in it—like a trajectory of keys: you establish a home key, and then you go away from it, and the question is, are you going to come back to it, and when, and how? It's a sense that something is unfolding at the moment that you listen to it. Something about Shostakovich's music, you could view it as 'theatrical' in the best sense of the term. That's why Phil had the idea of commissioning a theater piece based on it."

That theater piece was *The Noise of Time*, a March 2000 collaboration between the Emerson Quartet and Théâtre de Complicité, in which the musicians performed Shostakovich's music while director Simon McBurney—aided by his brother, the composer and music historian Gerard McBurney—told the story of Shostakovich's life. Though the production in the end used only the Fifteenth Quartet, Philip Setzer's initial (and, as he admits, excessively ambitious) plan had been to dramatize all of them. He got the idea, he insists, from the nature of the string quartets themselves. "In a basic way," he said, "the quartets have a narrative feel to them. There's an opening, the lights come up. Usually things start in a Chekhovian way, without too much conflict, with people discussing inanities—innocently unfolding. The Third is a perfect example. The Fifth is also a good example: that opening could be music for a Noël Coward play." For Setzer, an important part of what makes Shostakovich's music dramatic, in a very literal sense, is that it isn't *always* intense or *always* profound. So where others have consistently interpreted such quotidian moments as "ironic," Setzer thinks something more theatrical is going on: "Sometimes he was just setting up, like Chekhov. You can't have turmoil going on all the time. Sometimes he's being ironic, but sometimes he's just biding his time to set up something dramatically powerful.

"I started to see the quartets as little plays, as little dramas, basically, with four characters," Setzer told me. "Especially as the quartets mature, you start to see little solos, or pairs, or trios. In the Eighth, for instance, three people are holding sustained notes and one is 'crying.' . . . I wrote it all out, just a way of staging all fifteen quartets. Originally the idea was to tell his story through these quartets: it was really like an autobiography in fifteen chapters."

What Setzer was responding to, in part, was the way Shostakovich's quartets lend themselves to a kind of analysis which is perhaps more literary than musicological. They ask to be absorbed and understood not merely as elegantly constructed, technically virtuosic artifacts, but as individually produced artworks freighted with meaning. That meaning, which is emotional as well as intellectual, will never be completely available to us, and it will alter over time, as we move further and further from the original circumstances of the work's creation. Sometimes the distance will make it harder for us to see what is happening in the artwork, and sometimes it will make it easier, but we will never arrive at the exact answer to the riddle, because there *is* no exact answer, and in some ways there isn't even a riddle. The artwork is not a question the artist has asked us, or even himself; it is a self-contained outpouring of all his conscious and unconscious capacities, shaped by his intentions but not limited to them. So its meaning can never be a single meaning alone. The power of the artwork as both aesthetic experience and social communication inheres largely in that multiplicity, that layering, that depth. Everyone has always understood this about Shakespeare. Perhaps we simply lack sufficient distance to see that it is also true of Shostakovich.

One explanation that is often given for why Shostakovich wrote the way he did—melodically but idiosyncratically, in his strange, emotionally expressive language—is that he was cut off from the twentieth century's dominant musical currents. As a Soviet composer trapped mainly within his country's borders, he was not a part of the international classical-music world that shaped Pierre Boulez or Elliott Carter or Aaron Copland or Iannis Xenakis or Olivier Messiaen, and thus he did not end up sounding like any of them. But this theory loses a little steam once we consider that none of them ended up sounding much like each other. Besides, Shostakovich did have access to a great deal of Western music, especially in his youth but also intermittently later on: he received records and scores from European and American composers throughout the late 1950s, 1960s, and early 1970s, and he was still traveling to London and New York, and hearing concerts there, during the last five years of his life. It's also quite clear that, as he grew older and turned more often to chamber music, he was able to experiment with a number of compositional techniques that would have been considered dangerously "modern" and even "atonal" if they had appeared in his middle-period symphonies.

So the theory needs to be refined a bit. It was not so much that he was actively prevented from choosing, at least in his most personal music, between some form of Stravinskian modernism and some variety of Schoenbergian serialism (the choice that most Western composers of his age found themselves making); it was more that he did not have to do this in order to make a musical career for himself. In the Soviet Union his career requirements were other, and in some ways more onerous: he had to write for the movies, he had to come up with popular songs, he had to compose symphonies on national themes. But none of these governmentally imposed restrictions was liable to become confused in his own mind with what he wanted to do musically. The external requirements of the job and the internal impulse to write music remained separate for him, especially in the string quartets, and that was in part what enabled him to produce the music he did—music that carried so clearly the sound of his own voice rather than simply the general compositional habits of his day.

As a result of this, Shostakovich was in many ways *less* isolated than his Western counterparts. For whereas he was patently eager to communicate with his audience—an audience that shared many of his doubts and despairs but was unable to express them except through the wordless communion of the concert hall— many mid-century European and American composers were at best uninterested in and at worst virulently disdainful of the people who came to listen to classical music. In 1958, just a couple of years before Shostakovich composed his expressive and emotionally received Eighth Quartet, the American composer Milton Babbitt published a piece in the magazine *High Fidelity* that became a kind of credo for the rest of his profession. Printed under the title "Who Cares If You Listen?" (a title chosen by the editor to highlight Babbitt's extreme position), the article suggested that "the composer would do himself and his music an immediate and eventual service by total, resolute and voluntary withdrawal from this public world to one of private performance and electronic media, with its very real possibility of complete elimination of the public and social aspects of musical composition." In such circumstances, the modern composer "would be free to pursue a private life of professional achievement, as opposed to a public life of unprofessional compromise and exhibitionism."

This kind of breathtaking but far from atypical narcissism did not, I think, end up being very helpful to either American composers or their potential audiences. What Babbitt calls "unprofessional compromise" can be a commendable or even necessary attempt to acknowledge reality. And the longing for total withdrawal seems a strange wish for any artist who really has anything to say. Shostakovich knew what it was to be forcibly withdrawn; having experienced it twice, he dreaded it almost more than anything else. His intense desire to hear his quartets played aloud, even in the depths of the Zhdanov period, was not simply a self-centered need to hear his own latest production: he wanted to have his music played to an audience because only then did it fully come to life. Nor were Shostakovich's personal friends and musical acquaintances the only ones who could hear what he was saying in these works. All the audiences to the quartets, then and now, in the Soviet Union and elsewhere, have responded as if the communications were intended for them, too. As Philip Setzer has pointed out, "He wanted people to understand what he was saying."

But the power of the string quartets rests partly on the degree to which they never wholly give up their secrets. In this respect, a certain kind of isolation—one might call it, perhaps, seclusion— remains central to Shostakovich's enterprise. He speaks to us urgently and fervently, but from an ever-increasing distance, as if his very desire to communicate, the intensity of his wish to connect, were hampering our reception. This description makes him seem rather like Cassandra, doomed to be misunderstood; and yet what we are doing, when we take in the quartets, is not precisely "misunderstanding." We are understanding as much as we are able to of a medium that asks *not* to be too facilely comprehended nor too easily translated into our own everyday language. Shostakovich's quartets may speak to us of the world in which they were created and the man who created them, but that is only partly what they do, and they only partially do it. Just as important as the message that is sent is the fact that we can never fully receive it.

With his passion for cryptograms, punning references, and musical quotations from his own and other people's works, Shostakovich was clearly a master of implication and allusiveness. He delighted, for instance, in tucking personally significant names or initials into the sequences of musical notes he devised, and he was inveterately fond of quoting, either blatantly or secretly, from the works of other composers. Yet to assert that he loved allusion does not get us very far in the direction of untangling his meanings. Should we interpret all the DSCH passages in the Eighth Quartet, for instance, as a sign that Shostakovich was writing about his own life, or do they imply (as Philip Setzer has suggested) that "It's us, it's Russia—it's the tragedy of Russia too"? Does the repeated quotation from the *William Tell* overture in the first movement of the Fifteenth Symphony refer to freedom (as Kurt Sanderling has proposed), or to the fact that Rossini "lived slightly too long" (as Shostakovich once put it in a letter)—or is it simply the composer's way of acknowledging a beloved predecessor whose captivating melodies were "in his luggage"? None of these meanings excludes the others, so they could all be correct, but it's also possible that they're all wrong and Shostakovich meant something else entirely. It is in the nature of allusiveness to produce uncertainty in this way, and perhaps that's why the always watched, often persecuted Soviet composer was drawn to it.

Nor is all quotation necessarily allusion. "An allusion predicates a source," Christopher Ricks has observed in his book *Allusion to the Poets*, ". . . but identifying a source is not the same as postulating an allusion, for a source is not necessarily called into play by its beneficiary. What goes to the making of a poem does not necessarily go to its meaning." He then offers the specific example of Keats:

> Sometimes readers will disagree as to whether a line of Keats had its source in, say, *Hamlet*; sometimes, readers may agree that such was a source but disagree as to whether he was alluding; and often readers will disagree as to just what they should make of what Keats made of that which he alluded to. This, not because in criticism anything goes, but because much goes. Poems have a way of being undulating and diverse.

And so, we might add, do string quartets.

It is the inevitable disagreement among those of us receiving the message that lends multiplicity to the artist's meaning, and in helping to create that meaning, we ourselves become implicated. This is the central argument put forth by Richard Taruskin, who has repeatedly and very effectively defended Shostakovich from both the embraces and the assaults of those who would prefer to simplify him. While Taruskin has been notoriously hard on the interpreters who, following Volkov, have found an anti-Stalin code in practically every bar of Shostakovich's music, he does not deny that the music contains messages, including political messages. All he claims, in deploring the simplistic "Rosetta Stone" approach, is that we cannot reduce any given work or portion of a work to a single, inarguable meaning, either for Shostakovich or for us. It's not just that our access to the composer's intentions is necessarily incomplete. Such intentions, even if we could know them, would not be equivalent to the work's meaning, which depends on numerous different factors that will vary over time. And this, as Taruskin points out, is not at all a bad thing, for it accounts for the music's enduring significance to each one of its listeners. "We can never simply receive its messages," he observes; "we are always implicated in their making."

To be involved almost to the point of being guilty: that is what "implicated" suggests in this context, and it is a richly effective formulation, for it begins to explain why Shostakovich's quartets strike such an intimate note, why they seem to make us and the composer into co-conspirators, even if we have no clear sense of what, at this late date, we might be conspiring against. Or for. We are his collaborators in that respect, too: the joint effort involves not just the things we are resisting or hopelessly giving in to, but also whatever it is we might be constructing together at this precise moment in history, this twelve or twenty or thirty-five minutes during which we are gathered at the concert hall. It is this particular sense of "implication"—this mutual commitment on all our parts—that gives Shostakovich's quartets their vital power in live performance, and that makes any interpretation seem incomplete until it is played before an audience.

This is why the Emerson Quartet players, despite their awareness that it would be risky, decided to make their monumental
recording of the fifteen quartets at a series of live performances.
"When we were first learning some of these quartets, we were
struck by the simplicity of the method in some of them," Eugene
Drucker told me. "And then when we were performing them,
we were struck by the emotional logic, and the narrative logic, of
the music. And this awareness came to us most strikingly in
front of an audience. It was an emotional awareness more than
an intellectual one."

Ignat Solzhenitsyn has noticed the same quality even in some
of Shostakovich's larger-scale pieces. "The full greatness is not
revealed until performance," he observed. "There are passages in
the Tenth Symphony that, when I conduct them in rehearsal,
don't quite grab—they don't quite work—and then in performance it all makes sense." But isn't this true of other composers
as well? "It's not true to the same extent," said Solzhenitsyn.
"With the music of Beethoven, it becomes evident very early on
which passages are the most transcendent, and then it becomes a
lifetime's work figuring out how to make that happen. But I can't
think of another composer where the meaning only fully comes
out in performance."

The word "transcendent" caught my ear, and I asked Solzhenitsyn whether he would ever use that same word about Shostakovich. "No," he answered. "Broadly speaking, I wouldn't. I don't
know that Shostakovich tries to transcend: transcend our nature,
the limitations of who we are. Beethoven's entire will is bent

upon that, I think, even from early on, and it becomes more evident as his life unfolds. With Shostakovich, I think more of adjectives like 'mesmerizing,' 'hypnotizing,' 'arresting'—because his music can have this utterly intangible magic, but it's centered around the human being sui generis, rather than the human's attempt to break free." And yet that embeddedness in the merely human, that location in the here and now, does not strike Solzhenitsyn as at all reductive in Shostakovich's case. "No composer is more a reflection of his times," the Russian-born conductor acknowledged, but all the same, he insisted, "what is completely obvious to me is that this is a genius for all time. I know that as I know the sky is blue."

If we want to see how deeply rooted Shostakovich was in the world of the merely human, we need look no farther than his palpable sense of shame. As an element in Shostakovich's music, the shame is perhaps not as audible as the melancholy or the dread, but it is ever-present nonetheless. One cannot point to a precise place in the music where you can hear it, but it underlies and supports most of the other painful emotions, and if it were removed from the mix, you would certainly notice the difference. The shame is apparent in the harshness with which Shostakovich treats himself and his own feelings; it saves the saddest quartets, like the Eighth, from self-pity, and it saves the more cheerful ones, like the Sixth, from any tincture of smugness or self-assurance. Shostakovich's sense of shame is not the grandiose, embarrassing, self-dramatizing emotion manifested by a Fyodor Karamazov or a Semyon Marmeladov; on the contrary, it is a deeply internal and undemonstrative feeling, much closer in tone to Chekhov than to Dostoyevsky. It is linked to the sense of doubt that Paul Epstein detected in the Fourteenth Quartet, and because it is specifically *self*-doubt, it prevents the quartets from ever sounding at all bombastic or overconfidently authoritative. In this way it distinguishes the quartets from at least some of the symphonies and most of the commissioned patriotic songs, and it is probably what helps persuade us that the quartets are telling us the truth.

Shostakovich had a great deal to feel ashamed about, and it would appear that he was acutely susceptible to this particular emotion. According to Kurt Sanderling, who was recalling with unfaded ire "that swine Nabokov" and his behavior at the 1949 Waldorf-Astoria conference, Shostakovich "told Mravinsky that the worst moment of his life was when he was asked whether he shared the Zhdanov opinion of Stravinsky, and he was forced to say yes." Even if that "worst" is an exaggeration, it still suggests how painfully aware he was of the public travesties he had lent himself to. To call this sentiment regret would be to downplay its importance: it was deeper, more elemental, less cerebral than re-gret, and it was inexpungible.

The composer Sofia Gubaidulina, who is exactly one generation younger than Shostakovich, explained the impact of Shostakovich's betrayals and compromises on her circle of musicians. "When Shostakovich joined the Party in 1960, our disappointment knew no bounds," she told Elizabeth Wilson. "That such a man could be broken, that our system was capable of crushing a genius, was something I could not get over. We were left wondering why, just at this time when the political situation had relaxed somewhat, when at last it seemed possible to preserve one's integrity, Shostakovich fell victim to official flattery. What forced him into this action?"

Both Sanderling and Gubaidulina used the word "forced" to explain Shostakovich's compliant behavior. Can one, or should one, feel ashamed of actions about which one had no choice? The answer that Bernard Williams gives in *Shame and Necessity*, his philosophical study of Greek tragic figures such as Ajax, Achilles, Oedipus, and Agamemnon, is basically yes. As Williams illuminatingly suggests, even the acts which these classical heroes committed under duress (that is, when operating under the influence of the gods, fate, madness, or other uncontrollable factors) warranted, and were met with, a feeling of personal shame.

There were no gods in Shostakovich's case, and he was not exactly a hero, but his situation was remarkably similar to the one Williams describes when he summarizes the ancient Greek idea of supernatural necessity: "an idea that the structure of things is purposive, playing against you. Things are arranged in such a way that what you do will make no difference to the eventual outcome, or will even help to bring about what you try to prevent." The ancients clearly felt that a man who lives under such conditions can still be held responsible for his own actions— perhaps more to the point, can still hold *himself* responsible.

"Living in a world in which such forces or necessities operate does not, then, mean that you cannot do anything, or that you think you cannot do anything," Williams points out. "You can act; you can deliberate; and so you can think about what different things would have happened if you had acted differently." And in the midst of such thoughts you can, if you have the proper sensibility, experience shame. In this respect, shame is a symptom of freedom—not actual freedom, maybe, but the kind of existential freedom through which a human being asserts that he is still a self-determining individual rather than a mere movable force.

For Gubaidulina, something of this feeling seemed to enter into Shostakovich's music, enabling it to speak in a special way to and for his compatriots. What gave the composer this moral authority was not just that he had been subjected to terrible trials and unbearable cruelties, but that he had (in her words) "succumbed to weakness" and had thus become "pain personified, the epitome of the tragedy and terror of our times." In language that eerily echoed both Aristotle's view of Greek tragedy and Christianity's take on *its* central tragedy, Gubaidulina observed:

> Indeed, I believe that Shostakovich's music reaches such a wide audience because he was able to transform the pain that he so keenly experienced into something exalted and full of light, which transcends all worldly suffering. He was able to transfigure the material into a spiritual entity, whereas Prokofiev's music lacks the contrast between terrible darkness and ever-expanding light. We listened to Shostakovich's new works in a kind of exaltation.

We who listen now cannot feel exactly the same way, of course. But we too have our shames, our responsibilities, both personal and political. Until we leave off being human, we will always—if we are morally astute enough—retain a salutary awareness of the difference between what we did do and what we might have done. And Shostakovich's music speaks to that capacity in us.

Yet if Shostakovich is in some ways our representative man, it is not just because of his self-lacerating side. His shame may speak to one aspect of our complicity in human error, but his notorious sense of humor addresses us in another, more companionable, possibly somewhat lighter way, though in his case even the lightness can be extremely dark.

Practically all humor is in one way or another based on the discrepancy between truth and falsehood, between things as they are and things as they are not. While this is obviously the case with irony and satire, it also applies to punning, exaggeration, mimicry, and even slapstick (where, for instance, the honest fact is that we enjoy laughing when someone else slips on a banana peel, while the tendered falsehood is that such injuries don't really hurt). Humor is thus an invaluable tool for someone who lives in a period when lies are routinely put forth as truth and vice versa. I do not know of anyone who has *not* lived in such a period, but the version of it that Shostakovich experienced was more extreme than most.

That the man himself was very witty we know from countless

anecdotes. His deep sense of irony was manifested in his letters, his daily encounters, and his annual New Year's toast. He was also, apparently, an inveterate mimic, as many people have testified, including Krzysztof Meyer, a Polish composer who became Shostakovich's friend toward the end of his life. "He had an idiosyncratic sense of humour and a love of acting," Meyer wrote in an obituary article after Shostakovich's death. "I remember visiting him once at his home and finding a militiaman there. . . . When eventually the man left, Shostakovich spent nearly half an hour laughing and imitating his salutes, bows and mannerisms. Another time he enacted for me the scene of a misunderstanding with an optician who had prescribed spectacles which were too strong for him. He enjoyed all this like a child."

Mimicry can be a form of humor in music, and that may be partly what those quotations are doing in the Fifteenth Symphony and elsewhere. But this is not what most musicians mean when they talk about Shostakovich's humor. Mainly they are referring to his well-known sense of irony. "If the music didn't have irony, it would be lacking some important aspect—perhaps more in his work than in any other composer," Eugene Drucker told me. Philip Setzer, on the other hand, took a slightly different view. "With Shostakovich everything has been made to be 'ironic,' and I don't think it's so much that way," Setzer said. "I think he has many different kinds of humor, like any great humorist—which he was. Shostakovich had a wicked sense of humor. You don't see much humor in the Fifteenth Quartet, but even in the Fourteenth and Thirteenth, it's humorous, some parts are humorous, the way Beethoven can be: in a kind of de-monic way." Yet even this comparison, according to the Alexan-ders' Frederick Lifsitz, overstates the hilarity in the quartets. Re-ferring to Shostakovich's "dark and sarcastic" sense of humor, Lifsitz argued, "It is not on the level of true laughable humor that Haydn, Mozart, Beethoven used. His surroundings and his reac-tions to them were just too depressing to break out on that level."

"The sick humor—a dark, dark humor" is what the young players of the Vertigo Quartet listed foremost among the "char-acter traits" they could discern in Shostakovich's music. And when I asked them to elaborate on what was meant by humor in his music, the violinist José Maria Blumenschein said, "I think it's more sarcasm. 'You idiot, you have to play this now.' Like in the Twelfth, where you play 'Bum-bum. Bum-bum. Bum-bum. Bum-bum.'" What he was quoting was the same pizzicato sec-tion which Dmitri Tsyganov, its first performer, described as "the funereal episode . . . where one seems to hear the tread of death itself." But even if one man's sarcasm is another man's funeral march, both are agreed that the prevailing color is black. As Kurt Sanderling pointedly observed, "Shostakovich is not joyful, in the Brahms sense. Sometimes he has idyllic moments, but he is not joyful."

We know from literature—not just Russian literature, but also Dickens and Shakespeare—that sadness and humor, tragedy and satire, can often go hand in hand. But musicians, on the whole, seem loath to allow that the two can be mixed. Asked whether Shostakovich's irony was allied to his sadness, Eugene

Drucker said, "No, I think of them as being different parts of his musical personality." And other string players, such as the members of the Guarneri Quartet, decided not to play Shostakovich at all because one or more of them found the music too unfeeling, too empty in its apparent mockery. The charge of irony, in other words, is always a charge, and one begins to see why Philip Setzer was so eager to protect Shostakovich from it.

But this ignores the extent to which Shostakovich's ironic sense and his tragic sense are inextricably linked. Those jokes in the music are meant to hurt us. It is we who slip on the banana peel, in those juddering starts and stops, and we who feel ourselves suddenly let down when, at the end of the second movement of the Fourteenth Quartet, "instead of really writing an ending, he has it sort of humorously peter out," as Setzer put it. After he described that moment to me, I asked him whether he thought Shostakovich's irony was meant to jab you, or whether it was the sort of irony that enclosed you within itself and made you complicit. "I think you're meant to be jabbed by it," Setzer acknowledged. So the jokes (if they can even rightfully be called that) are at everyone's expense, his *and* ours; and their source, it would seem, lies as much in his resigned sense of melancholy as in any kind of conviviality.

Was Shostakovich himself a melancholy person? "To the highest degree," affirmed Kurt Sanderling. "But not by nature: due to the circumstances under which he was forced to survive. As a composer, he started young and boyish, and the older he got, the more tragic he got." Galina Shirinskaya conveyed a similar impression, of a man who was simultaneously, or at any rate sequentially, witty and melancholic. "He was both," she said. "He was a very sarcastic person, but very gloomy at the same time. You see, life breaks all of us, and it broke him like not many others. But in his early work there is such wit—his musical wit can be compared with Beethoven's wit: powerful wit, he laughs at what he hates. But you can laugh at the idiocy up to a certain point; when it is everywhere, it makes you sick, and then you become a melancholic."

The tendency, if you are at all inclined to such habits, is to hear precisely this psychological progression in the cycle of string quartets. During Shostakovich's centennial year, the fifteen quartets were often played in a single chronologically ordered series, and to those who heard them in this fashion, as well as to the musicians who performed them, something additional seemed to accrue to the individual pieces when they were linked together in this way. "I do feel that there is a thread or story line that travels all through the quartets, which creates an overall epic effect," commented the Alexanders' Frederick Lifsitz, and Philip Setzer employed the same metaphor when he said, "I think if you're trying to share the story of his life and this narrative thread that runs through—I think it's more moving to hear them and play them in that way. But," Setzer added, in regard to the Emersons' performances, "we prefer to do Bartók and Beethoven chronologically, too."

The difference, though, is that people do not tend to read Bartók's and Beethoven's lives quite so firmly into their quartets. For Richard Taruskin, this is the great disadvantage of programming Shostakovich's quartets as a cycle. "As long as we have only one context, namely the biographical, in which to interpret Shostakovich's music," Taruskin writes, "that music will continue to make a limited, and diminishing, appeal to our imaginations. And as long as we hear his quartets only as a cycle, we will have no other context." I do not think the situation, even now, is quite that dire; I think that audiences, if not professional musicologists, are already able to hear the multiple layers in the quartets and appreciate them as individual pieces of music, and this capacity is likely to become even greater as our distance from Shostakovich's own time increases. But there is a lure to the biographical that Taruskin is right to resist, if only because the rest of us so easily submit to it. Given the prominence of Shostakovich's own narrative gift, we cannot help feeling that he has actually planted that thread or story line in the cycle of quartets. ("You have to think that he was thinking about them as a volume," as Philip Setzer has remarked.)

The story of Shostakovich's life is a very powerful one, and he was a master storyteller in music, so it is not surprising that we should confuse the two. Perhaps he sometimes confused them himself, and perhaps he infused autobiographical elements into some or all of the quartets. Finally, though, such indeterminables don't really matter. Like the interpretation we impose on a work of art in order to bring its alien majesty closer to our understanding, the narrative arc is a device we impose on a life to make it more comprehensible, more graspable. But our interpretation of a life (as of an artwork) could easily be wrong, and in any case it can never be wholly true, for a life is as complicated as a work of art—more so, in some ways, because of its arbitrariness. In life, things happen out of order, and that is what makes it particularly difficult to distinguish cause from effect, personal choices from impersonal givens, and random incidents from significant foreshadowings.

Consider, for instance, the curious case of the one-act opera called *Rothschild's Violin*. Based on a Chekhov story of the same name, the piece was originally sketched out in 1939 by Veniamin Fleishman, a young Russian Jewish composer who was studying with Shostakovich at the Leningrad Conservatory. But poor Fleishman, who joined the Soviet army as soon as Hitler invaded Russia, was killed in 1941 at the age of twenty-eight. Shostakovich eventually rescued his unfinished manuscript from the Leningrad Composers' Union and finished it, in Kuibyshev, in late 1943 or early 1944. According to Shostakovich, the vocal lines had all been written out by his student, and he merely expanded and orchestrated the work. The opera was belatedly released into the world in the 1960s (first in a concert version in 1960, and then with a full staging in 1968) as the only known composition of Veniamin Fleishman.

And yet to my ear it sounds eerily like Shostakovich—not just the Shostakovich of the Fourth and Fifth Symphonies, which had preceded this exercise, but also the composer of the later symphonies and, especially, the quartets. These foreshadowings are both structural and melodic, both musical and textual. For example, from the Chekhov story (and, one presumes, the Fleishman libretto), this relatively early work borrows the theme of Russian anti-Semitism that was to resurface over twenty years later in Shostakovich's Thirteenth Symphony. Still more tellingly, the klezmer band that lies at the heart of both the story and the opera lends the score a distinctively Jewish sound—a sound that Shostakovich was to reuse almost immediately in his Second Piano Trio and his Second Quartet.

So here is a mystery solved, or perhaps just made more complicated. The proximate cause of that sorrowful but also convivial klezmer sound in the two 1944 chamber pieces was not, or not only, the sudden death of Ivan Ivanovich Sollertinsky. For many months before Sollertinsky died, Shostakovich had been thinking about and working on Fleishman's opera, and this was how the echoes of a Jewish village orchestra entered his own music.

"What he said he liked about Jewish music was that it was so sad, even the happy music sounded sad," Eugene Drucker has commented, seconding what many others said about Shostakovich. *Rothschild's Violin* expresses that combination exactly. In Chekhov's story, as in Fleishman's opera, the main character—a coffin maker called Bronza who occasionally plays the fiddle in the local klezmer band—asks on his deathbed that his most prized possession, his violin, be given to Rothschild, the Jew he has previously scorned and beaten. Using this instrument,

Rothschild repeatedly performs the plaintive air he first heard Bronza playing, a tune that is at once "so sad and sorrowful that his audiences weep," and so popular that the town's "merchants and officials used to be continually sending for Rothschild and making him play it over and over a dozen times." It is on this characteristically mixed note that the Chekhov story ends.

And here is where the notion of order—in a biography, in a cycle of works—truly comes into question. As an incident in the well-constructed narrative of Shostakovich's life, the opera *Rothschild's Violin* is completely out of place. There it is, written at the moment when the composer's reputation is at its highest, a year or so after he has completed the Leningrad Symphony and become the toast of the world. Yet it speaks of failure, and sorrow, and a life that has not been lived as one might have wished to live it. It speaks of these things through the masks of its other creators, so that Shostakovich can hide (as he was wont to hide, in later days) behind Chekhov, behind Fleishman—but he is nevertheless present as a kind of anticipatory ghost of himself. One senses in the music his poignant involvement in the only opera he was ever able to finish after *Lady Macbeth*, even if it is not, nominally or actually, his own opera. And one also detects a version of Shostakovich, an older, sadder version, in the voice of the beloved storyteller, that writer who was to remain so important to him up to the very end.

The Chekhov of "Rothschild's Violin" speaks of the world not as Shostakovich understood it then, in 1943, but as he would ultimately come to understand it by the time of the Fifteenth

Quartet. The story is like a warning that an older self sends back to his younger self, knowing it cannot possibly be heeded. "A man's life meant loss: death meant gain," Chekhov's coffin maker thinks to himself as he is dying. "This reflection was, of course, a just one, but yet it was bitter and mortifying; why was the order of the world so strange, that life, which is given to man only once, passes away without benefit?" And then, as Bronza's sole episode on earth draws to a close, even his mournful thoughts fall silent.

"Silence in music is a bit like the white part of the canvas," Philip Setzer told me. In Shostakovich's music, we are even more aware of that underlying whiteness than we are with most other composers—though in his case we might prefer to call it emptiness, it is so dark. It's not just that, as he got older, he left more and more of the canvas bare. It's also the fact that, for Shostakovich, silence seems to be yet another kind of voice, another strand in the melody, a special variant that can be combined with the notes played by the four instruments to create a new sound for the string quartet.

Naturally, there were silences at the ends of his quartets; and until he began eliminating the breaks, as he first did in the Fifth Quartet, there were also the silences that came between movements. But because of Shostakovich's intense theatricality, even the normal gaps between movements demand to be performed with more enunciation—that is, with a greater degree of quiet and stillness—than is usual in string quartets. And that demand becomes even stricter when the breaks occur in the middle of a movement. Technically, this doesn't happen until the Eighth Quartet, where Shostakovich gives us our first complete bar of silence. But even before that he knew how to create apparent silences, in the form of those nearly inaudible passages where one or more of the strings carry on with a very high, very soft, practically tuneless series of notes. As a violinist who is often called upon to play such passages, Setzer associates such moments in the music with the dread-filled waiting that Shostakovich endured in his life; and he and his Emerson colleagues are strongly aware in performance of "the tension that creates, dramatically. How we do that is we have to be extremely still."

Shostakovich's silences, though, are not always about impending disaster. At times, as Eugene Drucker has observed, "there's the silence with excitement, where your heart will leap into your throat." At other times the silence is companionable, signaling a wordless sense of communion, almost a telepathic feeling of connection—among the players and, by extension, between the players and their audience. "There's something magical about the end of the Eighth, the end of the Fifteenth, where you hold that note and all somehow know where to end it," Philip Setzer pointed out. "I don't think that kind of thing happens in a lot of other music, even great music."

If silence was a crucial element in Shostakovich's music, it was also a central factor in his life. And, just as in the music, its meaning could vary enormously. It could represent ease and companionship, the absence of any need to speak, as numerous anecdotes about his wordless "conversations" attest. Zoya Tomashevskaya, a friend and neighbor of Mikhail Zoshchenko's, offered one remembrance of how the writer would be called upon to keep the composer company in moments of stress:

> Dmitri Dmitriyevich would sometimes phone him up, and in his tragic, quick-voiced patter asked him to come immediately to see him: "I need to talk." Mikhail Mikhailovich would go. Dmitri Dmitriyevich would sit him down in an armchair, and then start to pace up and down in a frenzy. Gradually he would calm down, and finally, soothed and radiant, would say to Zoshchenko in a tired voice, "Thank you, thank you dear friend, I so much needed that talk with you."

And Elizabeth Wilson reports similar stories about his silent visits with Anna Akhmatova and Mstislav Rostropovich, all of which imply that for Shostakovich silence *was* conversation.

But there was a darker side to his silence as well, for it also represented submission to the powers that controlled Soviet life. This was the expressive silence that prevailed whenever there was any danger of being overheard, the speaking silence that came between the lines of a potentially interceptable letter. It was the silence of conspirators, even when there was no explicit conspiracy. In the face of lies and terror, this kind of silence was the only thing that could bring a modicum of truth and safety into one's life—and even so, it was never a sure solution.

And then there was the version of silence that was a passive form of lying, an avoidance or even renunciation of the truth.

This silence, the failure to speak out, was possibly the darkest and most tragic of all the ones Shostakovich faced. (Except death, which was often the other choice.) Yet even this foul silence, as practiced throughout the composer's life, was better than the alternative, the active lie—as Shostakovich well knew, because he had been forced to engage in both, the active lie as well as the passive one, and of the two he preferred silence. But he did not always have even that paltry option, or so he believed, and the result was that he knowingly and repeatedly brought shame on himself. "O Lord, if only they knew at least how to keep silent!" Boris Pasternak said when Shostakovich publicly confessed to his shortcomings at the time of the Zhdanov Decree. "Even that would be a feat of courage!"

But in his music he did know how to keep silent, and it is through those silences, in particular, that we are now able to hear him speak. They are *our* silences as well, for as audience members we do not have any other role in the music: for us, it is silence or nothing. In fact, I would go so far as to say that it is finally our silence, rather than our applause or anything else, that most strongly affirms our understanding of what Shostakovich is trying to say to us in the string quartets. "I don't remember applause at those rehearsals," Galina Shirinskaya has said of the late-stage run-throughs, held in the Shirinskys' reception room or else in Shostakovich's own study, at which she and a few others were allowed to hear the finished quartets. "Usually there was silence in the end, dazed silence, because it always was a revelation, a discovery of something."

In that dazed, revelatory silence lay the essence of what Shostakovich was communicating in his string quartets. It was the thing itself—the only unquestionable message, the sole uncontradicted point. Like the whiteness of the canvas, it underlay everything else. Surrounded by its opposite, it existed in a profound yet companionable solitude. It asserted itself with a shy forcefulness. It spoke eloquently to all who heard it. And if you listen very closely at a live performance, in that brief moment between the music's end and the start of the clapping, you can hear it still.

Notes

All the passages in this book that are direct quotations from other written sources or from interviews are cited in the notes below. For ease of reading, no numbers have been attached to the quotations in the text. The reader who wants to know where a particular quote comes from can simply locate the opening and closing words of the quote, keeping in mind that all quotations appear in the order given and are divided up according to the chapter in which they appear.

Each reference is given in full the first time it appears. For sources that reappear frequently, an abbreviated version is used in every subsequent case (that is, Elizabeth Wilson's *Shostakovich: A Life Remembered* is cited as "Wilson," Isaak Glikman's *Story of a Friendship* is cited as "Glikman," and so on).

Dostoyevsky epigraph, p. ix: From the preface to *The Brothers Karamazov* (translated by Richard Pevear and Larissa Volokhonsky), San Francisco: North Point Press, 1990, p. 3.

CHAPTER 1. ELEGY

Mikhail Zoshchenko epigraph: Laurel Fay, *Shostakovich: A Life,* New York: Oxford University Press, 2000, p. 121. [Hereafter cited as Fay.]

"diary . . . story of his soul": Irina Antonovna Shostakovich, in a conversation with the author, Moscow, June 4, 2008. [Hereafter cited as Irina Antonovna interview.]

"a committed Communist": *New York Times,* August 11, 1975, pp. 1, 30.

"most intelligent man . . . generation": Preface to Solomon Volkov, *Testimony: The Memoirs of Dmitri Shostakovich* (translated by Antonina Bouis), New York: Limelight Editions, 2006, p. xvi.

"Let's drink . . . better!": Elizabeth Wilson, *Shostakovich: A Life Remembered,* Princeton: Princeton University Press, 2006 (rev. ed.), p. 214. [Hereafter cited as Wilson.]

"a stream of sounds . . . end in tears": "Muddle Instead of Music," unsigned article in *Pravda,* January 28, 1936; this translation (by Marina Frolova-Walker and Jonathan Walker) taken from "Newly Translated Source Documents," published by Carnegie Hall in conjunction with the symposium "Music and Dictatorship: Russia under Stalin," Weill Recital Hall, New York, February 22, 2003, pp. 7–8.

"I think . . . really happy": Galina Vishnevskaya, as reported by Larissa Chirkova in a conversation with the author, St. Petersburg, June 8, 2008.

"Where this fear . . . sisters": Wilson, p. 349.

"Contradictions do not . . . wrong": Ayn Rand, *Atlas Shrugged,* quoted in Mark Crees, "The Company of Stone," *Times Literary Supplement,* July 27, 2007, p. 17.

"We were rehearsing . . . broke out": Wilson, pp. 156–57.

"In the break . . . deliberate": Wilson, p. 354.

"If once . . . cacophony": "Muddle Instead of Music," p. 7.

"knew his Bible": Isaak Glikman, *Story of a Friendship: The Letters of Dmitri Shostakovich to Isaak Glikman, 1941–1975* (translated by Anthony Phillips), Ithaca: Cornell University Press, 2001, p. 268, in regard to a parable alluded to by Shostakovich on p. 78. [Hereafter cited as Glikman.]

"You ask . . . pure music": Wilson, p. 481.

"*fortissimo* and in the major": Fay, p. 103.

"a lengthy . . . crowned by victory": Fay, p. 99.

"formation of a personality . . . all-conquering optimism . . . *pianissimo* and in the minor": Fay, pp. 102–3.

"real and fresh piece of music": Wilson, p. 152.

"tedious intimidation": Fay, p. 103.

"waste matter": Fay, p. 103.

"the practical creative . . . just criticism": Fay, p. 102.

CHAPTER 2. SERENADE

Tatiana Litvinova epigraph: Wilson, p. 198.

"Until I started . . . and listen": Wilson, p. 13.

"Nadejda remembers . . . the window": Victor Ilyich Seroff, *Dmitri Shostako-vich: The Life and Background of a Soviet Composer,* New York: Alfred A. Knopf, 1943, pp. 64–65.

"I tried . . . springlike moods": Fay, p. 112.

"joyful, merry, lyrical": Fay, p. 112.

"In the process . . . know how": Fay, p. 112.

"After all . . . difficult genres": Fay, p. 111.

"captivated": Fay, p. 112.

"You should write . . . play it": Fyodor Druzhinin, as reported by Olga Dombrovskaya in a conversation with the author, Moscow, June 3, 2008. [Hereafter cited as Dombrovskaya interview.]

"simple and popular . . . accessible to all": "Muddle Instead of Music," p. 8.

"Do you know . . . wanderer": Glikman, p. xxxiii (and Glikman's appended remark, same page).

"My husband and I . . . intelligentsia": Wilson, p. 197.

"Nobody . . . his movements": Wilson, p. 196.

"It will be . . . unalloyed joy": Glikman, p. 23.

"the music . . . become popular": Fay, pp. 137–38.

"And what . . . said about this?": Fay, p. 141.

"about the origin . . . and something else . . . wonderful new friend": Wilson, p. 73.

"They had . . . chuckling": Wilson, p. 73.

"When they . . . with time": Wilson, p. 73.

"My guess . . . more than the music . . . Sollertinsky . . . out of the blue": Kurt Sanderling, in a conversation with the author, Berlin, June 13, 2008. [Hereafter cited as Sanderling interview.]

"Dear Isaak . . . write to me": Glikman, p. 24.

"Sollertinsky . . . describing it": Irina Antonovna interview.

"Neither Shostakovich . . . Jewish melodies": Sanderling interview.

"I can't . . . I'll go on": Samuel Beckett, *The Unnamable,* in *Three Novels,* New York: Grove Press, 1958, p. 414.

"distinguished thing": from Henry James's greeting to death ("So here it is at last, the distinguished thing!"), as reported by Edith Wharton in *A Backward Glance,* New York: Charles Scribner's Sons, 1985, p. 367.

"Yes, indeed . . . for you": Wilson, p. 501.

"In general . . . fabulous mood": Glikman, p. 32.

"bourgeois degeneracy": Wilson, p. 232.

"Dear Iosif . . . Shostakovich": Wilson, p. 229.

"Calm unawareness . . . for what?": Paul Epstein's program notes to Emerson Quartet performances of Shostakovich quartets, Alice Tully Hall, New York, spring 2006. The detailed information about the absence of any evidence for the titles comes from Laurel Fay's review of the third edition of Derek Hulme's *Shostakovich Catalogue,* published in *MLA Notes,* September 2003, pages 178–80, and an e-mail message from Fay to the author on March 26, 2010; see also Judith Kuhn, *Shostakovich in Dialogue: Form, Imagery and Ideas in Quartets 1–7,* Farnham, UK: Ashgate, 2010, p. 105.

"We were rehearsing . . . open and defenseless": Wilson, p. 502.

"Life is beautiful . . . will triumph": Alan George's liner notes to the Fitzwilliam String Quartet recordings, London/Decca, 1998; see also Fay, p. 137, for the context of this quotation.

"directness . . . message": Alan George's liner notes to the Fitzwilliam Quartet recordings.

"For some reason . . . all the same": Wilson, pp. 280–81.

"What the pen . . . cut out": Glikman, p. xxii.

"He listened . . . other people": Dombrovskaya interview.

"Silently . . . I envy him": Wilson, p. 260.

"Death is . . . the grave": Wilson, p. 471.

"Shostakovich hated . . . what I've said": Wilson, pp. 423–24.

"There is no . . . other things": Sanderling interview.

CHAPTER 3. INTERMEZZO

Vasily Grossman epigraph: Vasily Grossman, *Life and Fate* (translated by Robert Chandler), New York: NYRB Classics, 2006, p. 51.

"While still . . . firing squad": Wilson, pp. 437–38.

"a piercing . . . gas-chamber": Wilson, p. 242.

"many failures . . . critical instruction": Fay, p. 157.

"formalist distortions . . . tendencies": Fay, p. 158.

"When, today . . . Soviet composer": Fay, p. 160.

"At that time . . . jealous of him": Michael Ardov, *Memories of Shostakovich: Interviews with the Composer's Children* (translated by Rosanna Kelly and Michael Meylac), London: Short Books, 2004, p. 64.

"not his friends . . . distanced themselves": Sanderling interview.

"We have a . . . for the Party and the country": Sanderling interview.

"Shostakovich told us . . . tactful way": Wilson, p. 261.

"How could . . . same way": Sanderling interview.

"Half-conscious . . . its expression": Sanderling interview.

"Jewish songs": Fay, p. 168.

"a cut-out paper doll on a string": Wilson, p. 335.

"At the end of February . . . freely performed": Wilson, pp. 244–45.

"At the appointed time . . . Comrade Stalin": Fay, p. 172.

"And then . . . a full check-up": Ardov, *Memories of Shostakovich*, pp. 70–71.

"A voice unbelievably . . . on the telephone": Grossman, *Life and Fate*, p. 762.

"one of his more gruesome . . . hope": Laurel Fay, in a conversation with the author, New York, March 18, 2008.

"There was just . . . before whom": Grossman, *Life and Fate,* p. 768.

"I fully agree . . . *Pravda*": Alex Ross, *The Rest Is Noise: Listening to the Twentieth Century,* New York: Farrar, Straus and Giroux, 2007, p. 377.

"the worst moment of his life": Sanderling interview.

"if the finale . . . Andantino": Alan George's liner notes to Fitzwilliam recordings.

"But they were tense . . . ice didn't break": Ardov, *Memories of Shostakovich,* pp. 99–100.

"came from Leningrad . . . lie in music": Wilson, p. 281.

"This Quartet . . . November 13, 1953": from the published score of the Fifth Quartet.

"There's a sense in Shostakovich . . . was waiting": Philip Setzer, in a conversation with the author, New York, November 4, 2008. [Hereafter cited as Setzer interview.]

"When I listen to my father's work . . . his nervousness": Galina Shostakovich, in *Shostakovich against Stalin,* a film by Larry Weinstein, 2005.

"the opening theme . . . violent events": Paul Epstein's program notes to Emerson Quartet performances, Alice Tully Hall, New York, spring 2006.

"There can be no question . . . Remarried. Mitya": Fay, p. 80.

"I have to say that Nina . . . Shostakovich circles": Wilson, p. 125.

"I was full . . . calm character": Wilson, p. 189.

"When somebody . . . sign anything . . . Nina laughingly . . . off": Wilson, pp. 188–89.

"a brilliant . . . intuitive judgment": Seroff, *Dmitri Shostakovich,* pp. 18–20.

"who were not . . . academic studies": Seroff, *Dmitri Shostakovich,* p. 149.

"Of course . . . love is free!": Laurel Fay (editor), *Shostakovich and His World,* Princeton: Princeton University Press, 2004, p. 5.

"Our first impulse . . . Mother has died": Ardov, *Memories of Shostakovich,* p. 103.

"When we got . . . into tears": Wilson, pp. 264–65.

"I remember sitting . . . comfort him": Ardov, *Memories of Shostakovich,* p. 104.

"It was during . . . place for me too": Ardov, *Memories of Shostakovich,* pp. 103–4.

"I only remember . . . burst into tears": Wilson, p. 310.

"In the grief-laden . . . wept silently": Glikman, p. 55.

"The music . . . Levon Atovmyan": Ardov, *Memories of Shostakovich,* p. 105.

"I have very . . . small comfort to me": Wilson, p. 308.

"problem of tone," "deceptive cheer": David Fanning, *Shostakovich: String Quartet No. 8,* Aldershot, UK : Ashgate, 2004, p. 40; "emotional ambivalence": Kuhn, *Shostakovich in Dialogue,* p. 213.

"some frightening rumors . . . particularly after Nina": Wilson, pp. 310–14.

"Nothing special . . . no memories of her": Dombrovskaya interview.

"Without a word . . . looked when they played": Isaiah Berlin, letter to Rowland Burdon-Muller, June 28, 1958, in *Enlightening: Letters 1946–1960* (edited by Henry Hardy and Jennifer Holmes), London: Chatto & Windus, 2009, and published in the *New York Review of Books,* July 16, 2009, p. 22.

"Everywhere were portraits . . . Day of Celebration": Glikman, pp. 72–73.

"The deceased . . . admirably grounded": Glikman, p. 69–70.

"a celebratory dinner . . . nuptials": Glikman, p. 76.

"It's possible . . . Komarovo": Glikman, p. 81.

"When I think . . . a coward": Wilson, p. 345.

"Another reason . . . his children": Wilson, p. 346.

"The Beethoven Quartet . . . April 1960": Glikman, pp. 89–90.

"Altogether life . . . earthly activities": Glikman, p. 67.

CHAPTER 4. NOCTURNE

David Fanning epigraph: Fanning, *Shostakovich: String Quartet No. 8,* p. 47.

"music for dummies": Fanning, *String Quartet No. 8,* p. 15.

"Dresden was . . . self-critical hangover": Glikman, pp. 90–91.

"When we finished . . . the way you did": Wilson, p. 282.

"It was his . . . meaning of the Quartet": Wilson, p. 381.

"in memory of . . . war": from the published score of the Eighth Quartet.

"Ridiculous! . . . fascism? . . . I can't answer . . . content for him": Sanderling interview.

"The fact . . . Russia too": Setzer interview.

"rich in cinematographic continuity techniques": Fanning, *String Quartet No. 8,* p. 40.

"It is tactful . . . is implied": William Empson cited in Christopher Ricks, *Allusion to the Poets,* Oxford: Oxford University Press, 2002, p. 2.

"transcendence": Fanning, *String Quartet No. 8,* p. 131.

"He was treated . . . blackmailed . . . the Zhdanov period": Irina Antonovna interview.

"How is it possible . . . forced to shout": Sanderling interview.

"I don't know how not to be afraid": Wilson, p. 425.

"He was only . . . concerned others": Sanderling interview.

"strongly suggests . . . line in the sand": Fay, p. 219.

"I didn't join . . . surrendering my mind": Aleksander Wat, *My Century* (edited and translated by Richard Lourie), New York: NYRB Classics, 2003, p. 16.

"Today I feel dreadful and disgusting": Glikman, p. 117.

"like giving speeches . . . for other people": Sanderling interview.

"a broad avenue . . . designer boutiques": Angela Charlton, *Frommer's Moscow and St. Petersburg,* Hoboken, NJ: Wiley Publishing, 2008, p. 89.

"Apartment 23 . . . we are leaving": Glikman, p. 101.

"Once . . . help him in his life . . . give in to compromise": Wilson, pp. 397–98.

"It was the first . . . domestic peace": Wilson, pp. 398–99.

"My wife's name . . . a girl with a past": Glikman, pp. 102–4.

"He loved them . . . same street . . . that he felt safer": Irina Antonovna interview.

"the *russe* style": Introductory notes to the published score of the Unfinished Quartet, Moscow: DSCH Publishers, 2006, p. 6.

"I finished . . . burnt all my manuscripts": Glikman, p. 99.

"working on . . . about two weeks": notes to Unfinished Quartet, p. 7.

"Shostakovich's music . . . persecution of truth": Wilson, p. 419.

"the hypersensitivity . . . an ever-open wound": Wilson, pp. 418–20.

"depending on whether . . . so many sketches": Dombrovskaya interview.

"the kind of music . . . pain in the stomach": Fay, p. 239.

"They smell of vodka . . . a knock at the door . . . he had a family": from the printed libretto, translated by Andrew Huth, that accompanies the recording of Symphony No. 13 conducted by Bernard Haitink, Decca, 1993.

"pure music": Wilson, p. 416.

"I knew that . . . unprincipled turncoat": Wilson, p. 417.

"At the end . . . go on forever": Glikman, p. 283.

"if it is indeed a symphony?": Glikman, p. 105.

"honeymoon": Glikman, p. 102.

"He used to say . . . fate was tragic": Irina Antonovna interview.

"audition": Glikman, p. 260.

"My music . . . second time": Glikman, p. 109.

"Weinberg was . . . prominent, and older": Dombrovskaya interview.

"There was a bet . . . more quartets": Sanderling interview.

CHAPTER 5. FUNERAL MARCH

Shostakovich/Rostropovich epigraph: Wilson, p. 417.

"But why . . . when I look at his eyes": Larissa Chirkova, in a conversation with the author, St. Petersburg, June 8, 2008.

"I have come . . . *Song of the Earth*": Glikman, p. 112.

"I should like . . . the Metro": Glikman, p. 158.

"Well, Sergei . . . even better life?": Wilson, p. 429.

"When my teacher . . . these quartets": Wilson, pp. 438–39.

"The relaxed atmosphere . . . smile and joke": Wilson, p. 439.

"He bent down . . . too early for him": Galina Shirinskaya, in conversation with the author's representative, Daria Rhyzhkova, using the author's questions as a guide; Moscow, August 23, 2008. [Hereafter cited as Shirinskaya interview.]

"His authority was absolutely indisputable . . . talent as a composer": Shirinskaya interview.

"They performed . . . And the examining . . . Soviet leaders": Shirinskaya interview.

"Starting with . . . In my opinion . . . being individuals": Irina Antonovna interview.

"He makes it sound . . . Suzuki exercise": Eugene Drucker, in a conversation with the author, New York, October 7, 2008. [Hereafter cited as Drucker interview.]

"So much roughly speaking . . . maintained": Samuel Beckett, *The Lost Ones,* New York: Grove Press, 1972, pp. 62–63.

"The Eleventh . . . tools and ingredients": Setzer interview.

"It implies a lot without saying very much": Elizabeth Wilson, in a telephone conversation with the author, February 6, 2009.

"poor, bare, forked animal": *King Lear,* act 3, scene 4, line 99.

"Now my charms are all o'erthrown": *The Tempest,* epilogue, line 1.

"the authorities . . . in the sonnet": Irina Antonovna interview. [The verse quotations are from Shakespeare's Sonnet 66.]

"a very interesting person . . . to the Quartet": Shirinskaya interview.

"I am terribly nervous . . . on strike altogether": Glikman, p. 129.

"28 May was . . . ill during the night": Glikman, p. 131; the published English translation, which specified "the Small Hall of the Conservatoire," has been corrected here on Laurel Fay's advice to "the Small Hall of the Leningrad Philharmonic," as in the Russian edition.

"I am thinking . . . terrible things to happen": Glikman, p. 140.

"They both pronounced . . . slippery pavements": Glikman, pp. 134–35.

"my legs seem . . . Here is . . . out of order)": Glikman, pp. 146–47.

"the lifelong happiness . . . two-thirds of a man": Mark Twain, "Aurelia's Unfortunate Young Man," in *Sketches New and Old,* New York: Harper & Brothers, 1875, p. 308.

"It's funny . . . left unfinished . . . Dmitri Dmitriyevich . . . high spirits at the time": Glikman, p. 152.

"entry point . . . the Twelfth": Laurel Fay, in a conversation with the author, New York, March 18, 2008.

"In no other work . . . force and intensity": Wilson, p. 460.

"the ultimate examination . . . elsewhere in the series": Alan George and Christopher Rowland, "Interpreting the String Quartets," in Christopher Norris (editor), *Shostakovich: The Man and His Music,* London: Marion Boyars, 1982, p. 30.

"splendidly": Wilson, p. 461.

"Very typical . . . any real beauty": Dmitri Shostakovich, *The Power of Music,* New York: A Music Journal Publication, 1968, p. 39.

"*This dogma* . . . quite pathetic": Shostakovich, *Power of Music,* p. 50.

"But one finds examples of it in Mozart's music": Wilson, p. 461.

"A. A. Zhdanov's . . . melodious and graceful": Glikman, p. 66.

"wrong" notes: Michael Tilson Thomas, in his PBS documentary about the Fifth Symphony, has a similar take on Shostakovich's wrong-note approach. "Just changing one or two notes can change the entire meaning of the piece," MTT observes, "and that's the essence of one of Shostakovich's methods. He evokes memories and associations of music the audience would already know, but changes the musical language just enough to suggest what *he's* feeling, what *they* are feeling, but that no one would dare speak aloud." From *Keeping Score: Shostakovich Symphony No. 5,* a PBS television program created by Michael Tilson Thomas with the San Francisco Symphony, 2009.

"I get a blister . . . play it so loud": Drucker interview.

"You have to really . . . it's dull": José Maria Blumenschein, in a conversation with the author, New York, September 30, 2007.

"the charged . . . involved in the drama": George and Rowland, "Interpreting the String Quartets," p. 30.

"Shostakovich praised . . . my musical nature": Wilson, p. 461.

"Dear Mitya . . . play the Fourth Quartet": quoted in Oksana Dvornichenko's recent biography of Shostakovich, available only in Russian; this passage located and translated for the author by Helga Landauer.

"extended recitatives . . . other time . . . constant recourse . . . strong dramatic vein": George and Rowland, "Interpreting the String Quartets," p. 17.

"Yes, indeed it was, Mitya. I wrote it for you": Wilson, p. 501.

"I remember him . . . wonderful professor": Shirinskaya interview.

"The shackled genius . . . could not hold a pen": Fay, p. 270.

"very fond . . . He loved his music . . . Something else I should say . . . not really in the cards": Ignat Solzhenitsyn, in a conversation with the author, Philadelphia, March 24, 2009. [Hereafter cited as Solzhenitsyn interview.]

"It is incredible . . . one of the wittiest": Glikman, p. 159.

"It cannot really . . . a soprano and a bass": Glikman, p. 159.

"All-powerful is death . . . cries within us": libretto accompanying the recording of Symphony No. 14 conducted by Simon Rattle, EMI, 2006.

"eternal problem . . . resigned to this event": Glikman, p. 160.

"I have been sent . . . full of the joys of life": Glikman, p. 114.

"Dmitri and Irena . . . foil for him . . . quick nip of vodka": Wilson, p. 453.

"Despite obvious differences . . . feel at home": Ross, *The Rest Is Noise,* pp. 435–36.

"turning point": Glikman, p. 161.

"The Thirteenth . . . disturbed by it": George and Rowland, "Interpreting the String Quartets," p. 27.

"No . . . with a strong character": Irina Antonovna interview.

"The world Union . . . chairman"; "If asked . . . Everything": Hindemith and Shostakovich comments both quoted in the liner notes for the recording *Vadim Borisovsky: Viola, Viola d'amour,* Vista Vera, 2005.

"It's as if you're on . . . feeling that this conveys": Drucker interview.

"that very sinister . . . jam session from hell": Drucker interview.

"I wrote . . . joke middle . . . in a concentration camp": Shirinskaya interview.

"It may have . . . replace a chin rest": Drucker interview.

"I remember we joked . . . they are coming": George and Rowland, "Interpreting the String Quartets," p. 29.

"the last act . . . the coffin lid": Wilson, p. 498.

"a piercing road-drill": Wilson, p. 242

"It's fugal . . . at the same time": Drucker interview.

"Britten, moved and shaken . . . Shostakovich's hand": Wilson, p. 500.

"I have been warned . . . distressing to me": Glikman, p. 182.

"sent it into the world . . . what they were hearing": Sanderling interview.

"he had a wonderful . . . 'in his luggage'": Irina Antonovna interview.

"Freedom . . . a symbol of freedom, possibly": Sanderling interview.

"I don't myself quite know . . . *not* include them": Glikman, p. 315.

"He has become . . . even more . . . if Maksim is . . . intended to": Glikman, p. 183.

"I should like you . . . tears come to my eyes": Glikman, pp. 184–85.

"as though . . . much-beloved composer": Glikman, p. 185.

"incurable": Fay, p. 276.

"without our second violinist . . . played with one finger": Wilson, p. 500.

"my Italian bit": Wilson, p. 500.

"We think of that . . . landscape of his late works": Drucker interview.

"very contemporary . . . expertise but uncertainties": Paul Epstein's program notes to Emerson Quartet performances, Alice Tully Hall, New York, spring 2006.

"He had to provide . . . all his life": Shirinskaya interview.

"He was a delightful man . . . much loved by his pupils": Elizabeth Wilson, in an e-mail message to the author, February 7, 2009.

"'old school' teacher . . . staying at the dormitory": Mark Maryanovsky, in an e-mail message to the author, August 5, 2008.

"Berlinsky wrote . . . great mark on the person": Shirinskaya interview.

"Oh, plenty of hope . . . but not for us": Franz Kafka, in a conversation with Max Brod, as quoted by Walter Benjamin in *Illuminations,* New York: Schocken Books, 2007, p. 116.

"Shostakovich dedicated . . . 'Well, I can die now'": Shirinskaya interview.

"they found a cyst . . . immaculate cyst-free lungs": Glikman, p. 188.

"Don't waste your efforts . . . allowed to breathe!": Wilson, p. 487.

"Shostakovich's signature . . . genius and villainy are compatible": Fay, p. 278.

"Dmitri Dmitriyevich came . . . felt the same way": Wilson, p. 489.

"in regard to . . . much else besides": Wilson, p. 484.

"Andrei Yefimich loves reason . . . signs the account just the same": Anton Chekhov, *Ward No. 6,* in *Seven Short Novels* (translated by Barbara Makanowitzky), New York: W. W. Norton, 2003, pp. 118–19.

"His heavy head . . . would be another person": Chekhov, *Ward No. 6,* p. 127.

"Where had Nikita taken . . . and see him in a bathrobe": Chekhov, *Ward No. 6,* pp. 152–53.

"I am almost completely helpless . . . broken in my brain": Glikman, p. 188.

"Things are very bad . . . 'Three Blind Mice'": Glikman, p. 191.

"At the moment I am in hospital . . . legs are very weak": Glikman, p. 195.

"In whose hands are you leaving me to die?": Fay, p. 279.

"Just writing that passage had to be very painful to him": Setzer interview.

"I have the feeling . . . an elegy to himself": Drucker interview.

"I don't know . . . one in each key": Irina Antonovna interview.

"Who can know? . . . couldn't dedicate it to anyone": Sanderling interview.

"In a garden . . . incomprehensible to us mortals": Anton Chekhov, "The Black Monk," in *A Woman's Kingdom and Other Stories* (translated by Ronald Hingley), Oxford: Oxford University Press, 1989, pp. 74–75.

"Play it so that flies . . . from sheer boredom": Wilson, p. 531.

"a tall black column like a whirlwind or a sand-storm": "The Black Monk," p. 95.

"He was very fearful of death": Sanderling interview.

"the first time in my life . . . this is the aim of remembrance": Theodor Adorno, *Essays on Music* (selected and introduced by Richard Leppert, with new translations by Susan H. Gillespie), Berkeley: University of California Press, 2002, p. 612.

"but on the way to the bus stop . . . the last hour of his life": Shirinskaya interview.

"And yet another's . . . in the evening he was no more": Glikman, p. 199.

"When Shostakovich . . . I remembered from long ago": Glikman, p. 199.

"Fedya, I have buckled down . . . so we can talk": Wilson, p. 531.

"He came flying over . . . on his birthday, 25 September": Wilson, p. 532.

"It's good . . . best medicine for him": Olga Dombrovskaya (editor), *Dmitri Shostakovich: Pages of His Life in Photographs,* Moscow: DSCH Publishers, 2006, p. 202.

"My mother was there . . . nothing special as far as I know": Shirinskaya interview.

"She made her way. . . . Nobody stopped her . . . death emphasized that": Helga Landauer, in a conversation with the author, Berkeley, August 6, 2008. [Hereafter cited as Landauer interview.]

"When Shostakovich died . . . almost no enemies": Lev Ginzburg, in an e-mail message to the author, April 5, 2009.

"After break . . . out of the hall in total silence": Mark Maryanovsky, in an e-mail message to the author, August 5, 2008.

CHAPTER 6. EPILOGUE

Taruskin epigraph: Richard Taruskin, *Defining Russia Musically,* Princeton: Princeton University Press, 1997, pp. 476–77.

"It is not interpretation . . . just on a different scale": Maxim Shostakovich, in a telephone conversation with the author, April 3, 2009.

"I think the quartets . . . messages to mankind": Sanderling interview.

"are becoming more a part . . . in their own terms": Frederick Lifsitz, in an e-mail message to the author, February 16, 2009.

"Shostakovich was popular . . . adolescence and so forth": Lily Francis, in a conversation with the author, New York, September 30, 2007.

"In certain ways Shostakovich . . . notes really mean . . . certain intimate quality": Nicholas Canellakis, in a conversation with the author, New York, September 30, 2007.

"musicologists love to engage . . . into a dismissive posture": Solzhenitsyn interview.

"For so many years . . . tremendous intellect behind them": Setzer interview.

"When we put a Shostakovich . . . immediacy of the music": Drucker interview.

"Like most things . . . make something that was great": Setzer interview.

"You cannot lie in music": Wilson, p. 281.

"Music cannot lie . . . it is not music": Shirinskaya interview.

"Music was the last retreat . . . not totally scrutinized": Landauer interview.

"If music cannot lie, then music also cannot tell the truth": Gerard McBurney, in a conversation with the author, Chicago, December 11, 2008.

"I think in Shostakovich . . . the *y* axis is something else": Drucker interview.

"As much as I love Shostakovich . . . please the authorities": Setzer interview.

"intimate diary . . . without a trace of his soul": Lev Ginzburg, in an e-mail message to the author, April 5, 2009.

"He abided by . . . communicate how he truly felt": program note by the Jupiter Quartet accompanying a concert in Alice Tully Hall, New York, March 15, 2009.

"I don't hear that . . . to something else . . . With the quartets . . . he's not found out": Setzer interview.

"Man is least himself . . . he will tell you the truth": Oscar Wilde, "The Critic as Artist," in *The Artist as Critic: Critical Writings of Oscar Wilde* (edited by Richard Ellmann), New York: Vintage Books, 1970, p. 389.

"There's the whole question . . . one who tells the truth": Setzer interview.

"Writing quartet music was the closest . . . always on his side": Landauer interview.

"None of his predecessors . . . who wants to experience them": Barbara Everett, article on Shakespeare's sonnets in the *London Review of Books,* May 8, 2008, p. 12.

"wild ride . . . inevitable . . . unpredictable": Sandy Wilson, in an e-mail message to the author, February 15, 2009.

"His music tells a story . . . theater piece based on it": Drucker interview.

"In a basic way . . . dramatically powerful . . . I started to see the quartets . . . fifteen chapters": Setzer interview.

"the composer would do himself . . . unprofessional compromise and exhibitionism": Ross, *The Rest Is Noise,* p. 406.

"He wanted people to understand what he was saying": Setzer interview.

"It's us, it's Russia—it's the tragedy of Russia too": Setzer interview.

"lived slightly too long": Glikman, p. 140.

"in his luggage": Irina Antonovna interview.

"An allusion predicates . . . undulating and diverse": Christopher Ricks, *Allusion to the Poets,* Oxford: Oxford University Press, 2002, p. 157.

"We can never . . . implicated in their making": Taruskin, *Defining Russia Musically,* pp. 476–77.

"When we were first learning . . . than an intellectual one": Drucker interview.

"The full greatness . . . comes out in performance . . . No. Broadly speaking . . . the sky is blue": Solzhenitsyn interview.

"that swine Nabokov . . . forced to say yes": Sanderling interview.

"When Shostakovich joined . . . forced him into this action?": Wilson, p. 348.

"an idea that the structure . . . Living in a world . . . acted differently": Bernard Williams, *Shame and Necessity,* Berkeley: University of California Press, 1993, p. 141.

"succumbed to weakness . . . Indeed . . . a kind of exaltation": Wilson, p. 348.

"He had an idiosyncratic . . . all this like a child": Wilson, pp. 522–23.

"If the music didn't have irony . . . any other composer": Drucker interview.

"With Shostakovich everything . . . kind of demonic way": Setzer interview.

"dark and sarcastic . . . It is not . . . break out on that level": Frederick Lifsitz, in an e-mail message to the author, February 16, 2009.

"The sick humor . . . character traits": All the members of the Vertigo Quartet, in conversation with the author, New York, September 30, 2007; then, more specifically, José Maria Blumenschein ("I think it's . . . 'Bum-bum'"), on the same occasion.

"the funereal episode . . . the tread of death itself": Wilson, p. 461.

"Shostakovich is not joyful . . . he is not joyful": Sanderling interview.

"No, I think of them . . . musical personality": Drucker interview.

"instead of really writing . . . meant to be jabbed by it": Setzer interview.

"To the highest degree . . . the more tragic he got": Sanderling interview.

"He was both . . . you become a melancholic": Shirinskaya interview.

"I do feel . . . an overall epic effect": Frederick Lifsitz, in an e-mail message to the author, February 16, 2008.

"I think if you're trying . . . Beethoven chronologically, too": Setzer interview.

"As long as we have . . . no other context": Richard Taruskin, *On Russian Music,* Berkeley: University of California Press, 2009, p. 356.

"You have to think . . . as a volume": Setzer interview.

"What he said he liked . . . happy music sounded sad": Drucker interview.

"so sad and sorrowful . . . over and over a dozen times": Anton Chekhov, "Rothschild's Fiddle," in *Later Short Stories, 1888–1903* (translated by Constance Garnett, edited by Shelby Foote), New York: Modern Library, 1999, p. 255.

"A man's life . . . passes away without benefit?": Chekhov, "Rothschild's Fiddle," p. 253.

"Silence in music . . . white part of the canvas": Setzer interview.

"the tension that creates . . . have to be extremely still": Setzer interview.

"there's the silence . . . heart will leap into your throat": Drucker interview.

"There's something magical . . . even great music": Setzer interview.

"Dmitri Dmitriyevich . . . needed that talk with you": Wilson, p. 362.

"O Lord . . . would be a feat of courage!": Ross, *The Rest Is Noise,* p. 256.

"I don't remember applause . . . discovery of something": Shirinskaya interview.

Recommended Listening

There are a number of excellent recordings of the complete Shostakovich string quartets, including:

Emerson String Quartet (Deutsche Grammophon): This is a good place to start, not only because the Emersons are expert at the Shostakovich quartets, but also because these performances, which were recorded before live audiences, manage to be simultaneously intense and restrained.

Beethoven String Quartet (Doremi): These recordings, made between 1956 and 1974, constitute the essential document of the composer's relationship with his trusted friends, who were the first players of almost all the quartets and the dedicatees of six of them.

Borodin Quartet (Chandos): There is a complete edition of the quartets by a later version of the Borodins, but the one I recommend is a recording of the first thirteen quartets by the original Borodin players, made while Shostakovich was still alive.

Fitzwilliam String Quartet (London): These were practically the first players to perform the quartets outside of Russia, and Shostakovich himself listened to and worked with them on some of the later quartets.

Alexander String Quartet (Foghorn Classics): Available in two volumes, this complete recording features strong, appealing performances, plus a bonus in the form of the Unfinished Quartet (which preceded the Ninth).

For those not ready to invest in a complete boxed set, there are many individual recordings that are very good, including but not limited to:

Jerusalem Quartet (Harmonia Mundi): Two separate recordings, one featuring Quartets No. 1, 4, and 9, the other Quartets No. 6, 8, and 11.

St. Lawrence String Quartet (EMI): Quartets No. 3, 7, and 8.

Juilliard String Quartet (Sony): Quartets No. 3, 14, 15 (plus the Piano Quintet, op. 57, with Yefim Bronfman).

Philharmonia Quartett Berlin (Thorofon): Quartets No. 3, 7, and 12.

Vogler Quartet (RCA): Quartets No. 10 and 11 (plus other quartets by Debussy and Janáček).

Gidon Kremer, Daniel Phillips, Kim Kashkashian, and Yo-Yo Ma (CBS): Quartet No. 15 (plus *Rejoice!*, a work for violin and cello by Sofia Gubaidulina).

Finally, there are two other chamber works—the 1944 Trio for Piano, Violin, and Cello, op. 67, and the 1975 Sonata for Viola and Piano, op. 147—which in some ways bracket the string quartets, and which seem to me intimately linked to them. The viola sonata is somewhat hard to come by: the best version I have been able to obtain is by Yuri Bashmet and Sviatoslav Richter (Regis). As for the piano trio, I strongly recommend the original recording featuring the composer himself on the piano, Dmitri Tsyganov on the violin, and Sergei Shirinsky on the cello; this is available on *Legendary Treasures: Composers Performing: Shostakovich, Vol. 1* (Doremi). Among its other virtues, this recording gives us Shostakovich's own speaking voice as he sounds out the section titles for a series of piano exercises called *Children's Notebook:* it is worth the price of the disc just to hear him say (in Russian, of course) "March," "Waltz," "The Bear," "Funny Story," "Sad Story," "Clockwork Doll," and "Birthday."

Acknowledgments

Four tutelary figures presided over the birth of this book. Laurel Fay, with a generosity unequaled in my experience, offered me her knowledge, her connections, her opinions, and her time; her book *Shostakovich: A Life,* which remains the essential starting point for anyone interested in a fact-based account of the composer's life, was the foundation against which I continually checked my own work. Elizabeth Wilson's wonderful *Shostakovich: A Life Remembered* proved to be a major source for documents and interviews translated from the Russian; in addition, its author kindly spoke with me about the string quartets and their original players. Vera Chalidze organized my trip to Russia, put me in contact with crucial interview subjects, and—as she put it in a loose translation from the Russian—"checked for lice" in my earliest finished draft. Ara Guzelimian gallantly read through two and in some cases three drafts of each chapter, scrupulously pointed out musical inanities, and made invaluable suggestions about prose style. Without these four, the book would not exist, though of course none of them bears any responsibility for its flaws.

Those who generously allowed themselves to be interviewed on the subject of Shostakovich and his quartets included José Maria Blumenschein, Nicholas Canellakis, Larissa Chirkova, Johannes Dickbauer, Olga Dombrovskaya, Eugene Drucker, Lily Francis, Lev Ginzburg, Helga Landauer, Frederick Lifsitz, Gerard McBurney, Mark Maryanovsky, Kurt Sanderling, Philip Setzer, Galina Shirinskaya, Irina Antonovna Shostakovich, Maxim Shostakovich, Ignat Solzhenitsyn, and Sandy Wilson. Other kinds of help and advice were provided by Martin Bauer, John Branch, Kathryn Crim, Svetlana Harris, Thomas Laqueur, Lisa Little, Gloria Loomis, Katharine Michaels, Christopher Ricks, Pamela Rosenberg, Alex Ross, Oliver Sacks, Richard Sennett, Yuri Slezkine, Ileene Smith, Mark Stevens, Elizabeth Tallent, Erik Tarloff, Richard Taruskin, Marie Unger, and Brenda Wineapple. Daria Ryzhkova, my intrepid and resourceful interpreter in Moscow, went far beyond the call of duty in conducting the interview with Galina Shirinskaya after I had already left town. Jason Royal read a draft of the book to correct the musical errors, and his thoughtful comments profoundly influenced my interpretations. Arthur Lubow did his usual perspicacious editing. Richard Rizzo gracefully endured the intrusion of Shostakovich into our lives, joined me on my travels, attended concerts with me, and otherwise made the whole project a companionable rather than a solitary one.

I am very grateful to both the Dedalus Foundation and the Leon Levy Center for Biography for supporting this book with year-long fellowships. My membership in the New York Institute for the Humanities (a boon in many ways) allowed me access to New York University's libraries, my main bibliographic resource. And, finally, I owe a permanent debt to concert hall press officers worldwide—but particularly to Eileen McMahon of Lincoln Center Presents, Marlisa Monroe of the Chamber Music Society of Lincoln Center, Justin Holder of Carnegie Hall, and Christina Kellogg of Cal Performances—who made it possible for me to hear Shostakovich's music repeatedly played live.

Index